'This book highlights the continuous cultural lineage that underpins current activism for an ecologically viable and spiritually nourishing life now and in the future. For permaculture practitioners and activists focused on building ecologically smart, localised economies, this book highlights how rethinking our attitudes and behaviour toward consumption can be a fruitful pathway to social and ecological harmony.'

– **David Holmgren**, *Permaculture: Principles and Pathways beyond Sustainability*

'*Simple Living in History* challenges the mentality of waste and extravagance that defines modern industrial lifestyles, reminding us that the answers we need have been here all along, waiting for us to notice them.'

– **John Michael Greer**, *The Wealth of Nature* and *Green Wizardry*

'This engaging book raises one of the key questions of our times, presenting a rich tapestry of perspectives on what it means to live simply.'

– **Rob Hopkins**, *The Transition Handbook: From Oil Dependency to Local Resilience*

CONTENTS

Acknowledgements   *ix*

Preface by the Editors   *xi*

FOREWORD by David Shi   *xvii*

1. **BUDDHA** – Peter Doran   1

2. **DIOGENES** – William Desmond   11

3. **ARISTOTLE** – Jerome Segal   19

4. **EPICURUS** – Michael Augustin   27

5. **THE STOICS** – Dirk Baltzly   37

6. **JESUS** – Simon Ussher   45

7. **WESTERN MONASTICISM** – William Fahey   53

8. **THE QUAKERS** – Mark Burch   67

9. **THE AMISH** – Steven Nolt   75

10. **HENRY THOREAU** – Samuel Alexander   83

11. **JOHN RUSKIN** – David Craig   93

12. **WILLIAM MORRIS** – Sara Wills   101

13. **GANDHI** – Whitney Sanford   113

14. **DITCHLING VILLAGE** – William Fahey   121

15. **THE AGRARIANS** – Allan Carlson   129

16. **THE NEARINGS** – Amanda McLeod   139

17. IVAN ILLICH – Marius de Geus   149

18. JOHN SEYMOUR – Amanda McLeod   159

19. VOLUNTARY SIMPLICITY – Mary Grigsby   169

20. RADICAL HOMEMAKING – Shannon Hayes   177

21. INTENTIONAL COMMUNITIES – Bill Metcalf   185

22. PERMACULTURE – Albert Bates   195

23. TRANSITION TOWNS – Samuel Alexander
and Esther Alloun   203

24. DEGROWTH – Serge Latouche   211

25. THE SIMPLER WAY – Ted Trainer   217

26. MINDFULNESS – Mark Burch   225

Notes on the Contributors   237

Lately in the wreck of a Californian ship, one of the passengers fastened a belt about him with 200 pounds of gold in it with which he was found afterwards at the bottom. Now, as he was sinking, had he the gold? Or had the gold him?

– John Ruskin

ACKNOWLEDGEMENTS

We owe a debt of gratitude to all those who helped bring this project to fruition. First and foremost, we would like to thank the contributors for their time, efforts, and expertise. This book would not exist but for their generosity.

The chapter by Serge Latouche in this volume was submitted in French. We would like to thank Esther Alloun, Guillaume Dutilleux, Sandy Taddeo, and Michael Singleton for translating the article for us. Their time was very much appreciated.

We would also like to acknowledge the fine work of our cover designer, Andrew Doodson, who also designed the cover for *Entropia*. Once again, he achieved all that was asked of him and more. A picture is worth a thousand words.

None of the chapters in this volume have been published before, except for chapter seventeen, by Marius de Geus, and chapter twenty, by Shannon Hayes. A version of chapter seventeen was published in the Belgian journal, *Oikos* (51, 2009: 54-65), and a version of chapter twenty was published in *Yes! Magazine* (February, 2010). We appreciate the opportunity to reprint.

PREFACE BY THE EDITORS

SAMUEL ALEXANDER AND AMANDA MCLEOD

This book is framed by the realisation that consumerism –
that is, the high consumption way of life which defines the
most 'developed' industrial societies – has no future.
Consumer lifestyles have no future because our planet simply
cannot sustain the weight of their energy and resource
intensive burdens. Earth's ecosystems are trembling under
the weight of one or two billion high-end consumers, so it is
nothing short of delusional to think that our planet could
sustain four or six or eight or ten billion people living this
way. There are limits to what Earth will tolerate.

And yet, it is precisely the fantasy of universal affluence
that shapes national and international conceptions of
'progress' and 'development'. Across the ideological spectrum
it is assumed that with sustained economic growth the
poorest people on the planet can attain the consumerist ideal,
while at the same time it is assumed that the richest people
can continue to achieve ever-higher levels of affluence. We
are continually told that technology and 'free markets' will
solve the grave ecological problems caused by this mode of
development, all the while our old growth forests disappear,
the oceans are emptied, the topsoils erode, our rivers are
polluted, the holocaust of biodiversity continues, and the
climate is destabilised. As the consumer class expands, we
see the face of Gaia vanishing.

While the ecological impacts of the consumerist way of
life are severe, the social justice implications are equally

challenging. In order to support the high consumption lifestyles enjoyed by a minority of humankind, the global economy must be structured so as to siphon resources away from the 'developing' world, where the majority of humankind live. While it can be acknowledged that 'development' has indeed lifted millions out of extreme poverty, people are being forced off the land into the wage slavery of factory life, in order to make consumer trinkets which are then shipped off to the rich world, only for those trinkets to be promptly disposed of, creating mountains of consumer waste that are sometimes shipped back to the developing world for dumping. The issues are more complex and nuanced than this, of course, but the point is that beneath the nice-sounding political rhetoric calling for justice and sustainability lies a form of development that is too often oppressive and degrading, and which insidiously promotes narrow and unimaginative conceptions of the good life. We are told that in time 'sustainable development' will enrich the poorest people and nations, all the while economic inequality worsens, the rich get richer, and the destitute, by in large, remain impoverished. We are told to wait for progress, as if in a Kafkaesque novel, but we are not told how long we must wait.

If the social justice and ecological implications of consumerism are disturbing, what is perhaps most unsettling of all is the fact that even those who have attained the consumerist ideal often do not seem satisfied with it. The social and ecological costs are tragic, and yet the promised benefits are constantly deferred. As we get caught up in the stressful 'work-and-spend' cycle of a growth-orientated world, too often our communities and families fragment into a materially rich but culturally poor society of isolated and alienated individuals – individuals who seek contentment in 'nice things', but who do not find it. It seems the treadmill of consumption is failing to live up to its promise of a fulfilling life, failing to satisfy the universal human craving for meaning, and yet our televisions and newspapers bombard us with the message that more consumption is the only solution to our malaise. When we get that new kitchen, and replace the carpet; when we upgrade the car or house and purchase that new watch or dress – then we will be happy; then our peers will respect us; then we will be loved. So do not question the status quo; fall quietly in line; and be grateful for a life of comfortable unfreedom.

This is the Grand Narrative of our times.

We know, deep down, of course, that something is very wrong with this narrative, that there must be better, freer, more humane ways to live. But we live in a corporate world that conspires to keep knowledge of such alternatives from us. We are told that consumerism is the peak of civilisation and that there is no alternative, and over time, as these messages are endlessly repeated and normalised, our imaginations begin to contract and we lose the ability to envision different worlds. We begin to think that the future must look more or less like the past, and we find ourselves becoming part of the problems we would like to solve.

As tragic as this picture of industrial civilisation may be, there is a silver lining to our predicament upon which grounded hope can be found. If it is the case that human beings simply do not find the limitless pursuit of ever-more consumption a very satisfying mode of existence, then this should provoke us all – if only out of self-respect – to ignite our imaginations in search of alternative ways to live. Indeed, if it is the case that consumer lifestyles are unable to make us truly happy or fulfilled, then we need not feel aggrieved by the scientific literature telling us that it is impossible to universalise affluence due to ecological limits. We should explore alternatives, then, not simply because soon we will be ecologically compelled to live differently, but because we are human and deserve the opportunity to flourish within sustainable bounds. This does not however mean regressing to something *prior* to consumerism; rather, it means drawing on the wisdom of ages in order to advance *beyond* consumerism; in order to create something better, freer, and more humane.

This book is a humble contribution to that great, ambitious, but necessary endeavour. If the consumerist way of life is a temporary, fossil-fuelled perversion that has no future, it follows that the future will be defined necessarily by less materialistic, 'simpler' ways of living. Fortunately, although the roots of consumerism are shallow, the roots of simplicity are deep, and this book will invite readers to put their hands in the soil of history to examine those deep roots, to feel them and learn from them, in the hope of enriching the present as we move into an uncertain future. With that in mind, this anthology brings together twenty-six short essays discussing the most significant individuals, cultures, and social movements that have embraced forms of 'simple living' throughout history.

But what does it mean to 'live simply'? Granted, this is a concept that means different things, to different people, at different times; nevertheless, it can and should be given some definitional content. Broadly speaking, simple living refers to a way of life based on notions such as frugality, sufficiency, moderation, minimalism, self-reliance, localism, and mind-fulness. It can be understood to refer to 'the middle way' between overconsumption and under-consumption, where basic material needs are sufficiently met but where attention is then directed away from continuous materialistic pursuits, in search of non-materialistic sources of satisfaction and meaning. Practically this might involve growing one's own organic food, wearing second-hand or mended clothes, minimising energy consumption, riding a bike, sharing or making instead of buying, avoiding superfluous possessions, spending conscientiously, and minimising waste. But none of this should imply hardship or sacrifice. By minimising wasteful consumption and embracing sufficiency, people living simply tend to have more time for the important things in life, like family and friends, home production, creative activity, self-development, civic engagement – or whatever one's private passions may be. In contrast to the consumer lifestyle, one could say that simple living is about privileging time over money, or freedom over stuff. In short, simple living is about knowing how much is 'enough' and discovering that 'enough is plenty'.

Anyone who has attempted to actually live simply, of course, will know very well that doing so is not very 'simple' at all, in the sense of being easy. This is especially so in the consumerist cultures that have arisen today, which are dominated not only by materialistic values but also by growth-orientated structures that often lock people into high consumption lifestyles. To be sure, it is hard to swim against the current of consumerism. What this suggests is that the significance of simple living is not just about personal lifestyle choice, but has wider and deeper implications on how we think about the structures of our societies. As we will see, this raises political and macroeconomic issues, as well as ethical, cultural, ecological, and even spiritual issues. It seems, then, somewhat paradoxically, that simple living is actually an extremely complex notion that exhibits a multitude of dimensions and defies simplistic definition. We hope that this anthology helps to convey the richness of simplicity, and perhaps even goes some way to unravelling its defining paradox – the paradox that less can be more.

While materialistic values have always been present and usually dominant in the evolution of human civilisations, so too have there always been brave souls and counter-cultures that have rejected those values in favour of less materialistic, 'simpler' ways of living. The purpose of this anthology is to review those diverse examples – those pioneers of the deep future. The early chapters of this book include discussions of momentous figures such as Buddha, Diogenes, Aristotle, Epicurus, and Jesus, while movements and cultures such as the Stoics, the Quakers, and the Amish are also reviewed. The middle chapters include discussions of such figures as Henry Thoreau, John Ruskin, William Morris, Gandhi, and Helen and Scott Nearing, as well as movements related to agrarianism, voluntary simplicity, and radical homemaking. The later chapters take a look at other contemporary expressions of simple living, including those based on notions of permaculture, intentional communities, degrowth, and transition towns. The anthology closes with a discussion of 'mindfulness', which is perhaps the one element common to all manifestations of simple living – and perhaps the most challenging element too.

This book reviews these great moments in the history of simple living, and many more, but again it only looks backwards in order to shed light on the present and the future. We were motivated to publish this book because of our belief that a sustainable, just, and flourishing society is one that learns many of the lessons of simplicity and adapts them to our times. Little else needs to be said by way of introduction, because the following *FOREWORD* by David Shi – the pre-eminent historian of simplicity – eloquently provides some more intimate context to this anthology. We will simply conclude with the following remarks.

Our civilisation has experimented with a particular relationship to the material world – and it is always good to experiment with life. But the consumerist experiment turned out to be a dead end. We should not feel obliged to continue down this path any further, and should instead imagine and undertake new experiments in living, explore different paths into the future, before darker alternatives are imposed upon us. As Henry Thoreau fairly insisted, 'there are as many ways [to live] as there are radii from one centre', and the choices made by previous generations need not bind us today. Let us think for ourselves, then, and be brave enough to create our own fate. That is the urgent task that confronts us today, the task of creating something new, as we find ourselves swept along by the currents of a destructive, industrial civilisation. With that creative task in mind – which is a task both of opposition and renewal – may the following stories of simplicity inspire you as they have inspired us.

FOREWORD

DAVID SHI

The simple life is almost as hard to define as it is to live. It has also been with us for thousands of years. Simplicity is an ancient and universal ideal. Most of the world's great religions and philosophies have advocated some form of simple living that elevates activities of the mind and spirit over material desires and activities. The great spiritual teachers of Asia – Zarathustra, Buddha, Lao-Tzu, and Confucius – all stressed that material self-control was essential to the good life. Greek and Roman philosophers also preached the virtues of the golden mean. Socrates was among the first to argue that ideas should take priority over things in the calculus of life. People were 'to be esteemed for their virtue, not their wealth', he insisted. 'Fine and rich clothes are suited for comedians. The wicked live to eat; the good eat to live.'

Aristotle refined this classical concept of leading a carefully balanced life of material moderation and intellectual exertion. 'The man who indulges in every pleasure and abstains from none', he observed, 'becomes self-indulgent, while the man who shuns every pleasure, as boors do, becomes in a way insensible; temperance and courage, then, are destroyed by excess and defect, and preserved by the [golden] mean'.

A similar theme of simple living coupled with spiritual devotion runs through the Old Testament, from the living habits of tent dwellers in Abraham's time to the strictures of the prophets against the evils of luxury. 'Give me neither poverty nor wealth but only enough', prayed the author of Proverbs. Jesus of Nazareth led and preached such a life of pious simplicity. He repeatedly warned of the 'deceitfulness of riches' and the corrupting effects of luxury, noting that gaining wealth too easily led to hardness of heart toward one's fellows and deadness of heart toward God.

Simplicity has been an especially salient theme in Western literature. Chaucer repeatedly reminded readers of Jesus's life of voluntary simplicity. Boccaccio took cheer in an open-air search for the spontaneous; Dante called upon his readers to 'see the king of the simple life'; and Shakespeare offered the happiness of the greenwood tree. The Romantics of the eighteenth and nineteenth centuries likewise promoted a simplicity modelled after the serene workings of nature.

So much for simplicity as an historical ideal. In practice, the simple life has proven far more complex, varied, and challenging than such summary descriptions imply. The necessarily ambiguous quality of a philosophy of living that does not specify exactly how 'simple' one's mode of living should be has produced many different practices, several of which have conflicted with one another. The same self-denying impulse that has motivated some to engage in temperate frugality has led others to adopt ascetic or primitive ways of living. During the classical period, for instance, there were many types of simplicity, including the affluent temperance of the Stoics – Cicero, Seneca, and Marcus Aurelius, the more modest 'golden mean' of Socrates, Plato, and Aristotle, the ascetic primitivism of Diogenes, and the pastoral simplicity of Virgil and Horace. In asserting the superiority of spiritual over worldly concerns, some early Christians gave away all of their possessions and went to live in the desert as hermits. Others joined monasteries, and a few engaged in prolonged stints of abstinence and mortification. At the same time, many officials of the early church preached simplicity while themselves living in considerable comfort and even luxury.

Over the centuries, simplicity has also been embraced as a stylish fad. Benjamin Franklin's self-conscious decision to wear an old fur cap and portray himself as a plain Quaker while serving as an American diplomat in Paris reflected his shrewd awareness that rustic simplicity had become quite fashionable among the French ruling class. Marie Antoinette's famous playground, Hameau, constructed on the grounds of Versailles, was a monument of extravagant simplicity. The toy village had its own thatched cottages, a dairy barn with perfumed Swiss cows, and a picturesque water mill. When the lavish life at court grew tiresome, the Queen could adjourn to Hameau, don peasant garb, and enjoy the therapeutic effects of milking cows and churning butter.

For such bored aristocrats, simplicity was clearly an affectation. But there have been many through the years who have practised simplicity rather than played at it. The names of St. Francis, William Blake, John Wesley, Leo Tolstoy, Mahatma Gandhi, and Mother Teresa come readily to mind. For them and others, simplicity entailed what William Wordsworth called 'plain living and high thinking'. The degree of plainness differed considerably from individual to individual, as did the nature of the 'high thinking'. They simplified their material activities in order to engage in a variety of enriching pursuits: philosophy, spiritual devotion, artistic creation, revolutionary politics, humanitarian service, or ecological activism.

In the Western experience, this ethic of plain living and high thinking has demonstrated similar diversity. As a way station between too little and too much, the ethic has encompassed a wide spectrum of motives and behaviour, a spectrum bounded on one end by religious asceticism and on the other by refined gentility. In between there is much room for individual expression. Some proponents of simplicity have been quite conservative in appealing to traditional religious values and or classical notions of republican virtue; others have been liberal or radical in their assault on corporate capitalism and its ethos of compulsive consumerism. In addition, class biases, individual personality traits, and historical circumstances have also combined to produce many differing versions of simple living in the Western experience.

The American history of simplicity has been a festival of irony, for the ideal of enlightened restraint has always been linked in an awkward embrace with the nation's phenomenal abundance and relentless work ethic. Since the colonial era, advocates of simple living have been professing a way of life at odds with an American environment full of bountiful resources, entrepreneurial opportunities, and increasingly powerful institutions that combine to exalt the glories of self-indulgence and war against contentment. Puritan and Quaker settlers who arrived in America during the seventeenth and eighteenth centuries brought with them a delicately balanced social ethic stressing hard work, self-control, plain living, civic virtue, and spiritual devotion.

Their goal was to create model societies in which simplicity of worship, dress, manners, and speech would be practised and enforced. Yet in both Puritan Massachusetts and Quaker Pennsylvania, the champions of collective simplicity soon found themselves waging a losing battle against the corrupting influence of rapid population growth, religious pluralism, and secular materialism. In 1733, for instance, a Boston minister bemoaned his colony's fall from grace when he said in a sermon that 'the powerful love of the world and exorbitant reach after riches have become the reigning temper in all persons of all ranks in our land'. Their original spiritual and social ideal was being 'abandoned, slighted and forgotten'.

The lesson in both Massachusetts and Pennsylvania seemed to be that pious simplicity as a *societal* ethic was impossible to sustain in the midst of unprecedented opportunities for economic gain and social display. Certainly that was the assumption of the many pietistic sects that settled in America in the eighteenth century and after. The so-called 'plain people' – Mennonites, Amish, Dunkers, Brethren in Christ, Moravians, Shakers, and others – shared a strong commitment to communal simplicity and a strict nonconformity to the ways of the larger world.

These various religious groups set themselves apart from mainstream society by establishing small, isolated, homo-geneous, and self-sustaining rural communities. Through mutual aid, intensive agriculture, thrift, and diligence, their settlements prospered. Some verged on asceticism, practising celibacy and renunciation of sensual and material pleasures;

others allowed cohabitation and a comfortable sufficiency. All of them, however, insisted upon the priorities of faith and family and community. In other words, these religious non-conformists required social conformity.

American history is strewn with dozens of communal efforts at simple living, ranging from the Transcendentalist utopias at Fruitlands and Brook Farm in the 1840s to the hippie communes of the 1960s and 1970s. Few of them, however, lasted more than a few months. Many of the participants in such alternative communities were naive about the hardships involved and lacked experience in the basic skills necessary for self-reliant living.

Yet the history of the simple life in the United States, as in the wider Western world, includes victories as well as defeats. That many of the 'plain people' have managed to retain much of their initial ethic testifies to their spiritual strength and social discipline. There have also been many successful and inspiring individual practitioners of simple living. As a guide for personal living and as a myth of national purpose, simplicity has thus displayed remarkable resiliency. It can be a living creed rather than a hollow sentiment or temporary expedient. During periods of war, depression, or social crisis, statesmen, ministers, and reformers have invoked the merits of simplicity to help revitalise public virtue, self-restraint, and mutual aid. In this way simplicity continues to exert a powerful influence on the nation's conscience.

The ideal of simplicity, however ambiguous, however fitfully realised, survives because it speaks to desires and virtues harboured by all people. Who has not yearned for simplicity, for a reduction of the complexities and encumbrances of life? In the American experience, for example, the simple life remains particularly enticing because it reminds us of what so many of our founding mothers and fathers hoped the country would become – a nation of practical dreamers devoted to spiritual and civic purposes, a 'city upon a hill', a beacon to the rest of the world.

Today, simplicity remains what it has always been: an animating vision of moral purpose that nourishes ethically sensitive imaginations. It offers people a way to recover personal autonomy and transcendent purposes by stripping away faulty desires and extraneous activities and possessions. For simplicity to experience continued vitality, its advocates must learn from the mistakes of the past. Proponents of simplicity have often been naively sentimental about the quality of life in olden times, narrowly anti-urban in outlook, and disdainful of the beneficial effects of prosperity and technology. After all, most of the 'high thinking' of this century has been facilitated by prosperity. The expansion of universities and libraries, the democratisation of the fine arts, and the ever-widening impact of philanthropic organisations – all of these developments have been supported by the rising pool of national wealth. This is no mean achievement. 'A creative economy', Emerson once wrote, can be 'the fuel of magnificence'.

Any virtue pressed too far can become counter-productive. Some simplifiers, for example, have pursued a fanatical survivalism; others have displayed a self-righteous, prickly individualism that has alienated potential supporters and impeded attempts at collective social or political action. Still others have adopted an affluent rusticity that seems more style than substance. Showy plainness is the red spider in the rose of simple living.

Americans, like their counterparts across the western world, have repeatedly espoused the merits of simple living, only to become enmeshed in its opposite. People have found it devilishly hard to limit their desires to their needs so as to devote most of their attention to 'higher' activities. This should not surprise us. Socrates pointed out centuries ago that 'many people will not be satisfied with the simpler way of life. They will be for adding sofas, and tables, and other furniture; also dainties, and perfumes, and incense, and courtesans and cakes'. He knew that all notions of moral excellence and spiritual commitment are by their very nature the province of a minority, since few can live up to their dictates for long. Thoreau likewise noted that simplicity was for the few rather than for the many. He recognised at the beginning of *Walden* that the simple life he described would have little appeal to 'those who find their encouragement and inspiration in precisely the present condition of things, and cherish it with the fondness and enthusiasm of lovers'. Many Americans have not wanted to lead simple lives, and not wanting simplicity is the best reason for not doing so. 'Simplicity', observed the Quaker reformer Richard Gregg, 'seems to be a foible of saints and occasional geniuses, but not something for the rest of us'.

Happily, most modern versions of simplicity demand neither an end to economic development nor a vow of personal poverty. If the decision to lead a simple life is fundamentally a personal matter, then so, too, is the nature and degree of simplification. There is no cosmic guidebook or universal formula to follow. Simplicity in its essence demands neither a vow of poverty nor a life of rural homesteading. Money or possessions or activities in themselves do not corrupt simplicity, but the love of money, the craving of possessions, the lure of conformity, and the prison of activities do.

As an ethic of self-conscious material moderation rather than radical renunciation, simplicity can be practised in cities and suburbs, townhouses and condominiums. It requires neither a log cabin nor a hairshirt but a deliberate ordering of priorities so as to distinguish daily between the necessary and superfluous, the useful and wasteful, the beautiful and vulgar. Wisdom, the philosopher William James once remarked, is knowing what to overlook. Mastering the fine art of simple living involves discovering the difference between personal trappings and personal traps. In this sense, simplicity is ultimately a state of mind, a well-ordered inner harmony among the material, sensual, and ideal, rather than a particular standard of living.

But is simplicity relevant to the complex corporate and consumer cultures that dominate modern life? Absolutely. Hidden beneath the surface appeal of life in the fast lane is the disturbing fact that the three most frequently prescribed drugs are an ulcer medication, a hypertension reliever, and a tranquiliser. In the United States, stress management has become one of the fastest growing industries. A hospital administrator recently observed that 'our mode of life itself, the way we live, is emerging as today's principal cause of illness'.

Today the typical corporate executive works three hours longer each week than in 1980, and he or she takes 20 percent fewer vacation days. In a special issue devoted to what it called 'The Rat Race', *Time* magazine announced that the work ethic has gone berserk in America. 'Simply to remain competitive', the editors noted, 'professionals – lawyers, doctors, accountants, and business executives – find that their lives are one long, continuous workday, bleeding into the wee hours of the night and squeezing out any leisure time or family interaction'.

For people living in a press of anxieties, straining desperately, often miserably after *more* money, *more* things, and *more* status, only to wonder in troubled moments how to get off such a treadmill, the rich tradition of simplicity still offers an enticing path to a better life. Those hesitant to change the trajectory of their runaway lifestyles might ponder a question posed by the poet Adrienne Rich: 'With whom do you believe your lot is cast? From where does your strength come?'

Those who choose an outwardly more simple and inwardly more fulfilling style of living discover that pressures are reduced, the frenetic pace of life is slowed, and daily epiphanies are better appreciated. Simpler living also benefits us all by reducing demands on our increasingly fragile and besieged environment. In addition, winnowing one's money-making and money-spending activities can provide more opportunities for activities of intrinsic worth – family, faith, civic and social service, aesthetic creativity, and self-culture. The saintly naturalist John Burroughs acknowledged this fact in 1911 when the superintendent of the New York City schools asked him to share with students the secret of his good life. 'With me,' he remarked,

> the secret of my youth [at age seventy-four] is the simple life – simple food, sound sleep, the open air, daily work, kind thoughts, love of nature, and joy and contentment in the world in which I live. ... I have had a happy life. ... May you all do the same.

CHAPTER ONE

BUDDHA

PETER DORAN

The historical figure, Siddhartha Gotama, probably lived and taught between the years 563 and 483 BCE in the foothills of the Himalayas. The iconic story of his birth into an economically and politically influential family in the village of Kapilavatthu and, at the age of 29, the tale of his subsequent renunciation of this relatively comfortable material existence in favour of the holy life of the wandering ascetic living on alms (*bhikkus*), has echoed down the centuries. The story has a special resonance in our own age because Siddhartha's quest – in common with other prophetic figures that would emerge across the world during the pivotal or Axial Age (800–200 BCE) (Armstrong, 2001) – was sparked by a restlessness and disillusion with received convention and tradition. Change was in the air.

Siddhartha's response to his time and place – marked by considerable social disruption – was characterised by a courageous and strikingly modern response to the stark realities and fleeting nature of our lives on earth. In a discourse to the people of Kalama who had become confused by conflicting doctrines and teachings, Siddhartha advised that it is proper to doubt, to be uncertain and to refuse to act on that which has merely been repeated or presented as tradition, even if it is offered as a sacred teaching (Batchelor, 2010: 98-99).

In the course of several centuries, the Axial period marked a decisive shift in collective human consciousness (of itself and of the world), with figures such as Confucius and Lao-Tzu, Zoroaster, Socrates and Plato, emerging within their own distinct worldviews to launch transformations in thought and understanding. The great thinkers of the Axial period shared a sense of a world gone awry and set about interrogating inherited truths, often turning inwards to uncover beauty, order and a new horizon of meaning.

It is useful to recall that recorded history only begins around 3,000 BCE. Siddhartha and the other great thinkers of the Axial period represent an important moment in the register of human consciousness itself – a formative moment when humankind began to articulate in a new way what had, up to then, been a dim memory of our long passage out of the Paleolithic era. In crossing this threshold of self-consciousness our species encountered finitude – most fundamentally, the reality of death and the passage of time. It has been suggested that it is precisely from this emergence into self-conscious knowledge and an awareness of time – both associated with our unique human predicament and a deep restlessness rooted in chronic insecurity – that we derive our myths of 'the Fall'. Loren Eiseley puts it rather beautifully: 'The story of Eden is a greater allegory than man has ever guessed.' For what was lost was the blissful ignorance of the natural animal that walks 'memoryless through bars of sunlight and shade in the morning of the world' (Eiseley, cited in Oelschlaeger, 1991: 333).

Siddhartha formed a desire to liberate himself from the transient life of the passions, attachments and delusions. He became convinced that it was possible in the midst of this predicament we call 'life' to experience a cessation of the sources of delusion and unhappiness, and pursue that which is free from ageing, death, sorrow, corruption and con-ditioning. And part of his solution was to retrace our steps to the still point of the 'beginner's mind' (Suzuki, 2001) that, in some respects, draws on the pre-conceptual experience (the 'first mind') of immediacy with wilderness (before 'the Fall' into consciousness of time).

We have entered the age of the Anthropocene – a new *turning point* in the history of humanity, in the ongoing story of creation and, in all probability, a turning point in human consciousness. Today we are confronted by the unprecedented extent to which our human technologies, institutions and collective imaginaries have emerged during the course of the past 500 years as the most decisive influences on the fate of our planetary home and the atmosphere. Our ecological crisis is above all a provocation to return to our own fractured narrative of *human-nature*.

Siddhartha's story is received today as a universal parable of a young man driven by a deep insight into the transient nature of life and its comforts, and a determination to embody a liberating path beyond the suffering associated with our human predicaments. It is an ancient story that prefigures an emerging *collective* narrative or imaginary around wellbeing and social change in our own time – one that points to a contemporary sense of our psychic exhaustion and disillusion with the surface features of modern lifestyles and institutions that are increasingly mediated by a political economy of hubris, celebrity, and habit formation – an economy of spectacle that underpins today's global circuits of production and consumption.

Little is known about the precise circumstances of Siddhartha's decision to abandon his home life and his family. What we can surmise is that at the point of his departure his existential dilemma – his conviction that an attachment to things and people bound him to an existence that seemed mired in pain and sorrow – was not dissimilar to the experience of many of his contemporaries who opted for the life of a forest monk. What is distinctive and resonant in the Buddha's life is his eventual response to the questions posed by the transience of life and its passing comforts: an ultimate rejection of the extremes of asceticism in favour of a 'Middle Way' dedicated to finally making peace – even falling into joy – with this fragile, all too brief sojourn on earth.

The Buddha referred to an unsettling characteristic of life as '*dukkha*', which is the Sanskrit term that refers to a 'wheel with an off-centre axle hole'. In stating that all things are marked by *dukkha*, the Buddha was simply observing that life can often be experienced as something that is out of kilter, always jolting or troubling us, always insisting on our attention. It is in this sense that Buddha framed his core teaching around acknowledgement and acceptance of suffering as the initial path to its cessation and the cultivation of wellbeing, in his *Four Noble Truths*.

To summarise the teachings of the awakened Buddha I will draw on the work of the Vietnamese Zen Master, Thich Nhat Hanh, who has done so much through his scholarship, poetry, teaching and work for non-violence since the Vietnam War, to translate the insights of the Buddha into a Western idiom. Today, his non-violent orientation to the world extends to a deep engagement with the underlying conditions of ecological collapse, and a translation of Vietnamese Zen Buddhist insights into a call for mindful care of the self as a foundational practice for ecological sustainability and a global ethic.

Nhat Hanh tells a story that is popular in Zen circles about a man and a horse. The horse is galloping quickly, and it appears that the man on the horse is going somewhere important. Another man, standing on the roadside, shouts, 'Where are you going?' and the first replies, 'I don't know! Ask the horse.' The story is about the human condition: the horse is habit energy pulling us along, and the rider is 'us', restless, always in a hurry, not quite sure where we are going, often at war with ourselves, and all too prone to falling into conflict with others.

This is why Buddhist meditation has two key aspects: shamatha ('stopping') and vipashyana ('looking deeply'). Meditation begins with the art of stopping – interrupting our thinking, habit energies, forgetfulness, and strong emotions that rush through us like a constant storm. The energy of mindfulness is cultivated to enable the meditator to recognise, be present to and transform these energies. The second function of shamatha is to calm the emotions by following the breath, and the third is resting.

As noted, the Buddha's teaching confronts our human condition. Part art, part science, the Buddha's approach is full of paradox: the first of his Four Noble Truths is 'dukkha', often translated as 'suffering' but literally referring to that dimension of human experience that is 'hard to face'. The word 'dukkha' is a compound of 'duh' which means 'difficulty', and 'kha' which can refer to the hole at the centre of a wheel into which an axle fits. So the word dukkha can mean a poorly fitting axle, something out of place, awry, or at odds with itself.

Mark Epstein (2013: 28) compares the observational posture of Buddhist meditation or 'bare attention' without reactivity (not clinging to what is pleasant and not rejecting what is unpleasant) to the quality of presence that a mother brings to a child:

> One of the central paradoxes of Buddhism is that the bare attention of the meditative mind changes the psyche by not trying to change anything at all. The steady application of the meditative posture, like the steadiness of an attuned parent, allows something inherent in the mind's potential to emerge, and it emerges naturally if left alone properly in a good enough way.

In his *Fire Sermon*, the Buddha used the metaphorical image of fire to describe the ubiquity of trauma in our lives: everyday life is on fire not only because of its fleeting nature but also because of how ardently people cling to greed, anger and egocentric preoccupations. He counselled that we are all feeding the flames of these metaphorical fires (also known as greed, hatred and delusion) motivated by our insecure place in the world, by the deep and felt experience of dukkha, of not fitting in. For the Buddha, the fires are defences against acknowledging *things as they are*, instinctive attempts at protecting ourselves from what feels like an impossible situation. It is from this imagery that we get the word Nirvana, from the Sanskrit 'cease to burn' or 'blow out'.

In Buddhist terms envisioning a model of 'simple living' is inseparable from the invitation to cultivate a deep transformation in our individual and collective orientation to the 'self' and to 'the world', and the embrace of a new or deeper materialism that implies a new intimacy, care and compassion. Buddha's core teachings point to practices that give us access to a mode of simple living that gives expression to an experience of liberation: a release from suffering, a discovery of wellbeing, and a restored intimacy with *all* things. Let us return now briefly to the Buddha's systematic teaching on liberation from suffering: *The Four Noble Truths*, and *The Noble Eightfold Path*. The Four Noble Truths are:

Suffering
Arising of Suffering
Cessation of Suffering (wellbeing)
How wellbeing arises

The passage from the naming and recognition of suffering through to a realisation of wellbeing is signposted by a series of teachings called the *Twelve Turnings of the Wheel of the Dharma* (teaching on what is). For each of the Four Noble Truths there are three stages: Recognition, Encouragement and Realisation.

This passage or pedagogical journey commences with the first Noble Truth: Suffering. The first turning, called 'Recognition' refers to a universal recognition that suffering – whether it is physical, physiological or psychological – is a companion of our life. The second turning is 'Encouragement' derived from recognition and looking deeply – with compassion, non-judgement and kindness – in order to understand the causes and conditions of suffering. The third turning is 'Realisation', marking the point of understanding.

The Second Noble Truth of 'Arising Suffering' commences with 'Recognition' of our tendency to increase our suffering through our initial reactive responses, whether these are words, thoughts or deeds. At this point in the process, attention is given to those elements or 'nutriments' that have helped feed our suffering. The Buddha identified four kinds of nutriments that can lead to our happiness or our suffering:

Edible food
Sense impressions
Intentions
Consciousness

The first one, 'Edible food' is familiar. The Buddhist teaching is that we must learn to distinguish between what is healthful and what is harmful, and practise *Right View* when we shop, cook and eat so that we preserve the wellbeing of our body, mind and planet. This entails looking deeply to see how our food is grown and processed, so that we eat in ways that preserve our collective wellbeing, minimise our own suffering and that of other species, and allow the earth to replenish itself. The second nutriment that demands our attention is 'Sense impressions'. In Buddhism the mind is regarded as one of the senses so we have to consider six realms of contact with sense objects, including media, advertising, movies, TV, social media and video games. Mindful approaches to these stimuli can protect aspects of our consciousness from unwholesome sense objects with the potential to feed our cravings, violence, fear and despair.

The third nutriment is 'Intention' or volition, also described as the will. In Buddhism, volition is considered the ground of all our actions. It is in this arena where mindfulness and bare attention can interrupt the energy driving us towards certain apparent satisfiers or promises of fulfilment in accumulation, status, revenge, possessions. Thich Nhat Hanh (1998: 35) writes:

> We need to cultivate the wish to be free of these things so we can enjoy the wonders of life that are always available – the blue sky, the trees, our beautiful children. After three months or six months of mindful sitting, mindful walking, and mindful looking, a deep vision of reality arises in us, and the capacity of being there, enjoying life in the present moment, liberates us from all impulses and brings us real happiness.

The fourth nutriment is 'Consciousness'. In Buddhism this is sometimes described as the 'seeds' sown by our past actions and the past actions of our family and society. These seeds can take the form of thoughts, words and actions that flow into the sea of our consciousness and create our body, mind and ultimately our world. There's an old saying, 'You are what you eat'. In Buddhism this applies equally, if not more so, to everything – every seed – that we allow to feed our consciousness. In a world where we are invited to export our attention – around the clock – to social media, 24-hour news cycles, advertising, and TV – the invitation to cultivate bare attention has never been more challenging and timely.

The Third Noble Truth encompasses a very popular concept in contemporary policy and news circles: wellbeing. The movement from realising the possibility of wellbeing to its actual realisation is a movement from transforming (not running away from) suffering, acknowledging its imperm-anence, and reaching out to touch those things that bring peace and joy: discovering that the true miracle is to walk on the earth! This is a stage that, above all, demands an alignment of mindfulness and *practice* or embodied realisation.

The Fourth Noble Truth is the path out of suffering towards wellbeing. It commences with a recognition of the *Eightfold Path* or practice manual which sets out those elements of learning, reflection and practice. The elements of the *Eightfold Path* are more than guidelines or ethical imperatives but describe the aspects of embodied practice (centred on the individual practitioner's own life experience) and behaviours sustained by a regular mindfulness practice:

Right View: The capacity for deep understanding and 'waking up' especially to the errors that accompany our experience of subjectivity and perception;

Right Thinking: Entails an alignment of mind and body, using the breath; interrupting fear-based thinking that leads to further suffering;

Right Speech: Closely related to Deep Listening with compassion and silence, Right Speech is truthful and aligned with the ends of social justice and non-exploitation;

Right Action: The basis of Right Action is mindfulness and the practice of non-violence towards self and others;

Right Livelihood: To practise Right Livelihood is to earn a living without transgressing the Buddhist ideals of love, compassion and non-violence;

Right Diligence: Nourished by joy and interest, Right Diligence lies in the 'Middle Way' – it is neither to be found in the extremes of austerity nor in sensual indulgence; it is associated with joy, ease and even humour;

Right Mindfulness: The Chinese character for mindfulness or 'remembering' is made up of two parts: 'now' and 'mind/heart'. Mindfulness is to be fully present and able to touch deeply what lies before us, with a 'beginner's mind' on the first morning of creation;

Right Concentration: Living each moment deeply sustains concentration, and this gives rise to insight.

The Buddha's narrative and teaching have been transmitted across many cultures over the centuries and are always – in effect – in translation. The generic idea of the 'buddha' incorporates awakening and teaching for a given time or era. In our own times, our conditions of life are giving rise to a sense of exhaustion that is both external (in terms of ecological stress, pollution, and our alienation from nature) and internal (in terms of the 'social recession' or pathologies associated with inequality and the colonisation of the life world by commercial and neoliberal logic). Out of this exhaustion – compounded by the onslaught of corporate-sponsored demands on our attention, there is a palpable demand for new forms of intimacy: the Sanskrit word for yoga is 'intimacy'. Yoga and mindfulness can be described as practices of intimacy, practices of becoming more intimately connected with our moment to moment physical experience, a radical act of paying attention.

For the Buddhist, living simply is simply living out a radical form of non-violence, a radical act of taking responsibility, for the moment-to-moment arising of all conditions. Caring for the self and caring for the world go hand in hand because, for the Buddhist practitioner, the quality and compassionate content of relationships (including our relations with the 'self', 'others', and the 'world') are always prior to the conditions and 'things' to which they give rise. Simple living can be an act of radical responsibility.

References

Armstrong, Karen. 2001. *Buddha*. New York: Penguin.

Batchelor, Stephen. 2010. *Confession of a Buddhist Atheist*. New York: Spiegel & Grau.

Eiseley, Loren. 1957. The *Immense Journey: An Imaginative Naturalist Explores the Mysteries of Man and Nature*. Random House: London.

Epstein, Mark. 2013. *The Trauma of Everyday Life*. Penguin Press: New York.

Nhat Hanh, Thich. 1998. *The Heart of the Buddha's Teaching*. Broadway Books: New York.

Oelschlaeger, Max. 1991. *The Idea of Wilderness*. Yale University Press: New Haven.

Suzuki, Shunryu. 2001. *Zen Mind, Beginner's Mind*. Weatherhill: New York.

CHAPTER TWO

DIOGENES

WILLIAM DESMOND

What is known or surmised about the life of Diogenes the Cynic can be quickly told. He was born around 400 BCE as a citizen of the Greek city of Sinope on the Black Sea. His father was an official in the mint but when he was accused of defacing the coinage – an act with potentially treacherous connotations – he and Diogenes fled. Diogenes came to mainland Greece where he consulted the Delphic Oracle and was told that to adapt to his new status as an exile and immigrant, he should 'deface the coin of custom' (*paracharattein to nomisma*). His interpretation of this riddle would make him into one of the great counter-cultural figures of the ancient Greek world as he relentlessly criticised the artificiality of many Greek customs, particularly in the large commercial cities of Corinth and Athens.

Diogenes was a near contemporary of such accomplished figures as Plato, Aristotle, Demosthenes and Alexander the Great. When he died around 323 BCE, he did not leave a world-empire or an *oeuvre* of complex philosophical and scientific work, yet he would remain famous in later antiquity and on into the medieval and modern period – for his wit, satire, and the startling simplicity of his lifestyle. He was possibly the first real ascetic in Greek history, and the austerity that he bequeathed to his followers would eventually become a prototype for Zeno and later Stoics, for Christian hermits, monks and friars (perhaps even for Jesus,

11

according to one school of thought), as well as for modern philosophers like Rousseau and Nietzsche.

In interpreting the Delphic Oracle, criticising Greek customs and demanding that people live 'according to nature', Diogenes embraced utter simplicity in his housing, diet, occupation, social relations and even style of speech. He took up residence free of charge wherever was most convenient and available – in temple porticoes, gymnasia, public baths, in the open air, or most famously, in a 'barrel' or 'tub', or to be more precise, a *pithos*, a large earthenware jar so commonly used by the ancients to store grains or liquids. With such a *pithos*-home, Diogenes had no mortgage, no rent, no worries, and by similar logic, he was known for being content with the minimum of clothing: no shoes, a single cloak for both summer and winter, a wanderer's staff and travelling bag for his frequent migrations. It was said that he initially carried a cup also, but when he saw a young boy bending to drink from the river with his mouth or cupped hands, he threw away the cup as so much extra luggage. Thus in paring life down to the necessary minimum, Diogenes criticised his contemporaries for hankering after land, houses, clothing, jewellery, gold, Tyrian purple and other luxuries. Such a love of things enslaves one to many masters: the money-lender, landlord, tax-collector, thief, chance and time itself continually threaten one's possessions and set one scurrying to guard one's hoard. Worse are the loan sharks, unscrupulous traders, money-changers, and tyrants, in whom the profit motive becomes particularly harmful. In criticising the corrosive effect of the narrow pursuit of wealth, Diogenes is reported to have said 'the love of money is the mother-city of all evil' – a generalisation which may well be the inspiration of the famous New Testament phrase. By contrast, Diogenes argued, a perfect indifference to wealth is the root of all virtue and happiness. Voluntary poverty and detachment alone allow one to find one's proper centre again and be truly free.

An even more basic need than shelter and clothing is food, and here too Diogenes pursued the utmost simplicity. From the scattered anecdotes told about him (especially in Diogenes Laertius' *Life*), one can construct a picture of a wanderer who tried to live as free as the birds of the air, surviving from day to day, even from meal to meal, sometimes begging, sometimes winning hand-outs or dinner invitations from amused hosts, sometimes foraging for wild plants. His diet was said to have consisted of simple foods – lentils, beans, figs, olives, lettuce, garlic, thyme as well as barley or wheat bread – and he is often depicted gathering the vegetables or herbs himself by the roadside or in the country. In judging this picture, some would emphasise those stories in which Diogenes begs sustenance of others and so becomes reliant, despite all his protestations, on the complexities of farming, markets, and trade within the Greek cities. This may very well be true, but a more generous reader might reflect that the ancient Greek landscape was less polluted and deforested than its modern counterpart. The countryside marched right up to the borders of even the biggest Greek cities and the fantastic richness of past ecosystems may well make more credible the many anecdotes which make Diogenes into a kind of nomadic grazer, who was able to survive partly or largely on what he gathered himself.

In any case, the trope that he would bequeath to later Cynics was that Nature always provides enough for her children – provided they are content with what they are given. Animals are wisely content with what they need, but it is the peculiar human animal who in his greed and pride transcends those limits, seeks out artificial stimulants, takes more than his share, and calls it 'honour' or 'merit' if he can to eat to excess while his neighbour starves. Diogenes seems not to have himself been a doctrinaire vegetarian or tee-totaler: he would enjoy meat, wine, honey-cakes or anything else if it happened to be at hand. But he preferred freedom to luxuries, and so preferred to drink free water rather than have to work, or pander, to get wine. He probably disapproved of cooking in principle, because it involves fire. Fire is the first technology that makes possible all others, including the working of metals like gold and iron – thus allowing for coined money, social inequality, slavery, and implements of war. In this dubious 'progress' of civilisation, fire also makes possible the rise of the professional cook, at whose hands many eat their way to self-indulgence, obesity and ill-health.

If such are some of the ideas that one can glean from the record of Diogenes the Cynic, it might seem that he was a puritanical kill-joy. In fact the very opposite seems to have been the case, and the anecdotes told about him have struck readers of many periods with their sense of antic fun and the ridiculous. For example, when Diogenes found a honey-cake among his olives, he threw it away with imperial hauteur, crying 'Out of the presence of the tyrant!' Or when all Corinth was in an uproar preparing for the next war, Diogenes too jumped up also so as to appear to be doing something and started to roll his *pithos* up and down a hill – thus ludicrously showing the Sisyphean folly of war. On another occasion, he met Dionysius who had been deposed as tyrant of Syracuse and was now living a meagre life in Corinth, no longer burdened by affairs of state and fear of assassination, and spending his time milling about town. Diogenes said to him 'O Dionysius, how little you deserve your present life!' Dionysius thanked him for his condolences, to which Diogenes launched forth:

> 'Condole with you!? Do you not suppose that, on the contrary, I am indignant that such a slave as you – who, if you had your due, should have been let alone to grow old, and die in the state of tyranny, as your father did before you – that you should now enjoy the ease of private persons, and sport and luxuriate here in our society?' (Plutarch, *Life of Timoleon* 15.7-10).

More famous is the story of how Diogenes went one day into the crowded market-place at noon, with a lighted lamp, looking for a 'just man': the lighted lamp suggested that he would not find one *there*.

Such anecdotes surely reflect how Diogenes' voluntary poverty, his indifference to wealth, status, honour and power, all afforded him the greater 'wealth' of time, which in turn allowed him to become one of the most famous wits of Greek and Roman antiquity. Wandering about the Greek cities, studying their various happenings, observing, cajoling and lampooning passers-by, Diogenes was able to hone his repartee to a fearful degree. Here one might say that Diogenes simplified his life so as to gain the leisure to think and speak freely. In his love of talk, he was quintessentially Greek: from Homer to Heraclitus, from Socrates to St John, Greek speakers of all periods worshipped speeches, good conversation and the *logos*. Talk is free yet good talk is one of the most significant sources of joy and enlightenment.

Spontaneity can wither away, however, before the relentless tyranny of customs, work, and overly complex social relations, and so Diogenes seems to have avoided all unnecessary complications. He had friends and 'disciplines' and can hardly be called misanthropic or antisocial, but he avoided marriage and had no children. He did not work, or if he did, it may have been like certain later Cynics who did temporary tasks to meet their basic daily needs, but there were no long days in the fields or on the work-bench, toiling extra to maintain land, house, family, pawn-brokers, political master, standing armies and other idle classes, or any personal addictions or expensive hobbies. Diogenes did not own slaves, and probably criticised slavery as a custom that degrades the master, for the master who relies on another's labour is not free. After his exile, he remained a stateless person and did not enjoy the rights of citizenship in any city, famously declaring: 'I am a citizen of the cosmos'. At the same time, he was unburdened by any of its complex responsibilities – deliberating, voting, serving on juries, fighting in battle.

Thus a radical detachment from social belonging as well as material things was the price of Diogenes' freedom, and his message of radical simplicity was a bitter pill for most of his contemporaries. The toughness of Diogenes' lifestyle somewhat shocked his fellow Greeks and we too may not want to follow him in throwing away all our 'cups'. In years to come, of course, the looming ecological crisis and population of ever growing billions may well force us to lower standards of living. But for now, at least in the developed world, a Cynic's austerity may not be as necessary for us as Diogenes felt it was in his time. In many ways technology and complex social organisation have made our lives *simpler* than ever: far fewer man-hours are needed now for building a house, ploughing a field, washing clothes, travelling or for making such intricate tools as a plough or a ship. The burdens that Diogenes shied away from are or should be less burdensome to us, simply because machines, when used wisely, can do much of the heavy labour. With control and power, appropriate technology actually affords greater freedom and leisure than was ever dreamed possible by a Plato or Aristotle.

Yet it may take a Diogenes to remind us that such freedom and leisure are the goals for which so many past generations struggled. Unfortunately, it seems to me at least we are in danger of ignoring or forgetting such basic truths. Certainly we hear little from our decision-makers about how all our labour-saving devices will save us from 60-hour weeks or 30-year mortgages, or how ever more efficient technical and social organisation could allow more people to develop their interests and talents more freely. At present, it would seem as if the euphoria surrounding technology threatens to become all consuming, as the drive mounts to digitize lives and relationships. And after e-friendships, e-messaging, e-gossip, e-books, e-games, there will soon be an internet of things, all 'communicating' with each other. There is much to be gained here, to be sure, but there are also countless artificial or superficial experiences that can amount to a real impoverishment – if we forget the human being at the centre of the tangled web.

In such a possible context, I am reminded of the old story of Alexander and Diogenes. Alexander the Great went to visit the strange philosopher in his *pithos* one day and offered him any gift that he might desire. 'Stand out of my sun' was Diogenes' reply. The response is even simpler in Greek, just two words: 'unshadow me'. It is a typical story in some ways: king vs. sage, worldly authority vs. spiritual insight, tangible wealth vs. the 'wealth' of virtuous character, physical force vs. the persuasive power of speech. It can also be as a parable of the essential truth of simple living. Alexander's immense achievements and historical import-ance have always inspired the euphoria of hero worship. Yet his life itself was a maelstrom of intrigue, battles, blood, conquests and plans for further conquests, as if in his accumulating power the king forgot the purposes ulterior to power. From this king of the world came an offer of adventure, gold, luxuries, armies, glory. Yet Diogenes refused it all, knowing that what Alexander offered at *that* moment were mere words, abstractions, superfluous goods, whose worth was not here *now*, but indefinitely deferred to some future point. Alexander's offer flickered with the light of some distant Indian sun, but what was this in comparison with the sunshine here *now*, warming the skin and the 'all-nourishing earth'? To be mindful of our own selves, the richness of the present moment, and all the golden things in it: Diogenes' refusal of Alexander may hold lessons for our times too.

Further Reading

Bracht-Branham, R. & M.-O. Goulet-Cazé (eds.). 2000. *The Cynics: The Cynic Movement in Antiquity and Its Legacy*. Berkeley: University of California Press.

Desmond, W., 2008. *Cynics*. Berkeley: Acumen / University of California Press.

Desmond, W., 2006. *Greek Praise of Poverty*. Notre Dame: University of Notre Dame Press.

Dobbin, R. (trans.). 2012. *The Cynic Philosophers: From Diogenes to Julian*. London: Penguin.

Hard, R. (trans.). 2012. *Diogenes the Cynic: Sayings and Anecdotes, With Other Popular Moralists*. Oxford: Oxford World's Classics.

Hicks, R.D. (trans.). 1925. *Diogenes Laertius: The Lives and Opinions of Eminent Philosophers, Vol. II, Books 6-10*. Cambridge: Harvard University Press.

Navia, L. 1998. *Diogenes of Sinope: The Man in the Tub*. London: Praeger.

CHAPTER THREE

ARISTOTLE

JEROME SEGAL

Born in 384 BCE, the Greek philosopher Aristotle made major contributions to almost every field of human knowledge. His *Politics* – the text most relevant to our theme of simple living – opens with a discussion of what he calls 'the art of acquisition', that is, how people make a living. He starts with the observation that there are a variety of modes of subsistence, and that this gives rise to a variety of ways of life. This is true among animals as it is of humans. Some animals live in herds, and others live in isolation. Some eat plants and others meat. Among human beings, Aristotle identifies five 'natural' ways of life: pastoral, farming, fishing, hunting and, interestingly, piracy. What he calls 'true wealth' is acquired through these activities and consists of the amount of household property that suffices for the good life. This he regards as a limited amount.

In distinction to these modes of acquisition which supply the household with its needs, there is a second form of the art of acquisition, which Aristotle (1961: 26) believes to be 'unnatural':

> The other form is a matter only of retail trade, and it is concerned only with getting a fund of money, and that only by the method of conducting the exchange of commodities.
> . . . the acquisition of wealth by the art of household management [as contrasted with the art of acquisition in

its retail form] has a limit; and the object of that art is
not an unlimited amount of wealth.

One approach to acquisition, then, views it as functional to
the life of the household. By contrast, the 'unnatural'
approach to acquisition can take on a life of its own, such that
it reproduces unchecked without regard to the larger life of
the organism, and ultimately undermines that life. Note that
this is the very description of what we now understand as
cancer – unlimited cellular growth that destroys rather than
supports the life of the organism.

What Aristotle presents in these lines isn't just an
academic distinction, but a clash between two different ways
of life, each captured by a way of thinking about money and
possessions. In the first, money and the things one can buy
with it play an important but limited role. Life is not about
money. It is not about getting rich. It is about something
higher, whether it be philosophy, or art, or the pursuit of
knowledge, or participation with one's fellow citizens in the
ever-absorbing process of governing the democratic polis.
Every person lives within a household, and the household has
its economic needs – but the point is to attain only what is
sufficient to enable one to turn away from money-getting and
undertake the real activities of life.

In this first vision of life, Aristotle views only some ways
of making a living as acceptable. His list of farmer, hunter,
fisherman, herdsman or pirate has an arbitrary quality to it.
What is important is what they are intended to rule out:
devoting one's life-activity to an open ended pursuit of higher
levels of income. Aristotle associates this with certain forms
of acquisition, being a businessman, a retail trader, a man or
woman of commerce. These all represent a kind of
slavishness to money. Nor (one would hope) do you find
yourself so destitute that you must work for someone else, for
that too, is a form of slavery. Ideally, for Aristotle, you are
born financially independent. The good life requires some
degree of good fortune.

But how do people manage to go so wrong about money?
How does it gain such control over their lives? Aristotle
suggests that this emerges from a deep misconception about

the nature of human happiness. It is this failure to understand the nature of happiness that leads to the focus on the pursuit of higher and higher levels of consumption and of the higher income necessary to sustain them.

Aristotle identifies what he terms 'external goods'. These externals include wealth, property, power, and reputation. These are the elements that make up the standard vision of success both then and now. To these, Aristotle (1961: 280) contrasts elements of character, what he terms the 'goods of the soul': fortitude, temperance, justice and wisdom. This is a familiar distinction, between inner and outer, between matters of worldliness and matters of virtue.

Aristotle tells us that happiness 'belongs more to those who have cultivated their character and mind to the uttermost, and kept acquisition of external goods within moderate limits' (Aristotle, 1961: 280). Those who lose in life are those 'who have managed to acquire more external goods than they can possibly use, and are lacking in the goods of the soul' (Aristotle, 1961: 280). We can better grasp this if rather than 'goods of the soul' we spoke about the impact that an excessive commitment to acquisition has on one's character or mental health.

Of course, one might ask, 'Why the either/or? Why not have both?' Why can one not have large amounts of wealth and property, but also sound character and flourishing mental health? But Aristotle, and many others, have thought that we really do have to choose. In explaining the relationship between externals and the good life, Aristotle (1961: 281) tells us that 'External goods, like all other instruments, have a necessary limit of size . . . any excessive amount of such things must either cause its possessor some injury, or at any rate, bring him no benefit'.

Here I think Aristotle is talking about two different aspects of wealth and acquisition. The first is whether or not higher levels of wealth or income result in greater happiness. The second is the impact on a person's wellbeing that emerges from the constant pursuit of higher levels of income.

His comments about the limits associated with increased amount of external goods – that there is a limit to their benefit – has been overlooked by those concerned with the history of economic thought. Implicitly, it is the first statement of the principle of diminishing marginal utility. We might remember from introductory economics, that marginal utility is the extra utility (or happiness, satisfaction, pleasure, fulfilment) that someone gets from each successive unit of something. And marginal utility generally declines. The pleasure, for example, from the first ice-cream cone is greater than from the second, and most of us can hardly eat a third.

Aristotle is saying that with all external goods, we find that the more we have, the less utility we receive from each additional amount, and that at some point 'any excessive amount' does us no good.

Actually, Aristotle's view of what nineteenth-century economists would identify as 'the utility curve' is quite radical. As we acquire more and more things, not only does the total utility (i.e. happiness, satisfaction) level fail to rise beyond an upper bound (as in classical presentations of the diminishing character of marginal utility), but the total utility level may actually diminish, implying that the marginal benefit attached to excessive amounts of external goods diminishes beyond the zero level, and actually becomes harmful. Here, however, I believe Aristotle has shifted his ground from considering the simple lack of benefit from having more, to the actual harm that *pursuing more* can do to the personality.

Translated into a thesis about money, Aristotle's formulation tells us that beyond a given level, having and pursuing additional increments of money is not only useless, but negative in its effect. Extended into a thesis about the society at large, it suggests that economic growth beyond a given point is actually harmful to human happiness. It is a straightforward rejection of the idea that 'more is better'.

The problem, as Aristotle understood it, is not merely of the sort that John Kenneth Galbraith described (twenty-three centuries later) in *The Affluent Society* (1958), where economic life is compared to life on a squirrel wheel, each of us fruitlessly expending time and resources but not getting anywhere as the wheel just spins faster and faster. For Galbraith the indictment is that we are wasting our time and energy, and thus wasting our lives.

For Aristotle the issue is even more serious than a life of wasted pursuit. The pursuit of higher and higher levels of income results in a distortion of the personality, such that we never come to be the persons that we most truly are; we are divorced from our truest selves. Instead, people are 'led to occupy themselves wholly in the making of money' (Aristotle, 1961: 26). Aristotle saw his own society as changing for the worse, even as it got (materially) wealthier. It was becoming a world in which people are 'using each and every capacity in a way not consonant with its nature' (Aristotle, 1961: 26); one in which the 'lower form of the art of acquisition has come into vogue' (Aristotle, 1961: 26).

Aristotle (1961: 27) offers examples of what he means by the distortion of capabilities:

> The proper function of courage, for example, is not to produce money but to give confidence. The same is true of military and medical ability, neither has the function of producing money: the one has the function of producing victory, and the other that of producing health. But those of whom we are speaking, turn all such capacities into forms of the art of acquisition, as though to make money were the one aim and everything else must contribute to that aim.

Consider 'medical ability' – Aristotle is talking about what it is to be a doctor. When we go to a doctor, we generally expect to encounter someone committed to the inner values of their profession, someone whose motivation centres around the inherent value of medicine – the health of the patient. What we do not expect and would be repelled by, is to encounter a business person in a white coat or an entrepreneur with aides who are specialists in billing practices. When this happens across the board, when everything is about money, a civilisation is cracking apart. Doctors are not concerned about patients, judges not concerned with justice, teachers not concerned about learning, scholars not concerned about truth. Instead, the focus has become an external good, primarily wealth, but also power, prestige and reputation.

It should be clear that Aristotle's critique is not merely about certain specific economic activities (e.g. retail sales as opposed to production). It is an indictment of a general outlook and form of life. In so far as these become dominant in society, the object of criticism is then the entire form of social life or civilisation.

Such civilisations – and I believe Aristotle would include much of the modern world in this category – is to be condemned as representing a distortion of human nature and a general thwarting of the possibility of human fulfilment.

When every human capacity gets placed at the service of obtaining money (or other external goods), *we ourselves are transformed and distorted.*[1] That is why 'you' can't have it all – who 'you' are changes through the choices you (and your household) make towards matters of acquisition, careers, and 'success'.

Within the Aristotelian framework, to say that our capacities, that is, our selves, are separated from their proper function, is to say that we are thus denied self-actualisation or human fulfilment. It is also to say that we are therefore denied the possibility of living well; for to live well for Aristotle is to express one's richest potentials at high levels of excellence.

It is easy to miss the full significance of this, as the Aristotelian vocabulary is not our own. But we can shift the language a bit. Perhaps we would speak of a life so absorbed in moment-to-moment gain and careerism that one loses, or never deeply develops, a sense of oneself and never lives the life once intended. And thus, in the end, one is left with a sense of emptiness and waste. It is captured in that bumper sticker: 'No one ever died wishing they had spent more time at the office.'

---

[1] Contemporary economic thought, taken in formal terms, can accommodate almost anything. Thus, if one claimed a distortion of personality, this would be viewed as an 'externality' generated by market transactions, adding to the real costs of every market interaction. But virtually no economists have expanded the idea of externalities to include such distortions of personality. It remains a formal possibility, but the consideration of such impacts, central to earlier eras, is largely outside the way we think of the economic realm.

These matters largely fall by the wayside in contemporary thinking about the economic realm. Instead we hear a very different story, an ideology of economics along the following lines. We come to the economic realm as well formed consumers. We have multiple wants and desires. There are limited resources. Producers compete for our spending by creating the products that best satisfy our desires. In an efficient system, we are told, the companies that serve people's desires most adequately and efficiently, make profits; the others disappear. The result is more and more consumer satisfaction, and thus happiness. But to participate in the process, we must sell our labour services to those who can make the best use of them. Thus, companies offer 'opportunities'. Being rational, we take jobs that pay more, and are enabled to buy more. When the system is working well, some of what is earned is re-invested, thus the economy grows, gaining greater capacity to produce. Incomes rise and the level of consumption rises within, making us even better off than we were before.

In contrast we can identify an approach that might be termed Aristotelian:

- There is no distinct economic realm.
- Economic institutions and policy must be judged in terms of how they affect the good life and the healthy personality.
- The central institution to be supported by economic life is the household (which in turn supports worthwhile activity in the larger world).
- The good life is not one of consumption, but of the flourishing of our deepest selves.
- Absorption in a life of acquisitiveness distorts the personality out of all recognition.
- What we need for our wellbeing is only a moderate supply of material goods. As we acquire more, material possessions are of diminishing value. Ultimately, the additional contribution of having more money to the good life reaches zero and its continued pursuit even becomes negative.

Aristotle, in his analysis of the limited place of money in the good life, and in his emphasis on how absorption in acquisition undermines both the healthy personality and the good life, can be seen as one of the intellectual fathers of a philosophy of simple living.

References

Aristotle, *Politics*, trans. Ernest Baker, 1961. New York: Oxford University Press.

CHAPTER FOUR

EPICURUS

MICHAEL AUGUSTIN

Epicurus was born in 341 BCE on the island of Samos, a Greek island in the eastern Aegean Sea. Little is known about his childhood and adolescence. He turned to philosophy at the age of fourteen, so the story goes, after becoming disgusted with his schoolmaster's inability to explain the meaning of 'chaos' in Hesiod's *Theogony*. At the age of eighteen, Epicurus travelled to Athens. But he left shortly after to join his father in the city of Colophon when Perdiccas – one of Alexander the Great's generals and regent of the empire following Alexander's death in 323 BCE – evicted the Athenians from Samos. In 309 BCE he left Colophon and established a philosophical school in the city of Mitylene, which was later moved to the city of Lampascus. Then in 306 BCE Epicurus returned to Athens, purchasing a garden just outside its walls. This became the permanent location of his philosophical school, which was aptly named 'the Garden', where he lived and taught philosophy continuously until his death in 270 BCE.[1]

---

[1] The principle sources for Epicurus's ethical thought are the following: the *Letter to Menoeceus* (*ad Men.*), the *Kuriai Doxai* or *Principle Doctrines* (*KD*), the *Sententiae Vaticanae* or *Vatican Sayings* (*SV*) and Cicero's *De finibus* or *On ends* (*De fin.*). Additional information concerning Epicurus's life and works is preserved in Book 10 of Diogenes Laertius's *Lives and Opinions of the Eminent Philosophers* (hereafter abbreviated 'DL 10'). I will use these abbreviations when citing these sources in the main text. Additional sources will be given in full at the end of this chapter.

Epicurus and his followers advocated living a moderately ascetic life as a means for attaining and maintaining *eudaimonia*. In a number of primary sources, Epicurus is presented as claiming that simple things produce as much pleasure as luxuries (*ad Men.* 130), and he is frequently portrayed as a model of simple living. In what follows, I wish to provide the reader with a sketch of how Epicurus conceives of the *eudaimon* life, and why simple living plays a central role in this conception. I shall focus chiefly on Epicurus's classification of desires. Ensuring that one lives well, for Epicurus, requires regulating one's desires such that one has only those desires that are *natural*. By examining Epicurus's classification of desires, we will come to understand one way in which simple living and the *eudaimon* life are connected in Epicureanism.

Let me begin with a few remarks on the Greek noun *eudaimonia* and adjective *eudaimon*, as they are central to understanding ancient Greek ethical thought. *Eudaimonia* is frequently translated as 'happiness', with the consequence that the phrase 'the *eudaimon* life' may be rendered 'the happy life'. Such translations are acceptable insofar as happiness is conceived in the correct way. Here happiness is *not* conceived of as a fleeting feeling, as when someone remarks, say, that she was happy fifteen minutes ago, but now she is sad. Rather, the conception of happiness referred to by the noun *eudaimonia* is a matter of one's life *as a whole* going well. It is the conception deployed when we reflect on how our lives are developing – we think about our overarching goals, how they fit together, and whether our choices and actions so far contributed to their realisation. So conceived, *eudaimonia* is something that we pursue for its own sake – it is *intrinsically* good. And because a *eudaimon* life is the only life we do not desire for some further end, *eudaimonia* is itself the end. Or, as the Greeks would put it: *eudaimonia* is the *telos*, the goal of life.

Epicurus operates within this structure. In so doing, he shares a common starting point with many other ancient philosophers, including Plato, Aristotle and the Stoics. Where Epicurus disagrees with them – and where they also disagree with each other – is over the question concerning what *eudaimonia* consist in. Epicurus declares that *eudaimonia* is identical with pleasure. As such, Epicurus is a hedonist, and his answer modifies the above structure in the following way: a life's being *eudaimon* is determined by whether one has experienced the most pleasure possible. Therefore, pleasure itself is the highest good. It is the thing that we pursue for its own sake and, as such, is the only intrinsic good. Consequently, pleasure is the *telos*.

Declaring that pleasure is the highest good has led many to misunderstand or ridicule Epicurus. Sometimes he is described as having lived luxuriously with frequent over-indulgence. Indeed, one report alleges that Epicurus vomited twice each day from overeating (DL 10.6)! However, such a portrayal misunderstands the particular flavour of Epicurus's hedonism. Two features are of interest to us here.[2]

First, mental pleasures are greater than physical pleasures. Examples of physical pleasures include the sensation of the sun's rays on my face or the aroma of my morning tea. An example of mental pleasure is participating in a philosophical conversation with friends. In what way is this latter pleasure *greater* than the former pleasures? Simply put, it is not tied to one's occurrent sense-experience; it spans the past, present and future. Memories of past painful experiences can themselves be painful, while memories of pleasurable experiences can themselves be pleasurable. For instance, remembering the death of my grandfather is still painful today, but recalling a philosophical conversation with friends is delightful. Likewise, anticipating future painful encounters can itself be distressing, while the confidence that my future will be pleasant facilitates tranquillity. If, say, I am preparing to attend a conference where speakers are routinely questioned in a harsh and combative manner, my anxiety leading up to the event may well produce more anguish than the event itself. But if I am told that this description is incorrect, and instead that audiences are supportive and offer constructive feedback,

---

[2] My exposition of these two features is much indebted to their treatment in Timothy O'Keefe's monograph *Epicureanism* (Durham: Acumen Publishing Limited, 2010).

then I will welcome the opportunity. Although some of these mental pleasures and pains will depend on bodily sensations, ultimately they require the use of memory or anticipation to be experienced.

In addition, Epicurus encourages his followers to train themselves to recall pleasant memories so that pleasure is always available to them (Cic. *De fin.* 1.57). That is, I can always remember previously pleasurable events, and thereby bring pleasure to the present moment. In fact, Epicurus claims, such training can prove very important, for it can help one to endure presently painful experiences. Sources report that on the last day of his life, while suffering terribly from strangury and dysentery, Epicurus wrote to Idomeneus that he was able to counterbalance the pain from these conditions by recalling their previous philosophical conversations (DL 10.22).

Second, Epicurus distinguishes two kinds of pleasures: *kinetic* and *katastematic*. Kinetic pleasures, as their name suggests, involve *movement*. Bodily kinetic pleasures consist in a stimulation of the senses. For instance, the flowery aroma of my tea as it enters my nostrils. In some cases, though, they are also associated with the process of satisfying some desire. If I am thirsty, my thirst is painful. And by drinking my tea, I satisfy my desire and my thirst is quenched. Likewise, mental kinetic pleasures consist in a stimulation of the mind. Here Epicurus's chief examples are joy and delight. I may experience such pleasures when, say, conversing with a friend over the nature of a *eudaimon* life. Kinetic pleasures, then, seem to be aligned with our commonsense understanding of pleasure.

When I finish drinking my tea, however, I am no longer suffering the pain of thirst. Many would consider this resulting state a neutral state, where I am experiencing neither pain nor pleasure. But according to Epicurus, everything that we take delight in is a pleasure, and everything that distresses us is a pain (Cic. *De fin.* 1.37). We delight not only in the titillation of our senses, but also when we are free from pain and want. Therefore, the state that results when I finished my tea is *not* a neutral state – it is the other kind of pleasure, a *katastematic* pleasure. Epicurus's conception of katastematic pleasure seems closely aligned with what we may regard as a homeostatic state of an organism. And not only is this state in fact a pleasure, of the two kinds it is the *greater* pleasure. For katastematic pleasure embraces the whole organism, whereas kinetic pleasures are localised in a particular sense-organ (*KD*, 9, 10). Finally, katastematic pleasure – a state where all pain and want are removed – is the limit of pleasure itself (*KD*, 3). Once this limit is reached, pleasure cannot be increased but only varied (*KD*, 18).

Bringing all this together produces the following: when the body is free from distress, it reaches the limit of bodily pleasure. And this katastematic bodily pleasure is called by the Greeks *aponia*. When one is confident that she can maintain *aponia* into the future and is free from any other source of mental distress, she then reaches the limit of mental pleasure. And this katastematic mental pleasure is called by the Greeks *ataraxia*. Now since mental pleasures are greater than bodily pleasures, and katastematic pleasures are greater than kinetic pleasures, then someone who attains and maintains *aponia* and *ataraxia* has reached the pinnacle of happiness. He or she attains *eudaimonia*.

Let us turn now to Epicurus's classification of desires. Several extant texts state that the chief impediments to *eudaimonia* are empty emotions and empty desires. Elsewhere this same idea is expressed slightly differently – fearing death and the gods, and failing to grasp the limits of desire are the root of all evil (*KD*, 10, 11). This suggests that regulating appropriately one's desires is only part of the task for attaining and maintaining *aponia* and *ataraxia*. But emotions too, such as fear and anger, involve particular types of desire. As such, one's desires play an even more important role in the attainment and preservation of *eudaimonia*.

Epicurus classifies desires in the following way: some are *natural* and some are *empty*. Of those that are natural, some are *necessary* and some are *non-necessary* (*ad Men.* 127). As such, desires come in three kinds: natural and necessary, natural and non-necessary, and empty. Allow me to comment briefly on each.

Desires are *natural* just in case they are *adiastrophos*, unperverted instincts. For example, if I am hungry, then I desire that my hunger be alleviated. But I do not learn to do this. Rather, it occurs naturally. In addition, natural desires have a natural limit. To use the example of hunger again, once I eat enough, then I am full and my natural desire to alleviate hunger dissipates. Natural desires are *necessary* just in case they satisfy one or more of the following conditions: it is necessary for *eudaimonia*, or for freedom from physical discomfort (*aponia*) or for life itself (*ad Men.* 127; *Pherc.* 1012, col. 67.1-10). Without food or water, for instance, I will soon die. And although I can live without adequate clothing and shelter, I will likely be cold and miserable. As such, I will not attain *aponia*, and therefore cannot attain *ataraxia*.

Epicurus's understanding of natural and non-necessary desires is captured succinctly in *KD*, 26 (see also *SV*, 21): *Of desires, all those that do not lead to pain if left unsatisfied are non-necessary; but their appetency is easily dissipated whenever they are hard to satisfy or seem productive of harm.* Let us take thirst as our example. If I am thirsty, then it is natural and necessary for me to desire that my thirst be quenched. But if I desire a particular kind of drink to satisfy my thirst, say a glass of champagne, this is not necessary. My desire that I am no longer thirsty can be satisfied by a simple glass of water. And where I do quench my thirst with a glass of water, my desire for a glass of champagne, though unsatisfied, produces no pain. For the original pain was not caused by a lack of champagne, but by thirst itself. In addition, were I to realise that acquiring a glass of champagne would be difficult, or that attempting to do so could result in harm, my desire for it would dissipate.

Now in cases where I desire some 'particular' as the *only* means to satisfying a natural desire, my instincts are perverted. For I believe (mistakenly) that the satisfaction of some natural desire can be fulfilled *only* by that particular. Recalling those conditions according to which a natural desire is necessary may prove helpful here. A natural desire is necessary only if it is necessary for *eudaimonia*, for freedom from bodily discomfort or for life itself. Desires for expensive champagne, luxurious foods, designer clothing or extravagant homes do not satisfy any of these conditions. As such, we may conclude that a natural and non-necessary desire is for a particular kind of thing, itself an outgrowth of a natural desire, but where the particular is not necessary for satisfying the desire.

Empty desires are contrasted with natural desires. While a natural and non-necessary desire is an outgrowth of a natural desire *simpliciter*, empty desires are the product of groundless beliefs (*kenodoxai*). Such beliefs are closely linked to what we may call value judgments (specifically, mistaken value judgments). If I desire crowns or statues erected in my honour, for example, it is because I judge (mistakenly), and so believe (mistakenly), that such objects are valuable. Among the causes of these groundless beliefs is traditional *paideia*, culture or education – it infects a person's mind, such that he or she comes to believe that fame or political power are desirable. Hence, Epicurus encourages the youth to steer clear of all *paideia* (*DL*, 10.6), and praises those who arrive untainted to the study of philosophy (Athenaeus *Deipnosophists* 13). While natural desires have a natural limit, empty desires do not. In fact, they often increase without limit and, for that reason, are difficult if not impossible to satisfy. Finally, trying to satisfy such desires will likely bring me into conflict with others, thereby making it even more difficult to satisfy them or exposing me to the possibility of incurring significant harm.

There is another dimension to empty desires that must be mentioned. It concerns the intensity with which one feels a desire. Recall that there are those natural desires that do not lead to pain if unsatisfied. Now, when an object of such a desire is pursued in an intense (*suntonos*) way, this intensity is produced by a person's empty opinion and fails to dissipate because of their empty opinion (*KD*, 30). Epicurus's contention here is that certain desires, which are not necessary, but which are outgrowths of unperverted instincts, may be classified as empty if they are felt and pursued in an excessively intense way. That is, while the *type* of this desire is natural and non-necessary, its *token*, if felt and pursued in an excessively intense way, is properly understood as an empty desire.

The above sets us up to understand in part how simple living and the *eudaimon* life are connected in Epicurus's philosophical thought. Empty desires require considerable effort to satisfy. And this will bring one into conflict with, and possibly incur harm from, others. Therefore, Epicurus advises his followers to eradicate them. Consequently, we should have only those desires that are natural. My hunger and thirst can be satiated by a simple meal and water. I can relieve and prevent bodily discomfort with simple clothing and a modest home. In so doing, I attain *aponia*, the limit of bodily pleasure. And because the goods needed to satisfy these desires can be acquired without difficulty, I can be confident that my present, content condition will continue into the future. As a result, I attain *ataraxia*, the limit of mental pleasure. Finally, by continuing to regulate my desires in this way, I maintain *aponia* and *ataraxia*. That is, I preserve *eudaimonia*.

In closing, two things should be noted about this picture. The first concerns the role of luxuries in an Epicurean life. While natural and necessary desires carry a certain primacy – for Epicurus regards self-sufficiency as a great good (*ad Men.* 130) – some natural and non-necessary desires will be permitted insofar as they too are easy to satisfy and without conflict. As such, luxuries are not to be avoided entirely. If a friend invites me to dinner at an expensive and fancy restaurant, I may join him or her if I so choose. Indeed, as Epicurus reminds Menoeceus, our aim is not to always live off a little, but to be able to do so if we do not have much. Moreover, Epicurus contends that those who need luxuries the least are the ones who derive the greatest kinetic pleasure from them (*ad Men.* 130). But whether I opt for a luxury is an important matter and must be handled with care. I should guard against the possibility of becoming attached to such luxuries, with the result that I develop an empty desire for them. The presence of such a desire would eventually disrupt my *ataraxia*.

Second, even with the occasional luxury, this kind of simple life advocated by Epicurus might seem *too simple*. One might worry that fulfilling my natural desires by living a simple life, and thereby facing the future serenely, would eventually become boring. To the uninitiated, the Epicurean life may indeed appear dull. But Epicurus contends that this is due only to the diseased state of their minds. Their education and cultural upbringing has led them to believe that *eudaimonia* requires obtaining and experiencing many and varied luxuries. Such people are afflicted with, among other things, ingratitude, which causes a greedy desire for unlimited variations in lifestyle (*SV*, 69). Everything needed for ensuring that one's life as a whole will go well is readily and easily available. And the person who realises this, and lives in accordance with it, will be content. We will live a *eudaimon* life.[3]

Further reading

For a general introduction to Epicurus's philosophical thought, I highly recommend Timothy O'Keefe's monograph *Epicureanism* (Durham: Acumen Publishing Limited, 2010).

A more in-depth treatment of various aspects of Epicurus's philosophy can be found in *The Cambridge Companion to Epicureanism* (ed. J. Warren. Cambridge: Cambridge University Press, 2009).

Our best source, though by no means an unbiased one, for Epicurus's ethical thought is Cicero's *De finibus* (*On Ends*). I recommend the edition edited by Julia Annas and translated by Raphael Woolf for the Cambridge Texts in the History of Philosophy (Cambridge: Cambridge University Press, 2001).

Much of our source material for Epicureanism, supplemented with invaluable commentary, is collected in *The Hellenistic Philosophers*, 2 vols. (eds. A. A. Long and D. N. Sedley. Cambridge: Cambridge University Press, 1987).

---

[3] I wish to thank Robert McIntyre, Jenessa Strickland, and Voula Tsouna for their comments on an earlier version of this article.

For a recent collection of essays that examines in detail the relationship between Epicurus and later Epicurean philosophers, see *Epicurus and the Epicurean Tradition* (eds. J. Fish and K. R. Sanders. Cambridge: Cambridge University Press, 2011).

CHAPTER FIVE

THE STOICS

DIRK BALTZLY

How much do you need to be happy? How much money? How much fame? How many designer labels carefully chosen to define who you really are? If you are reading this book, the chances are good that you already think that the answer to these questions is, 'less than most people suppose'. In this chapter, we will consider an even more radical answer. We do not need merely *less* of these things than most people suppose, but *none at all* – a position that obviously requires some explaining. The genuinely worthwhile life, according to the Stoics, is completely independent of such external things.

The Stoics were a group of ancient Greek and Roman philosophers, including Epictetus, Marcus Aurelius, and Seneca. Like all ancient Greco-Roman moral philosophers they treated the nature of the genuinely worthwhile life as the central question for ethical inquiry. They express this by asking, 'What is *eudaimonia*?' This Greek word is frequently translated as 'happiness'. Many scholars think this carries the potentially misleading connotation that this condition is merely a matter of how you feel. They prefer 'flourishing' to convey the fact that *eudaimonia* is not a passing state of mind, of the sort that we talk about when we say, 'winning the football match on Saturday made me happy'. If 'flourishing' sounds too biological, I think you could also understand *eudaimonia* as *real success* – not merely the conventional markers of success, but the sort of success it really makes sense to strive for. So the central question of ancient moral philosophy could be expressed in our times as 'What counts as real success?'

Since flourishing is an objective condition and not merely a subjective orientation toward life, we flourish by having 'goods' – that is, things that are objectively worth having or activities that are objectively worth doing. What things or activities are good according to the Stoics? They suppose that what is objectively good *inevitably* benefits the person who possesses it. What is good *always* makes you objectively better off.

Almost nothing, it turns out, passes this stringent test for what counts as good. Obviously money does not always make you better off if, for instance, you use it to develop a nasty drug habit. The Stoics argued that even being healthy could be a disadvantage in some circumstances. Imagine that you would be conscripted into an evil organisation like the Nazi SS – a situation in which you would undoubtedly be compelled to do horrible things – but for your heart condition. In this case, you are better off unhealthy. Since there are possible circumstances in which even health does not benefit us, it too is not really good.

The Stoics argued that only one thing passes this stringent test: virtue. You are always better off being virtuous (e.g. wise, courageous, self-controlled, and just). This is the sole good and its opposite, vice, the only thing that is objectively bad. Everything else they called 'indifferent' – neither good nor bad.

Since flourishing depends on the possession of what is objectively good, the Stoics' answer to the question, 'What is flourishing?' is easily stated but not easily understood. The short answer is that it is *virtuous living*. But this immediately invites the question, 'What is virtue?' and 'What does it mean to live virtuously?'

Here, as with the word *'eudaimonia'*, we need to make allowances for the fact that the English word 'virtue' is not an exact match for the ancient Greek word *'aretê'*. For us the notion of the virtuous choice is almost always the notion of a choice *opposed to* the chooser's self-interest. We tend to think that virtue is selflessness and self-sacrifice. We can choose happiness *or* virtue – not both. But by the Stoics' lights, the choice made *kat' aretên* or 'in accordance with virtue' is the one that embodies excellence in rational thought. What is done this way is inevitably done *well*. So the inevitable benefit that virtue brings is almost an analytic truth according to them. Given a choice, would you prefer to do something well or do it badly? Doing things well is always where your real self-interest lies since doing it *well* means doing it *successfully*. So the life of virtue, which means the life of reasoning well, is *eudaimonia* – real success.

What's so great about being rational? The Stoics described the life of excellent reasoning – i.e. the virtuous life – as one lived 'in agreement with nature'. This idea of agreement (*homologia*) with nature has two dimensions. First, in reasoning well they supposed that we fully realise our human nature. Rationality permeates all that we do. Even desire, they argued, is the result of reason's capacity to assent. When we desire a flashy new car it is because we have mentally said 'yes' to the impression that the car is desirable. So even in experiencing desire, we are exercising our capacity to make rational judgements. It just turns out that most of the time, we're using our reasoning capacity *badly* because we desire things that are not really good. So we are most fully ourselves when we reason well.

Second, rationality permeates the universe. The Stoics were pantheists who identified God with the chain of causes and effects that constitutes the history of the universe – a history that they supposed repeated itself, punctuated by a cosmic conflagration in which all things merged into divine fire and subsequently evolved from it. This causal order (i.e. God) is rational in the sense that all things happen through causes that a rational mind can understand. Understanding that, for instance, the bushfire that is about to engulf my home is necessitated by the previous history of the entire universe, I should not be troubled by it.

So we should reason well, but about what? If the only good is the excellent deployment of rationality, what should we deploy it to do? The Stoics thought that although things like health and wealth were indifferent – neither good nor bad – they also argued that (under normal circumstances) it was rational to *prefer* some of these indifferent things over others. Health, wealth and good reputation may not be good things, but the Stoics called them 'preferred indifferents'. Under most circumstances, it is rational to prefer health to sickness, shelter to homelessness, and so on. The only genuinely good thing is reasoning well, but when we ask what we should seek to reason well about, their answer is that this will be the conditional pursuit of preferred indifferents. Other things being equal, I reason well when I successfully pursue health or sufficient income to have a house to live in. Other people are also preferred indifferents. It can be rational for me to pursue food for myself (that's a thing that it is rational to prefer given my nature), but it is also rational for me to pursue food for other people (for others, insofar as they are rational, are also 'akin' or *okeion* to me), and it is rational for me to seek to promote what is akin to me. (The kinship we have with all rational beings provides the basis of our moral duties to others.)

But, since circumstances can wreck the most rationally laid plans, it is not the *getting* of these things that counts as happiness. It is excellent reasoning in the calm and measured pursuit of them. Real winning in the game of life is not necessarily putting runs on the board (or dollars in the bank or food on your family's table). It is playing well. Of course, playing well *usually* puts runs on the board, but not always. Likewise, reasoning well about the pursuit of preferred indifferents, like money to buy a house, often results in getting money. The Stoic's real goal is good rational form in playing the game. The actual achievement of rationally preferred indifferents often comes with that. But there are two important qualifications. First, the getting of the preferred indifferent is not what the Stoic plays for and, second, he or she experiences no frustration or disappointment if exhibiting good rational form is not sufficient to secure health or wealth or reputation.

This observation about frustration and disappointment brings us to another important aspect of Stoic thought. These are examples of what the Stoics call *pathê* – a term often rendered as 'passions'. Nearly all the things that we would describe as undesirable emotions – hatred, fear, envy – are all passions. So too are many things that we would regard as desirable emotions: sympathy, intense sexual desire, pride. The Stoic ideal is to transcend all these passions – to achieve *apatheia*. But *apatheia* is not apathy. It is better understood as tranquillity and control. To achieve the Stoic ideal of *apatheia* is to be always in control. You are the one who *acts* – not one to whom fortune or circumstance *does things*. The noun *pathê* is related to the verb for 'to undergo' or 'to get done to', *paschein*. So the Stoic ideal is the complete transcendence of passivity: you are someone to whom nothing *just happens*.

On the Stoic view, a passion like envy arises from a false judgement. It is the two-fold judgement that, first, when your neighbours have a new car they have something good and, second, that is right for you to have a certain kind of distress at this fact. The judgement is false in both its parts. The car is not itself moral virtue and so not good. It is merely a preferred indifferent. Moreover, it is false that it is right and rational for you to feel distress that yours is not as nice. Just as we can stop making other false judgements, however habitual they might be, so too we can stop experiencing passions like envy.

What can those of us who seek a simple life learn from Stoicism? I think that one grain of truth is that judgement plays a big role in both the desires and the emotions we experience. We are not, of course, *conscious* of making a judgement that it is reasonable to want that new car. But a lot of our judgements take place beneath the level of our awareness. It is like when you catch yourself engaging in some act of pre-judging (e.g. that some *female* acquaintance wouldn't be interested in the spare football ticket you have). In making that automatic assumption, you judged without being sufficiently reflective. That's what makes sexism so insidious: you can be sexist without trying to be. So one important lesson from Stoicism is the idea of bringing implicit judgements to full consciousness and assessing whether those are judgements we really want to endorse. A person raised in a sexist or racist culture can learn to police his or her own implicit judgements. We should adopt the same kind of strategy with materialism. Advertisers count on you not being reflective about whether you really need or want something.

Another important insight in Stoic moral philosophy is the idea of cosmopolitanism. Unlike Plato and Aristotle, the Stoics claimed that we are naturally akin or *oikeion* to *all* human beings – not merely to one's fellow Greeks. As a consequence, a truly rational concern for justice is a concern for justice globally. Such a commitment to global justice requires that we should live simply, of course, in order that others may simply live. The Stoics' theory of merely preferred indifferents would mean that such a simple life involves no *real* sacrifice. Our flourishing in no way depends on the possession of these things.

Their idea that a genuinely successful life is lived 'in agreement with nature' is attractive too. Their pantheism, coupled with their belief that the cosmic god and human beings are essentially rational, makes us 'at home' in our universe. Unfortunately, the Stoics themselves did not extend our kinship with the rational order of nature as a whole to kinship with specific pieces of it – particularly not with non-rational animals. They thought that the rational world order (i.e. God) made non-rational living things for the *use* of rational beings such as ourselves. So in fact the Stoics did not anticipate anything like the 'deep ecology' of Arne Naess. But perhaps one could accept some parts of their picture while rejecting others.

Among the ideas I think we ought to reject in Stoicism is the thesis that virtue alone is good and vice alone is bad. It is true that such a theory of value leaves our happiness or unhappiness entirely within our power. It is up to me – and no one but me – if I am courageous, just, wise, etc. But the Stoic theory of value has the consequence that the courageous, just, wise Stoic who sees all his friends and loved ones die in a famine suffers no *real* harm that could damage his happiness. If he is virtuous, he flourishes – no matter whether his family prospers or starves. This seems to me to be very implausible. I fear that I have no complex argument to back that claim up. This consequence of the Stoic view just strikes me as likely to be wrong. The naturalist approach of ancient Greek philosophy in general means that a theory's judgements about what happiness consists in are grounded in our experience of life. This consequence of the Stoic theory seems contrary to my experience of life.

I agree with proponents of the simple life that a genuinely satisfying life requires far less than Madison Avenue would have you believe. But it seems to me implausible to claim as the Stoics do that it requires *nothing* but my own rational excellence. For this reason, I think that Aristotle's moral philosophy is more likely to be correct. A good life requires *some* modest resources. Nevertheless, the enduring lesson we can take from the Stoics is that we all have the responsibility and the power to shape our own desires, including material desires, through reflection and self-discipline. By doing so, we can lead richer lives.

Further reading

Primary texts: Unlike Plato or Aristotle, the works of the earliest Stoic philosophers survive only in fragmentary evidence or testimonial reports. To read books, rather than fragments or reports, you will need to read the later Roman Stoics.

Marcus Aurelius, *Meditations*. Don't approach this as a treatise. It was actually a notebook that the emperor of Rome wrote to himself at night. It is personal and practical, focusing on how he might better live the Stoic life. http://classics.mit.edu/Antoninus/meditations.html

Epictetus, *Discourses* and *Handbook*. The latter is a pithy collection of reminders for the aspiring Stoic. The *Discourses* are longer, but have a similar 'pep talk' tone to them. http://classics.mit.edu/Epictetus/discourses.html and http://classics.mit.edu/Epictetus/epicench.html

To get a good overview of Stoic moral theory, you can read the work of scholars who have tried to reconstruct the thought of the early Stoic philosophers from our fragmentary evidence.

Tad Brennan, *The Stoic Life: Emotions, Duties and Fate*. Oxford University Press 2005. An engaging and clear book. I think it is best introduction to Stoic moral philosophy.

Dirk Baltzly, *The Stanford Encyclopedia of Philosophy* q. v. Stoicism. http://plato.stanford.edu has a good bibliography

Daniel Russell, *Happiness for Humans*. Oxford University Press, 2012. Russell defends an Aristotelian conception of happiness from the Stoic's competing view.

CHAPTER SIX

JESUS

SIMON USSHER

*'Hail, queen wisdom! May the Lord save
thee with thy sister holy pure simplicity!'*
— St. Francis of Assisi

At its heart the 'voluntary simplicity' movement is about a value shift. Adherents may display a commonality of practices, but no practice is common to all, and none capture the essence of what voluntary simplicity is at its core. The essence of the movement is not the practice; it is the informing principles.

Despite our eclectic backgrounds and motivations, voluntary simplicity tends to bring people together into a wonderful congruity. This way of life generally involves an eschewing of the messages of consumerism and materialism, and a reassertion of the value of people and time over money, environment over profit, and community over corporation. This association of seemingly unrelated values is not as arbitrary as it may appear, for the messages of consumerism and materialism do indeed risk eroding more than just our bank accounts.

In recent times social scientists such as Tim Kasser have highlighted how certain sets of values exist in conflict; that the values we espouse have something of a see-saw like quality, where an increase in one necessitates a decrease in a certain other. As materialistic values increase, often there is an accordant decrease in 'pro-social' values and concern for the environment. In contrast, those values that have been demonstrated to support psychological and physical wellbeing, termed 'intrinsic values' by Kasser and colleagues, tend to promote personal, social and environmental wellbeing and help to immunise people against materialism (Kasser, 2002).

And yet this insight is not as new as it may seem. Indeed, it is one of the few clear points of agreement amongst the great religious sages of history, and an uncompromising aspect of Jesus' ministry in particular. Jesus warned his disciples of this conflict in clear and literal terms: 'No one can serve two masters. Either you will hate the one and love the other, or you will be devoted to the one and despise the other. You cannot serve both God and money' (Matt 6:24 NIV). Jesus paints the same picture that Kasser does today: there is a direct conflict between the values of money, materialism and consumerism, and those of people, community and creation.

The Opposition of Materialism and the Kingdom

A clear theme throughout Jesus' ministry was the conflict between seeking God and seeking money (personified as Mammon in some gospel translations). The Gospels contain a glaring lack of discussion pertaining to sexual orientation, gender roles, church organisation, or other items of dogma, but return again and again to the subject of money and materialism. As we read in the gospels: 'What good is it for someone to gain the whole world, yet forfeit their soul?' (Matt 16:26 NIV).

Similarly, in the parable of the sower, Jesus discusses with his disciples those things that may render a life 'unfruitful'. Likening them to the various fates of seed sown by a farmer, he describes seed that 'fell among thorns, which grew up and choked the plants so that they did not bear grain'. He goes on to explain to his disciples that this seed represents those whose lives are rendered unfruitful by 'the deceitfulness of wealth and the desires for other things' (Mark 4:3-20 NIV).

On another occasion Jesus was approached by a wealthy young man, asking 'Good teacher, what must I do to inherit eternal life?'. Jesus responded by exhorting the young man to follow the commandments: 'do not murder, do not commit adultery, do not steal, do not give false testimony, do not defraud, honour your father and mother.' 'All these I have kept since I was a boy', responded the young man. 'One thing you lack', Jesus responded. 'Go, sell everything you have and give to the poor, and you will have treasure in heaven.' The young man left Jesus, saddened by his response and the dilemma he now faced. We do not have record of what the young man subsequently decided, but his reaction prompted Jesus to declare to his followers: 'It is easier for a camel to go through the eye of a needle than for someone who is rich to enter the kingdom of God' (Mark 10:17-25 NIV).

Perhaps this theme was at its most symbolic when Jesus entered Jerusalem and proceeded to the temple. Incensed by what he found, what follows is one of the most emotional scenes recorded in the gospels. Jesus physically drives out the money changers and those other traders selling sheep, cattle and doves, telling them they had reduced the temple from a 'house of prayer' to a 'den of robbers' (Matt 21:12-13 NIV). Notably, this is the only gospel record of Jesus ever using violence, albeit mild, in that he made a whip of cords and physically overturned the traders' tables – an exercise of force he did not show before or since. By contrast when he was arrested prior to his crucifixion he restrained his followers from violence, instead healing one of the arresting soldiers.

The Understanding of the Early Church

The first century church is often looked to for a sense of authenticity, given their chronological proximity to Christ. These early Christians clearly understood the inherent economic implications of the gospel, putting their poss-essions to the service of their fellows and practising a measure of communal ownership.

All the believers were one in heart and mind. No one claimed that any of their possessions was their own, but they shared everything they had. With great power the apostles continued to testify to the resurrection of the Lord Jesus. And God's grace was so powerfully at work in them all that there were no needy persons among them. For from time to time those who owned land or houses sold them, brought the money from the sales and put it at the apostles' feet, and it was distributed to anyone who had need (Acts 4:32-35 (NIV).

While not prescriptive or absolute, these practices revealed an attitude toward possessions that clearly valued the humane over the material; an ethos of stewardship rather than ownership. This ethos of stewardship was inseparable from life as a Christian, and the concept of a purely spiritual response to the Gospel was nonsensical. As Peter Oakes notes: 'In studying the first few centuries of the Christian movement, any attempt to isolate economics from other social factors such as politics would be doomed' (Oakes, 2009).

In the epistle of James, written sometime in the first or second centuries, we again read of the centrality of an economic response to the gospel. 'Religion that God our Father accepts as pure and faultless is this: to look after orphans and widows in their distress and to keep oneself from being polluted by the world' (James 1:27 NIV).

Many of these writings of the early Christians later became canonical, and thus informed all later expressions of Christianity.

St. Francis of Assisi

St. Francis was a monk who lived from 1182-1226 and to this day he remains one of the most venerated religious figures in history. The son of a wealthy silk merchant, he turned away from the wealth and privilege of his upbringing and embraced a life of poverty.

In losing his worldly wealth, he found delight in nature, in all creation, seeing in it the mirror of God. In one of his most popular writings, the 'Canticle of the Sun', St. Francis writes:

> Be praised, my Lord, through all Your creatures, especially through my lord Brother Sun, who brings the day; and You give light through him. And he is beautiful and radiant in all his splendor! Of You, Most High, he bears the likeness.
>
> Be praised, my Lord, through Sister Moon and the stars; in the heavens You have made them bright, precious and beautiful.
>
> Be praised, my Lord, through Brothers Wind and Air, and clouds and storms, and all the weather, through which You give Your creatures sustenance.
>
> Be praised, my Lord, through Sister Water; she is very useful, and humble, and precious, and pure.
>
> Be praised, my Lord, through Brother Fire, through whom You brighten the night. He is beautiful and cheerful, and powerful and strong.
>
> Be praised, my Lord, through our sister Mother Earth, who feeds us and rules us, and produces various fruits with coloured flowers and herbs.
>
> Be praised, my Lord, through those who forgive for love of You; through those who endure sickness and trial. Happy those who endure in peace, for by You, Most High, they will be crowned.

St. Francis' own life, as an expression of the gospel, highlights the inverse relationship between prizing wealth and possessions and prizing creation and our fellow brothers and sisters. Even on his deathbed, St. Francis requested that his clothes be removed and he be allowed to die naked, lying on the earth. A fitting departure for a life lived close to the creation, unimpeded by love of wealth.

John Wesley

Continuing the response of the early Christians and St. Francis, John Wesley understood that the gospel has inextricable social and economic implications. Wesley was an eighteenth century Anglican cleric who worked in England and the American colonies. He understood the gospel as intensely social, inherently manifest in our treatment of our fellow human beings, and that personal frugality underpinned the ability of individuals to contribute to this struggle.

'Do you not know that God entrusted you with that money', wrote Wesley, 'all above what buys necessities for your families, to feed the hungry, to clothe the naked, to help the stranger, the widow, the fatherless; and, indeed, as far as it will go, to relieve the wants of all mankind? How can you, how dare you, defraud the Lord, by applying it to any other purpose?' (Wesley, 1831).

In 1743 with the number of his followers grown too great to instruct personally, Wesley offered them a set of 'General Rules' to govern the 'United Societies' his followers had organised into. There was only one condition required of those who desired admission to these societies: 'a desire to flee from the wrath to come, and to be saved from their sins.' But Wesley noted that 'wherever this is really fixed in the soul it will be shown by its fruits', going on to list a large number of such fruits, many of which were economic, such as 'feeding the hungry', 'clothing the naked', 'all diligence and frugality', and avoiding evils such as 'laying up treasure on Earth', 'needless self indulgence' and 'the wearing of gold and costly apparel' (United Methodist Church, 1973).

Wesley's understanding of the teachings of Jesus was such that it could not be separated from the use of one's resources. 'Earn all you can, save all you can, give all you can', wrote Wesley. He understood that there was a fundamental conflict between the values of the Gospel and those of life as material consumption, and that these rippled out through the societies in which we live. As a result of this understanding, many of his followers became leading lights among movements such as abolitionism and prison reform, as well as sowing the seeds for modern Methodism, the Holiness movement, the Charismatic movement and all the social works that followed.

Modern Challenges

At the dawn of the third millennium since the birth of Jesus, over a third of humanity claim to follow Jesus, albeit to varying degrees. And yet, within this population of over 2.2 billion, Mammon still carries great influence.

Since the 1950s, there has been the spread of 'prosperity theology', a message advocating the godly life as a means to material success. The utter antithesis of the gospel, it is nonetheless popular and spreading.

An added challenge, many of the world's wealthiest and highest consuming citizens are counted among the Christians. As the interconnectedness of our economic and environmental actions are understood to an ever greater degree, we can hope that the understanding of how one ought to 'love thy neighbour' expands accordingly.

And indeed there is hope. In 2008, echoing the original 'seven deadly sins', the Vatican issued the 'seven social sins', including environmental pollution, contributing to wealth divides, accumulating excessive wealth and creating poverty.

Conclusion

Christianity in the twenty-first century is diverse in tradition and understanding of the gospel, but the centrality of Jesus is uncontested, and his words leave no doubt as to the obstacle that the love of wealth presents.

In the closing paragraphs of his work 'The Gospel According To The Son', Norman Mailer writes, in the voice of Jesus: 'God and Mammon still grapple for the hearts of all men and all women'. Indeed, the messages of consumerism contest for more than just our brand loyalty, and the noble lives of those practising voluntary simplicity stand in opposition, as ever, doing the Lord's work and living Jesus' message two thousand years hence.

References

Kasser, Tim. 2002. *The High Price of Materialism*. MIT Press, Cambridge, Massachusetts.

Oakes, Peter. 2009. 'Methodological Issues in using Economic Evidence in Interpretation of Early Christian Texts' in *Engaging Economics: New Testament Scenarios and Early Christian Reception*, edited by Bruce Longenecker and Kelly Liebengood. Wm. B. Eerdmans Publishing Company.

St. Francis of Assisi, as Quoted in Second Life (c. 1247) by Thomas of Celano as translated by Paschal Robinson in *The Writings of St. Francis of Assisi*, 1905.

The Holy Bible, New International Version (NIV). 2011. Grand Rapids: Zondervan Publishing House.

United Methodist Church (U.S.). 1973. *The Book of discipline of the United Methodist Church*. Nashville, Tenn: United Methodist Pub. House.

Wesley, J. 1831. *The Works of the Reverend John Wesley, A.M.* New York: Methodist Episcopal Church.

CHAPTER SEVEN

WESTERN MONASTICISM

WILLIAM FAHEY

The interest in monasticism – in high and popular culture – stretches from its apparent demise (e.g. Shakespeare's 'Bare Ruined Choirs') through the Romantic Movement of Europe, to the now ubiquitous 'monk-inspired' works in art, alternative medicine, mystery stories, and brewing. Western monasticism has outlived all reports of its death, and more provocatively, it has remained a consistent source of fascination and inspiration for those who consider themselves outside of any monastic tradition. For those seeking a deeper understanding of 'the simple life' as a response to consumerism, social atomisation, or the dehumanising effects of ill-considered technology or modern bureaucracy (whether governmental or corporate), monasticism offers students of simplicity a tested pattern of life for consideration and even imitation.

Over half a century ago, Cistercian Thomas Merton said that monasticism 'tends to present itself to the modern world as a problem and a scandal'. This was especially so in the West, which unlike the East, Merton sensed, had become a society oriented toward nothing 'beyond the mere transient quest of business and pleasure.... In a materialistic culture which is fundamentally irreligious the monk is incomprehensible because he "produces nothing"' (Merton, 1975: viii). Particular attention will be given over the next several pages to monasticism as a pattern of contradiction in relation to the material and financial world. Western monasticism, when it has been true to its calling, has always maintained that a simple life ordered toward God could educate men and women in joyfulness and answer a universal call to participate in a life beyond the flux and loss experienced in time.

St. Benedict famously wrote that the monk 'must prefer nothing to Christ'; this one principle was to order all his life. It is a misunderstanding of western monasticism to see its simple living as merely a turning away from everyday culture or, worse, a rejection of Creation. On the contrary, the unification of the mind and heart under a moderating rule allowed the monk to love all Creation properly and more abundantly. Monasticism is not chiefly a turning *from*, but a turning *toward*. It is the cultivation of a single-hearted desire to be united with God (Fahey, 2012: ix-xii). That desire, in the western tradition, demanded a lifestyle and structure, of which the principles endure to this day and offer to all a tested pattern for simple living.

The essential outline of monastic simplicity first arose outside the cities of the southern Levant, in Palestine and Egypt. Scholars have long debated the exact nature, location and even names of these communities, but there can be little doubt as to their contributions. The later western monasticism that gave early and medieval Christian culture much of its character was perceived by Christians themselves as arising out of the desert and, at times, explicitly in association with earlier communities – in particular, the Essenes of Judaea and the Theraputae of Egypt. According to ancient sources, both groups certainly existed in the first century A.D., and may have had their origins a century earlier.

Until recently, the Essenes were known to us only through passing references from the first century; yet even these reveal the heart of early monasticism. Pliny the Elder mentions them, but is likely to have derived his knowledge from the Jewish historian Josephus, who describes the Essenes as one of the three philosophical schools of Jewish philosophy. He describes them at length in a chapter of book II of his *Wars of the Jewish People*. The core of the tight-knit Essene community is revealed in Josephus's comment that they 'reject pleasures as an evil but esteem continence, and the conquest over our passions, as a virtue' (Josephus, 1979: 144).

An additional outside admirer was found in the Jewish mystic and philosopher, Philo of Alexandria. Philo placed the Essenes along with the seven wise men of Greece, the magi of Persia, and the gymnosophists of India – probably a reference to Hindu sannyasin – as exemplars of a small number of humans dedicated to the life-long pursuit of wisdom and justice. For Philo, the mark of the Essenes was the programmatic effort to become servants of God, not by sacrificing animals, but by 'rendering their minds holy', achieved in part by their ordered life and in part by their avoidance of the corrupting culture of cities (Philo, 1981: 249). In 1947, a chance find of an ancient communal library – the Dead Sea Scrolls – and subsequent excavations in cliffs near Qumran gave substance to the earlier accounts. The scrolls represent texts composed between 250 BC and AD 68, but the brotherhood that produced the scrolls was clearly a reformist group. Their documents either governed or inspired their way of life and worship (see Theodor Gaster's 'Introduction' in *The Dead Sea Scriptures*, 1964: 1-35). The community at Qumran was decidedly anti-establishment and held its membership up as the last hope for a true and redeemed Israel.

The Essenes then were chiefly – but not exclusively – men living a determined and common life in pursuit of truth. The scroll entitled *Serek ha-Yahad* or *The Manual of Discipline* may be a large portion of their 'rule' (*The Dead Sea Scriptures* 1964: 39-69). A second scroll – *The Zadok Document* – compliments *The Manual* but makes explicit the community's estrangement with Jerusalem and gives guidelines for small units, portions of a 'remnant', which will disperse until the priesthood of the Holy City is recovered by a messiah (*The Dead Sea Scriptures*, 1964: 70-97). Viewed alongside Joseph and Philo, these texts give us a tantalising glimpse of the first western monastic community. The opening of *The Manual* speaks of the intentional commitment demanded from those who truly wished to turn from Israel's corruption to a fuller life in 'the community'. 'All who declare willingness to serve God's truth must bring all of their mind, all of their strength, and all their wealth into the community of God, so their minds may be purified by the truth of his precepts' (*The Dead Sea Scriptures*, 1964: 46).

To achieve their goal, the Essenes established an order of life, reflected in simple but clear rules, a rhythm of life, and a planned community. Their 'order' was restrictive, with members undergoing a stringent probationary period before full incorporation. It was hierarchical, with a priesthood, Levites, and laymen. Marriage was not forbidden for the laity, but understood for the sake of regenerating the community and undertaken only after a three year period of observation. Absolute marital fidelity and modest behavior was assumed. Worship occurred at set times throughout each day, on the Sabbath, and other holy days. God's holy name was revered, and the books of sacred scripture and the writings of wise men steadfastly studied. The Essenes also pursued some philosophic studies – limited largely to ethics and cosmology. They had common buildings with meeting rooms, common dining, workshops, and bathing chambers for ritual purification. In strong contrast to contemporary Cynicism and even forms of Stoicism, the monasticism of the Essenes was not anti-social or individualistic. At its root, the simple life offered was one sought in common, through a redeemed community separated from the corruption of Jerusalem.

The common use of property is emphasised throughout these sources. Simplicity of life seems absolutely reliant on communal ownership or at least profound commitment to mutual financial support. Everyone was expected to master some small craft or work the land for self sufficiency. It was expected this work would generate enough surplus to assist the Essene community and, when needed, neighbours. *The Manual* stated explicitly that membership was to be 'understood in both a doctrinal and economic sense', although the priests seem to have a special reserve fund as well (*The Dead Sea Scriptures*, 1964: 54, 66).

Both Josephus and Philo emphasise the central importance that material modesty had in the common life of the Essenes. They avoided the language and customs of commerce and did not store wealth of any kind. Through 'studied action' they maintained a corporate level of modest security, but no more. 'They judge frugality and easy contentment to be... an abundance of wealth.' (Philo, 1981: 250) Organised around a single treasury and system of expenditure, the Essenes structured their communal life to avoid any 'occasion for cupidity', but instead firmly established principles for mutual support, which included caring for the sick, children, and the elderly (Philo, 1981: 250-251).

Yet the restrained approach to material culture was driven utterly by spiritual concerns. For Philo, the Essenes undertook all efforts out of a three-fold desire: love of God, love of virtue, and love of humankind. This systematic simplicity, rooted in love, led to an 'ineffable sense of fellowship, which is the clearest indication of a perfect and happy life' (Philo, 1981: 252). For Josephus, their adherence to the incorruptibility of the soul was the cornerstone of their life. The prophets – especially Elijah – stood behind the Essenes, but with the exception of Elijah the prophets of the Old Testament did not offer a corporate form of life to be imitated. With the Essene community, the solitary prophetic voice grew into a choir, praising God and, by its simplicity and fellowship, calling into question the material life of those in the cities nearby.

Philo also describes for us a community which is so similar to later monks and nuns that early Christians assumed him to be describing a Christian movement. These were the Theraputae of Egypt, whose name – literally, 'the healers' – betokened by their art of curing souls from the city formerly 'mastered by grievous and virtually incurable diseases, inflicted by pleasures and lusts, mental pains and fears, by acts of greed, folly and injustice' (Philo, 1981: 42). Like the Essenes, their life was highly structured, emphasising moderation in diet and dress, a regular prayer life based on the chanting of the Psalms, enriched by structured study of Scripture and literature, rooted in allegorical interpretation. It was, in short, a gentle and simple life pursued in common as 'citizens of heaven' seeing God's 'friendship... and the very summit of joy' (Philo, 1981: 57). On one point, they were more radical than the Essenes: they left aside private property entirely, contending that 'the management of wealth and possessions [was] time-consuming' and that 'to make money breeds injustice through the inequality entailed' (Phil, 1981: 44). Instead, through collective ownership and work, a new equality was established that could sustain their quest of seeking divine fellowship.

Both Essenes and Theraputae remained on the periphery of mainstream Jewish life and seemed either to have perished in the tumults of antiquity, withered away from lack of support, or to have been absorbed into Christianity, a religion for which monasticism seems to be intrinsic.

The history of Christian monasticism is rich and varied, but at the core of things, it sought an answer to one impulse: the desire for a perfect peace beyond temporal instability and human imperfection. This desire is, of course, at the heart of the Christian encounter with God, told in differing ways, but most evocatively in the recounting of one wealthy and pious Jew with Jesus (also described in the last chapter). Each of the synoptic Gospels presents the story of the young rich man, representative of many, who approached Jesus and asked 'What must I do to inherit eternal life?' (Matthew, 19:16-30; Mark, 10:17-31; and Luke, 18:18-30). The man was in absolute observance of the Commandments, yet he desired more. Jesus' answer – to distribute all that he had to the poor, be satisfied with spiritual treasure, and follow him – left the man sad for one reason: he had many possessions. In its essence, Christian monasticism is the attempt to relive that encounter, but not to depart in sorrow.

Christian monasticism takes its known historical form in the late third century. The initial call to the desert was, of course, influenced by the persecution of Christians, by a cultural heritage of philosophers rejecting the complexity and constraints of civilisation for personal freedom, and by economic crisis. But these and other social influences are minor. After all, the majority of Christians did not pursue monasticism; the majority were not intellectuals, the majority were not free to choose their economic destiny (nor did monasticism initially guarantee financial security). No, the conception of Christian monasticism was a response to an interior encounter with the divine and its growth was prompted by a persistent desire to strip away all obstacles to continuing in that encounter.

From the original monks of the wilderness, through the wandering Celtic ascetic movement, to the various forms of communal life influenced by St. Augustine and St. Benedict, the history of Christian monasticism has been determined by a regular cycle of simplicity, crisis, and return to simplicity. The Carolingian and Papal securities granted to the monastic life aimed at establishing spiritual simplicity at the centre of European society. The rise of Cluniac monks – with their zeal for perpetual prayer – created a monastic order in which life was radically restructured around the lavish praise of God in liturgy. The reactionary primitivism of the Carthusian, Cistercian, and other movements in the face of Cluny's stock-piling of wealth; the creation of Christian Chivalric orders (such as the Templars and Knights Hospitaller of St. John); the growth of lay brothers; the explosion of urban monastic 'beggars' (Mendicants such as the Franciscans and Dominicans); the rise of urban 'third orders' of lay men and women attached to the friars; the widespread appearance of laity and religious united under highly localised rules and living a simple, unified life of prayer and work (such as the frugal independent women known as the Beguines or the vocational 'guilds' that formed around baking, ship-building, weaving, and every conceivable medieval craft) – all these point to the one desire for more than material or even institutional religious satisfaction.

Scholars have given various projections for the percentage of the population involved in monastic orders (certainly under 5 percent during the middle ages). When one adds into the calculation the number of voluntary communal associations structurally and spiritually shaped by monasticism (such as lay confraternities, collegiate structures, third-order movements, and especially the guilds), one realises that medieval society was marked by an omnipresence of monastic culture – or 'corporate Christianity' (see, for example, Duffy 1992: 131-154). Every one of these communities had a dual focus – to provide spiritual formation and channel surplus wealth into religious and charitable activities. Guildsmen, for example, were expected to set aside a determined amount of their wealth to support religious ceremonies, the 'begging orders' (like the Franciscans), orphans and widows, and disabled members of their profession. All this was grounded in the monastic understanding of collective fulfilment of the Gospel vision for Christian life under rules that moderated production, consumption, and expenditure. The desire for spiritual perfection – for a living heart within society that beat out of a loving hunger for redemption and peace – was a mark of society prior to the modern age.

Christian monasticism shared much with its Jewish forerunners, including a detachment and, at times, hostility towards concepts of exclusively private wealth. It looked first to the wilderness and world of the rural villages for its centre, but developed forms of engagement with and within the city. It balanced a hierarchical sense of leadership with a fraternal approach to deliberation and governance. It focused on regular communal worship, centered on the singing of the Psalms. Corporate displays of unity – through common garments, ceremonial rites, and other marks of incorporations – were evident and celebrated, at times competitively so. Like the Essene movement, with its concern with restoring the true covenant, Christian monasticism seemed ever generating critics of ostentatious display, inequality, and spiritual laxity, who championed a return to some earlier, simpler form of living in the face of excessiveness, distraction, and social inequality. 'I am astonished that monks could be so lacking in moderation...' begins St. Bernard of Clairvaux in monasticism's greatest jeremiad against smug worldliness, a tongue lashing all the more astounding when one realises its target was Bernard's friend William of Saint Thierry (Casey, 1970). Bernard's depiction of the now majority of Benedictines as bloated, gaudy, and boozy helped make his letter a public cause célèbre that both helped advance both the Cistercian order and triggered a Benedictine reform movement.

In contradistinction to all pagan 'simplicity' movements (such as cynicism), and building upon nascent ideas of the Hebraic imagination, Christian monasticism embraced manual labour and craftsmanship. If the master worked as a simple carpenter, how could the disciple be any different? This was more than a theological difference with the pagan world. The pagan philosophical movements largely presumed the presence of a massive slave class which would sustain civilisation so that the few could seek contemplation. Without much fanfare, the Christian monks not only assumed a moderate amount of manual labour, but often described their spiritual ideals in terms of tools and the experience of hard work.

The fundamental difference between Jewish and Christian monasticism is found in the Christian belief in the Incarnation of God and its consequences. The simple living of the Christian monk was undertaken first and foremost to prepare the soul for divine union, and that union was formed by the simple path of imitating Christ, not merely obeying rules established by God for mortals. Furthermore, social and priestly reform – even the restoring of right relations between God and His people – were very much an afterthought to the primary quest for spiritual perfection along the path of mimetic humility. So, while *The Manual of Discipline* does state things resonant with Christian monasticism such as 'only through the holy spirit can one achieve union with God's truth and be purged of all his iniquities,' (Gaster, 1964: 50), *The Rule of St. Benedict* puts forward the fundamental Christian idea of moving beyond obedience to law or even correct knowledge of doctrine. Instead, the simple living of his monasticism creates the conditions by which one 'may share in the suffering of Christ through patience and thus be found worthy to be companions with Him in His kingdom' (Fahey, 2013: 104). Direct participation in divine life, in addition to some future reward, was always at the heart of Christian simplicity.

'The patience' described by Benedict, was the patience needed for the simple life. This sober truth is something that can be forgotten with the romance that accompanies the early stages of living a counter-cultural life. For the medieval world, simple living was not something driven by individual innovation. If it could be called 'voluntary', it was so only at the beginning. In fact, the will and unshackled self-determination was something to be uprooted. Through humility and living under the moderate requirements of the 'school of the Lord's service', monks were expected to live not for themselves. Indeed, nothing is seen so flawed and corrosive to happiness as the self-will in monasticism (see, e.g., Fahey, 2013: 101, 116-117).

Tradition and stability served as the essence of monasticism: the regularity of its structured life trained the monk to seek those things which were beyond change. The freedom sought by those entering monastic communities had been promised by, but not found in, an inconstant world. Monasticism offered them neither an earthly utopia nor an ideological opiate. In contrast, it offered a paradox: the seeming contradiction of freedom found through suffering and restraint. Dom Paul DeLatte, abbot of Solesmes at the beginning of the twentieth century, writing a harried mother who sought to pattern her life on the Benedictine masters, but who felt distracted and discouraged by the encroaching of the mundane, explained it this way:

> Worldly people generally demand a life without troubles; true Christians courageously take their portion of the dose of hidden bitterness God mixes into their life in order to put them in a position where they must lean on him. You will never have perfect peace; there will always be hard rubs and tribulation. It is certainly not by eliminating these annoying details that we will find peace; on the contrary, it is by accepting them in tranquility and making an effort to lean upon God. You are simply serving your apprenticeship as a creature (Totah, 1997: 93).

The restraint and renunciation of Christian asceticism was thus seen as the necessary precondition for spiritual creativity and peace, precisely because such self-denial did not hold out the false promise of freedom from suffering, but rather allowed one to transcend worldly concerns through a reliance on eternal sources. The monk, nun, or lay brother or sister lived out their 'apprenticeship as creature' through a simple life of prayer and work, patterned to communicate the transcendent world he or she so desired. That pattern most explicitly manifested itself in the form of a rule.

The *regula* – or rule – of monks is a word familiar to most. It is a Rule that one finds the particulars of the simple life of monks: dress, diet, the prescribed rhythm of the day and year, a communal constitution, etc. Although the *Rule of Benedict* remains the best known rule, dozens existed. Yet for all the word's familiarity, we tend to forget how essential this concept of 'rule' was to the pursuit of simple living. All Christian monastic communities took their inspiration from the first Christian community in Jerusalem, described in Acts, 2:43-47 and 4:32-35. To recreate that golden moment was always seen as the answer to life's struggle. St. Augustine noted that the common life offered by his *rule* aimed at living 'harmoniously in the house and to have one mind and one heart seeking God', echoing the very language of Acts (Kardong, 2010: 170). For St. Basil, the simple program that led to a life pleasing to God and to the monk began by discovering and following the right order of things that constituted a Christian life; without order and rule, love of God and man would be impossible (Holmes, 2000: 49-67). Even the wildly remote Irish monastic communities were in accord with the principle of *regula*. The eighth-century *Rule of Comghall* opened, 'Be faithful to the *rule*... for therein lies your salvation'; and the ninth-century *Rule of Mochudu Raithín* – a rule which governed not only monks but laity – opens with the self-referential words, '*This* is the path which leads to the Lord Jesus Christ... Let all people love God in heart and deed' (Ó' Maidin, 1996: 31, 61). For the monk, simple living was not envisioned as arising from spontaneity, but from structure.

Monastic orders and lay imitations each had their particular character, defined by the rules. Rules varied in length, tone, and specifics, yet they were united in presenting an essential structure to sustain western monasticism. Like the physical architecture of monastic houses – especially that of the inspired Cistercians – beyond all their variety, the rules shared in this: they provided a structure that encouraged men and women to dwell in a light-filled silence with their brothers and sisters, and there to discover God and find in God's simplicity that monks and their companions had been created in God's likeness and made for something beyond the dissolving complexities of this world.

Western monasticism has survived Christianity's disunion, the French Revolution's persecution, and modern consumerism's dismissal. It flourishes. There are approximately 18,000 Benedictines and 1,200 religious houses today. Nearly 25,000 lay people have become oblates, following the *Rule of St. Benedict* in their daily lives. Over the last half century the number of Cistercian monasteries has doubled. Monks and nuns of traditional orders – such as the Benedictines – are now found amongst Lutherans and Anglicans. Ecumenical groups such as the Community of Jesus have begun to appear in the presence of the most consumerist impulses. All this suggests that something singular continues to be offered in western monasticism to all seeking a peace that remains elusive in the world.

References and Further Reading

Casey, Michael (trans. & ed.). 1970. *Cistercians and Cluniacs: St. Bernard's* Apologia *to Abbot William*. Kalamazoo, Michigan: Cistercian Publications.

Duffy, Eamon. 1992. *The Stripping of the Altars: Traditional Religion in England, 1400-1580*. New Haven & London: Yale University Press.

Fahey, William (trans. & ed.). 2013. *The Foundations of Western Monasticism*. Charlotte, North Carolina: St. Benedict's Press.

Gaster, Theodor H (trans. & ed.). 1964. *The Dead Sea Scriptures*. 1964. Garden City, New Jersey: Anchor Books.

Holmes, Augustine. 2000. *A Life Pleasing to God: The Spirituality of the Rules of St. Basil*. Kalamazoo, Michigan & Spencer, Massachusetts: Cistercian Publications.

Josephus. 1979. *The Wars of the Jews*, in *The Works of Flavius Josephus*. 4 Vols. Grand Rapids, Michigan: Baker Book House. Original edition, Dublin, 1738-41.

Kardong, Terrence. 2010. *Pillars of Community: Four Rules of Pre-Benedictine Monastic Life.* Collegeville, Minnesota: Liturgical Press.

Kinder, Terryl N. 2002. *Cistercian Europe: Architecture of Contemplation.* Grand Rapids, Michigan: Wm. B. Eerdmans Publishing Co.

Lawrence, C.H. 1989. *Medieval Monasticism: Forms of Religious Life in Western Europe in the Middle Ages.* Second edition. London & New York: Longman.

Ó Maidín, Uinseann. (trans. & ed.) 1996. *The Celtic Monk: Rules and Writings of Early Irish Monks.* Kalamazoo, Michigan & Spencer, Massachusetts: Cistercian Publications.

Merton, Thomas. 1975. *The Silent Life.* London: Sheldon Press. Original edition, New York: Farrar, Straus & Cudahy, 1957.

Philo of Alexandria. 1981. *The Contemplative Life, The Giants, and Selections.* Translated by David Winston. Mahwah, New Jersey: Paulist Press.

Totah, Mary David. (ed.) 1997. *The Spirit of Solesmes.* Petersham, Massachusetts: Saint Bede's Publications and Tunbridge Wells: Burns & Oates.

CHAPTER EIGHT

THE QUAKERS

MARK BURCH

'Quaker' was a pejorative epithet applied in seventeenth century Britain to members of The Religious Society of Friends based on reports that they sometimes 'quaked' during their Meetings for worship. In the manner of Friends, and with perhaps just a touch of defiance, Friends adopted the title as a badge of distinction. Today Friends are still called Quakers.

Quakerism has been described as 'the Quaker understanding of the truth at the heart of the Christian faith' (Dale, 2000: 18) or 'a third form of Christianity – as distinct from Catholicism and Protestantism (Brinton, 1952: xvi). Describing what distinguishes these three strands of Christianity exceeds the scope of this chapter. Suffice it, however, that Quakerism is not a notion or a dogma, but a 'way' (Advices and Queries #2). Quakerism is simplicity itself. With no ordained ministry, no generally accepted creed, no established dogmas, no ceremonial or cultic rituals, and a minimalist organisational structure, perfectionist and individualistic, Quakers are a society of mystical empiricists whose practice of worship aims to plunge them toward the centre of the spiritual galaxy where the Light is strongest.

To understand the place of simple living in Friends' faith, practice and history, it is first necessary to understand the concept of 'testimony.'

Testimony is the lived experience of Friends' mystical intuitions. The concept of testimony fuses together the individual's evolving apprehension of inwardly revealed spiritual truth with the outward manner of his or her daily living. Stated a bit differently – Friends try to cultivate continuing awareness of spiritual truth. This truth is revealed both through their inward subjective experience of it and also through the outer relationships and events of everyday life. Friends desire that their choices and behaviour come into closer and closer alignment with their inner intuitions concerning the nature of Truth, or of Spirit, or of God. The congruence between spiritual intuition and outward behaviour is itself a Quaker testimony – the testimony to integrity. Today, the key testimonies of Quaker practice include the testimonies to Simplicity, Peace (nonviolence), Integrity, Community, Equality, and Sustainability (Earth care). In a sense, Friends might be described as people who strive to live out these values, first experienced as spiritual revelations, in all their daily affairs.

Simple living developed among Friends as a testimony when they recognised, both as individuals and as Meetings (i.e. collectively), that simple living was more in alignment with their intuitions concerning the truth, the nature of God, right relationships with others and with the Earth, than is a way of life characterised by affluence, waste, power, lust and luxury. In the seventeenth and eighteenth centuries, Friends adopted simple living partly from concern that materialism and commercialism posed major distractions to one's spiritual development. Wealth can become an idol rather than a tool. Moreover, the pursuit of luxurious living was seen as a major cause of war (hence contradicting the peace testimony), a system of oppression of aboriginal peoples and slaves (hence violating the testimony to equality), and the source of exploitative labour practices and unhealthy or dangerous working conditions for both people and animals (Woolman, 1793).

Some have described the history of simplicity among Quakers as continuous with the early mystical asceticism of the Patristic Age, monasticism, and contemporary groups like Mennonites, Waldenses, Lollards, Cathartists and Ana-baptists (Burdick, 2007). From this perspective, simplicity is the outer manifestation of the more fundamental testimony to integrity – conforming one's way of life to the model of Christ without compromise or admixture of motives. Seeking God first is what constitutes 'integrity before Christ'.

In the twentieth century, more emphasis has been placed on consumerism as a driver of economic injustice and war, neither of which Friends perceive to be in alignment with the divine nature (Binns-Young, 1938; Gregg, 1936). Most recently, Friends find themselves in increasing unity regarding simple living as the most congruent and constructive antidote for the effects of consumerism on the natural world. These effects are likely to include massive species extinctions, increasing risks to health, and unimaginable threats to the wellbeing both of those currently living in poverty and for future generations (Burch, 2000).

In Friends' experience, the testimony to simplicity has both an outer physical, and an inner subjective aspect. The outer manifestation of the testimony to simplicity has taken different forms, waxing and waning over the centuries. Early in Quaker history, Meetings sometimes enjoined sumptuary regulations on their members including practices that visibly distinguished Quakers from other members of the community. These included plain dress, plain speech, a general willingness to forego luxury consumption and other details of personal conduct. Simplicity was also expressed in the unadorned plainness of Friends' worship as well as a minimalist quality in the design and equipage of meeting houses (Shi, 1985). During the first century of Quaker history, such practices visibly marked Quakers as a self-described 'peculiar people', although secularising influences in the late eighteenth and early nineteenth centuries saw them diminish. Preoccupation with sumptuary concerns waxed again in the nineteenth century only to wane once more in the twentieth. Today, Friends in North America, Europe and Australasia are essentially indistinguishable in their manner of dress and speech from anyone else in their respective societies.

Apart from the relatively superficial matter of how one might dress, Friends' concern with how their outward way of life might reflect what they value is just as weighty a concern today as ever. As one's spiritual life deepens, at least at an empirical level, this makes little difference to the rest of humanity unless it manifests in some outward form that improves the world and brings it into closer alignment with the divine intention for human beings. Adoption of a materially simpler way of life liberates time and attention for the important work of spiritual growth and service to others.

Other voices speak from a more contemplative, interiorised perspective. For some (Burdick, 2007; Foster, 1981; Penn, 1668), simplicity is entirely a spiritual grace granted by God to whomever God chooses. The recipient of the gift of simplicity has little to say in the matter. One effect of the divine gift is to manifest in the outer form of one's life the material signs of the wholly inward and spiritual change that preceded it. Such a view has much in common with Calvinism and reflects the influence of resurgent North American Christian fundamentalism. It also more or less disregards the contribution that choosing a simple way of life can make to disposing us to receive the divine gift of simplicity should it be offered. The tradition of Friends practice sees human cooperation with divine action as essential to its fulfilment.

Another perspective of simplicity begins from the observation that we are inwardly divided (Prevallet, 1982; Whitmire, 2001). Our inner life is a cacophony of competing desires, impulses and opinions that cause suffering and inner turmoil. We are alienated from others and divided against ourselves. The spiritual meaning of simplicity thus refers to a process, entirely under divine guidance and mostly un-conscious, which gradually unifies and focuses our inner life and centres it in the divine intention for us. This process is decidedly not under our personal or conscious control, thus making it a supernatural work which we nevertheless invite, trust and to which we surrender. It is essential to its success that we choose to cooperate with the divine work and configure our lifestyle so as to support this inner process of spiritual evolution. The main vehicle for cooperating with the divine intention is the Quaker practice of worship. At the yonder end of this experience, we are 'made simple' by something we cannot control or fully understand but which gifts us with integrity, singleness of purpose, inner clarity, and freedom from compulsion such that we become truly free and able to choose what pleases God.

It seems clear that both the inner and outer perspectives of the testimony to simplicity represent two aspects of the same process. Inner change can manifest as an outward change in lifestyle. Choosing to live more simply, even out of our human strength, can also express an individual desire for, and the intention to welcome, the inner simplicity one's lifestyle makes visible.

All testimonies also have both an individual and a collective aspect (Dale, 2000). The seed of a testimony often appears first as a 'concern' arising from the spiritual intuition of an individual Friend, although it might also arise from the collective spiritual discernment of a Meeting as a whole. If a concern is pressing enough, it may find expression through the vocal ministry of an individual Friend during a Meeting for worship or in some other context. Once the concern is spoken out, it may become a matter for collective discernment. It becomes a question, a challenge, an experience, an invitation, a sensibility that enters the awareness of other members of the Meeting and is thence 'tested' against the spiritual intuitions of the other Friends present. This process may take a considerable time. For example, the discernment process that gradually evolved Friends' collective opposition to the institution of slavery took over a century to evolve completely (Brinton, 1952).

In any case, every testimony represents an intuition about the nature of spiritual truth which has usually first arisen as a fact of individual experience, but which is then assimilated by the Society as a whole, being tested and sifted against the Meeting's awareness of spiritual truth as well. As the testimony becomes part of Friends' spiritual culture, it then helps inform the consciences of children growing up under the care of a Meeting, and also those who may be joining the Meeting as adults. Exactly how the testimony to simplicity is lived out becomes another matter for individual discernment and can take a myriad of specific forms. But the spirit behind these many expressions displays unity of purpose and coherence of intent if it is a true testimony. Individual insight is parsed through the collective experience of the Meeting, while the collective sense of the Meeting is continually open to challenge by fresh individual experience.

All testimonies, including the testimony to simplicity, have both a notional and behavioural aspect. They certainly include intellectual content in as much as they can be approached through words and thoughts, but never reduced to mere words and thoughts. Most Friends would hasten to remind us that Quakerism is not a set of dogmas – 'a form of words' as they say – but a way of living. Most Friends recognise the limitations of language to formulate these matters clearly and therefore allow a wide margin in this regard. But Quakers would also be emphatic that the 'way' of Christianity formulated by Quakerism is a way of behaving – a practice more than a dogma. Historically, this practice has included relatively superficial aspects such as plain dress, plain speech, etc., which have changed with time and culture, but also profounder aspects such as the Quaker manner of worship, of attention to business, of cultivating clearness, and of taking individual members or their concerns 'under the care of the Meeting'.

The Religious Society of Friends first appeared in England in the mid-seventeenth century through the preaching of George Fox and others. From the beginning, Friends' peace testimony placed them at loggerheads with the military service demanded by the Crown. The testimony to equality expressed as a refusal to observe 'hat honour' and use formal titles when addressing those in positions of authority or higher social station rankled the upper classes. As more Friends were imprisoned, they inevitably endured, and came to be concerned about, the living conditions within prisons and the fate of prisoners themselves.

The conjunction of Friends' testimonies and political and social reform movements got carried into the American colonies in the late seventeenth century, a notable example being William Penn's attempt to establish a political state modelled on Quaker values, a territory which is the modern state of Pennsylvania. Other Friends such as John Woolman preached insistently on the evils of slavery, exploitation of aboriginal peoples, and the systemic oppression required to provide for luxury consumption. Elizabeth Fry worked tirelessly for the reform of prisons, and other Friends became key figures in the movement to abolish slavery.

By the eighteenth century, for a variety of reasons most of which were internal to the Society of Friends, Quakerism entered its 'quietist' period marked by a greater emphasis on contemplation and individual spiritual practice. But at the turn of the twentieth century, traditional concerns of Friends began to re-emerge, particularly the Society's opposition to war and the preparation for war, as well as a number of social issues such as poverty alleviation, international relief efforts, its continuing concern about prison reform and restorative justice. By the end of the twentieth century, Friends also recognised a growing concern focused on sustainability and Earth care. It is with respect both to the Earth care and peace testimonies that the testimony to simplicity has enjoyed somewhat of a renaissance.

In conclusion we can note once again that the very meaning of 'testimony' in the Quaker expression of Christianity fuses belief based on personal spiritual experience with action in the world of our daily human relationships. This fusion of inner conviction and real world social engagement is also present in the testimony to simplicity as it resonates more or less strongly in all the other Quaker testimonies.

References

Binns-Young, Mildred. 1938. 'Functional Poverty'. Wallingford, PA: Pendle Hill Pamphlet #6.

Brinton, Howard H. 1952. *Friends for 300 Years*. Wallingford, PA: Pendle Hill Publications.

Burch, Mark A. 2000. *Stepping Lightly: Simplicity for People and the Planet*. Gabriola Island, BC: New Society Publishers.

Burdick, Timothy James. 2007. 'The Testimony of Quaker Simplicity: CHTH 564 – Quaker History and Polity'.

http://www.scribd.com/doc/23899627/Testimony-of-Simplicity

Dale, Jonathan. 2000. 'Quaker understanding of testimony' In: Elizabeth Cave & Ros Morley (eds.) 2000. Faith in Action: Quaker Social Testimony. London, U.K.: Quaker Home Service, Britain Yearly Meeting.

Gregg, Richard. 1936. 'The Value of Voluntary Simplicity'. Wallingford, PA: Pendle Hill Pamphlet #3.

Penn, William. 1668. *No Cross, No Crown.* (Ed.) Ronald Selleck. 2007. BiblioBazaar LLC.

Prevallet, Elaine M. 1982. *Reflections on Simplicity.* Wallingford, PA: Pendle Hill Pamphlet #244.

Shi, David E. 1985. *The Simple Life: Plain Living and High Thinking in American Culture.* New York, NY: Oxford University Press.

The Yearly Meeting of the Religious Society of Friends (Quakers) in Britain. 1994. Advices and Queries. London, UK: The Yearly Meeting of the Religious Society of Friends (Quakers) in Britain.

Woolman, John. 1793. *The Journal and Major Essays of John Woolman.* (Ed.) Phillips P. Moulton 1989. Richmond, IN: Friends United Press.

CHAPTER NINE

THE AMISH

STEVEN NOLT

'How can we instil in our children the value of the plain life?' asked an Amish mother in *Family Life*, an Amish-published magazine edited in Aylmer, Ontario, Canada. 'We treasure the simplicity of our heritage and although we know it is not the key to eternal life, yet we feel plainness is a necessary fruit – evidence that we have set our affections on things eternal' ('Simple Living', 1997: 18).

The young woman's musings capture the sentiments of Amish people when it comes to simplicity. The simple life for them is not something optional nor is it a distant ideal. It is a concrete and attainable reality, embodied in families and local communities. At the same time, Amish people understand simplicity not as an end in itself, but as an expression and by-product of life lived in humble obedience to God.

Today the Amish – some 282,000 adults and children in the United States and Canada – are widely known around the world, in large part because their highly traditional way of life stands in stark contrasts to the individualistic, commercialised, and scientific-progressive North American culture in which they live. The Amish do not drive or own cars, are not connected to the electric grid of public utilities, wear 'plain' clothing and hairstyling that does not reflect current fashion, and stop their formal education with eighth grade schooling. Today only a minority makes a living through farming, but virtually all continue to live in rural areas where they support themselves with small shops catering to rural retail or the small-scale manufacturing of furniture and other goods.

There is a good deal of popularised and romanticised imagery of Amish life, much of which suggests that the Amish are unchanging or completely disconnected from the modern world. Such images are inaccurate since Amish life does adapt and change in measured and deliberate ways, and families interact with non-Amish neighbours and co-workers on a regular basis. Yet Amish life does stand in sharp contrast to dominant cultural values. Rejecting radio, television, and other electronic media, they are sheltered from the seductive blitz of advertisements that punctuate broadcast entertainment and pop up on computer screens.

The Amish are a sectarian Christian group that traces its roots to the Anabaptist movement of the sixteenth-century Protestant Reformation. Anabaptists rejected infant baptism, called for the separation of church and state, and most of them also eschewed violence, even in self-defence. As a diffuse and persecuted movement, Anabaptism developed different emphases in different places, spawning groups that included the evangelical Mennonites and communitarian Hutterites, among others. The Amish emerged as a distinct group in 1693 in Switzerland and the Alsace region of what is now eastern France. Nicknamed for their leader, Jakob Ammann, the Amish were Anabaptist, committed to distinguishing themselves from what they perceived to be 'worldly' society and the growing religious accommodation and cultural assimilation of other Anabaptists. To the degree that the Amish saw worldly society as profligate and indulgent, Amish life was constrained. In 1702 one observer noted that the Amish were distinguished by the fact that 'the men ... have a long beard and the men and women wear clothing made only of linen cloth, summer and winter'. In contrast, the Anabaptists who had not sided with Ammann had 'shorter beards' and dressed 'about like the Catholics' (Kraybill, Johnson-Weiner, and Nolt, 2013: 33).

Amish households immigrated to North America in the mid-1700s and again, in another wave, in the early to mid-1800s. The Amish church is organised only at the local level, with more than 2,000 church districts which form the locus of discernment and decision with regard to lifestyle choices and material acquisition. Each district includes around 150 people, about 40 percent of whom are baptised adults, with the balance being unbaptised children. There are no synods, conferences, or diocese to impose uniformity more broadly. Thus, Amish life varies in its details from place to place. Deference to tradition as codified in local, oral tradition provides the social glue that holds Amish society together rather than the organisation and bureaucracy that characterise modernity. The structure of local Amish churches is simple: members meet for worship in private homes, shops, or barns rather than in church buildings; there are designated male clergy but they are unsalaried. Worship includes *a cappela* singing, there are no choirs or liturgical art work, and the three-hour service follows a pattern unaltered over several centuries.

The Amish see Jesus as the touchstone for their practice. 'When Jesus was here, he left us an outstanding example of simple living,' explained one minister in *Strangers and Pilgrims: Why We Live Simply*. '[Jesus] gave us many teachings ... [about] the danger of material possessions and the importance of trusting God on a daily basis for our food and clothing. Concern for others also undergirds Amish simplicity: 'How can I eat cake, when my neighbor does not have bread?' he continued. 'How can I discard serviceable clothing because it is not in style, when my neighbor is shivering from cold? In short, how can I live in luxury when my neighbor lacks the necessities?' (Stoll, 2008: 5, 7).

Obedience to Jesus, submission to the church, and personal humility are values that underpin Amish commitments to simplicity. Amish people believe that the individual finds fulfilment in community. Anything that calls attention to the individual, or makes the individual stand above his or her peers is suspect. Thus, the Amish aversion to posing for photographs is an expression of their concern that portrait photography or consenting to be photographed is a sign of pride. A similar dynamic is at work in the general Amish refusal to be quoted by name in newspaper articles or books. No one wishes to speak for another or place themselves as speaking for the group or on behalf of others.

For the Amish, humility is the inseparable companion of submission. 'Unless we are truly humble, we are not truly plain,' said the Amish mother cited at the beginning of this essay. 'We must be willing to be something less than our neighbor across the road' ('Simple Living', 1997: 18). Plain clothing illustrates the combination. Clothing should avoid 'vain display in ornamentation, such as wearing of jewelry, fussing up the hair, and costly clothing', and it should not be left to individual choice. The humility evident in plain dress is matched by submission to the common dress standards that express the unity of the church (1001 Questions, 1992: 130).

Such commitments apply to more than clothing. Collective rejection of many consumer technologies and conveniences – from electric lighting to wall-to-wall carpeting – also imposes a rough egalitarianism on the local church. 'Our furnishings and way of life need to be plain and simple so as not to appear more wealthy than others', wrote one church leader (Kraybill, Nolt, and Weaver-Zercher, 2010: 133). Certainly there is some difference in wealth among Amish households; they are not a collectivist society that holds all property in common. Nonetheless, the thriving entrepreneur, the wage-labourer, and the small farmer all own the same kind of buggy, wear virtually the same clothes, sing the same slow-cadence hymns on Sunday mornings, and will be buried without eulogy in the same style of plain coffin under a uniformly simple headstone.

Amish people are frugal, thrifty, and practical. Clothing is reused and passed on to others. Strips of old cloth are fashioned into quilts or woven into braided rugs. Broken furniture is repaired, not tossed into the dumpster. A common Amish business is the so-called 'bent-and-dent' stores that purchase damaged and surplus products from national chain stores and then resell the items at deep discounts to Amish and non-Amish customers.

One of the signature ways that Amish society balances a commitment to simplicity with the needs of a dynamic social and economic life is by making a distinction between ownership versus access. Amish households may have limited access to a number of things they may not own. For example, although church members do not own or drive cars or trucks, they may ride in motor vehicles, pay for taxi service and arrange for a non-Amish driver to deliver goods or make a delivery. Similarly, an Amish family that rents a farmer's market stand in a large market house will use the electric lights and refrigeration made available by the building's non-Amish owner even though such amenities are forbidden in the family's own home. Some observers see hypocrisy in this use-but-don't-own approach, but the Amish see a deep consistency. The problem with ownership, from an Amish perspective, is the matter of individual autonomy and control. Having to arrange and pay for a driver means that the Amish car-rider does not have access to what the *automobile* promises: automatic mobility. Similarly, the terms of a market lease place the stand-holder in a subordinate position and communicate that some things may be possible on alien turf, but not in the sacred heart of Amish family life. In either case, the Amish are in debt to someone else – socially and financially – and must take another's time, schedule, and goodwill into account. On one level, this access-rather-than-ownership principle can insert extra costs into Amish life and might be seen as working against a definition of simplicity-as-efficiency. For the Amish, however, the bargain is one that places an accent on humility, submission, and practical limits, while allowing some flexibility in terms of economic innovation (Kraybill, Johnson-Weiner, and Nolt, 2013: 315-18).

Although simplicity is an esteemed value, it rests alongside fidelity to tradition and a willingness to forego innovation, in some cases, even if such innovation would make things simpler. For example, one Amish couple in Lancaster, Pennsylvania purchased a home that had been owned by a non-Amish family. The process of 'de-electrifying' the house in order to make it comply with Amish church expectations was not cheap. After replacing the electric lighting with bottled-gas lamps, they bought a propane-powered refrigerator (which cost twice as much as an electric one) and stove. Other changes followed until finally they faced their biggest issue: the electric water pump. The electricity to run the water pump cost a few dollars per month, but the Amish couple paid $14,000 to install a small diesel engine to replace the electric pump. The diesel engine creates pneumatic power to operate their water pump, washing machine, and sewing machine. 'It would have been cheaper for us to stay electric', the husband disclosed. As a result, the de-electrification process took four years. 'Our ministers were very understanding', the husband explained. 'The main thing was to be headed in the non-electric direction' (Kraybill, Nolt, and Weaver-Zercher, 2010: 11-12).

The four year process, in this case, also illustrates the way in which Amish practice of simplicity is comprised of many small decisions and choices, which also serve to communicate and pass on these values to Amish children. Since Amish youth are not routinely baptised into the church as infants and must choose, during their late teen years, whether to join the church (about 85 percent do so), parents feel a divine responsibility to train their children in simplicity so that those children will voluntarily adopt the Amish way.

The mother mentioned above reflected on her responsibilities as a parent, for 'eventually our children will see that the luxuries and complexities of the world are a hindrance to our faith.' In addition to curbing her own consuming desires, she offered these guidelines for teaching children simplicity: (1) keep toys few and simple; (2) dress and name dolls plainly; (3) teach basic sewing skills rather than embroidery and painting; (4) make new out of old in the course of hooking, braiding, and sewing rugs; (5) piece quilts from scraps of clothing; (6) remove needless fringes, ribbons, and tucks from dresses; and (7) remind children 'that the trend toward what is bigger, fancier, and more expensive leads rapidly in one direction – away from God' ('Simple Living', 1997: 19).

As pilgrims on a path to heaven that winds through a world of possession, Amish parents and children, alike, seek to live against a horizon of eternity. As an Amish minister explains:

> If we meant to stay here, it would make sense to accumulate and enjoy all the earthly comforts. If there were no eternity, then yes, the more fine food we can

eat, the more expensive clothing we can wear, the more leisure we can enjoy, the more wealth we can pile up. ... We came into this world with nothing, and we are going to leave it the same way (Stoll, 5).

References

1001 Questions and Answers on the Christian Life. 1992. Aylmer, Ont.: Pathway Publishers.

Kraybill, Donald B., Karen M. Johnson-Weiner, and Steven M. Nolt. 2013. *The Amish*. Baltimore: The Johns Hopkins University Press.

Kraybill, Donald B., Steven M. Nolt, and David L. Weaver-Zercher. 2010. *The Amish Way: Patient Faith in a Perilous World.* San Francisco: Jossey-Bass.

'Simple Living: How Can we Keep It?' 1997. *Family Life*, May, 18-19.

Stoll, Elmo. 2008. *Strangers and Pilgrims: Why We Live Simply.* Aylmer, Ont.: Pathaway Publishers.

CHAPTER TEN

HENRY THOREAU

SAMUEL ALEXANDER

Few individuals in history evoke images of 'the simple life' more distinctly than the poet-philosopher, Henry David Thoreau. In 1845, when Henry was 27 years old, he left his hometown of Concord, Massachusetts, and went to live alone in the woods, near Walden Pond, where he built himself a small cabin and for two years earned a simple living mainly from the labour of his own hands. He spent his days growing his own food, writing in his journal, and sauntering through the woods, observing and recording the seemingly infinite wonders of nature in a state of prolonged fascination. It was a period of immense personal growth for Thoreau, during which he struggled productively with the question of how much material wealth – or, rather, how little – a person actually needs to live well and be free.

The main literary product of Thoreau's time living in the woods was a book called *Walden*, a dense, unclassifiable text that is part autobiography, part nature writing, and part 'simple living' manifesto, but which is now widely regarded as one of the true classics of American literature. Not only that, *Walden* offers a penetrating critique of materialistic culture, one all the more piercing due to the fact that Thoreau was both a ruthless social critic and a literary genius. It makes for engaging and challenging reading, especially at those times when we see ourselves in the object of Thoreau's often scathing cultural critique.

In today's era of overlapping ecological, economic, and cultural crises, *Walden* is a text that is more relevant than ever before. As well as providing early insight into the destructive and oppressive nature of many processes of industrialisation, it also warns people of the self-imposed slavery that can flow from mindlessly dedicating one's life to the never-ending pursuit of 'nice things'. If nothing else, Thoreau's life and work serve as a fiery, poetic reminder that there are alternative, simpler ways to live – ways which are far freer and indeed more fulfilling than those governed by consumerist values and practices. Thoreau's message, in short, is that a simple life is a good life, and in our age of ecological overshoot, this is a message deserving of our closest attention.[1]

Thoreau on Materialistic Culture

In order to understand what drove the young Henry Thoreau out of his township and into the woods, it is necessary to acknowledge the context in which he was living. The middle of the nineteenth century was a time when the Industrial Revolution was really taking hold in the United States, but from Thoreau's perspective, his contemporaries were getting seduced by the extraordinary productive power of industry and machines, without putting their minds to the question of why or to what end they were expending all their efforts and labours – or at what cost. In Thoreau's eyes, the railroad was the defining emblem of industrialisation, and he often wrote of it metaphorically, as a representation of the emerging economic system that was fast changing the face of the United Sates and indeed the world. 'We do not ride upon the railroad,' he asserted, 'it rides upon us' (345).

---

[1] In what follows I quote extensively from Thoreau's writings, but to avoid cluttering the text with full citations I simply use brackets to reference page numbers from Carl Bode, ed., *The Portable Thoreau*, 1982. New York: Penguin. Most of the quotes are from *Walden* or Thoreau's essay, 'Life without Principle'.

Thoreau had travelled widely in his province, but everywhere, in shops, offices, and fields, the inhabitants seemed to him to be living lives of 'quiet desperation' (263), committing themselves to 'nothing but work, work, work' (632) in order to pay for their rising material desires. 'The twelve labors of Hercules were trifling in comparison with those which my neighbors have undertaken; for they were only twelve, and had an end; but I could never see that these men slew or captured any monster or finished any labor' (260). Thoreau likened people's materialistic cravings to the heads of a hydra, noting that 'as soon as one head is crushed, two spring up' (260).

The ancient Chinese philosopher, Lao-Tzu, once said: 'He who knows he has enough is rich' (Vanenbroeck, 1991: 116). Thoreau was telling his contemporaries that they had enough, but that they did not know it, and so were poor. Always wanting more luxuries and comforts, and never content with less, Thoreau felt that people did not understand the meaning of 'Economy', did not understand that 'the cost of a thing is the amount of ... life which is required to be exchanged for it' (286). 'Most [people],' he insisted, 'even in this comparatively free country, through mere ignorance or mistake, are so occupied with factitious cares and superfluously coarse labors of life that its finer fruits cannot be plucked by them' (261). By a 'seeming fate', there was 'no time to be anything but a machine' (261).

And for what? People's lives were being 'ploughed into the soil for compost' (261) just to obtain 'splendid houses' and 'finer and more abundant clothing ... and the like' (270). But as Thoreau would insist: 'Superfluous wealth can buy superfluities only' (568). Indeed, he claimed that 'most of the luxuries, and many of the so-called comforts of life, are not only not indispensable but positive hindrances to the elevation of mankind' (269). More concerned about accumulating nice things or climbing the social ladder than they were about their own destinies, people astounded Thoreau with how 'frivolous' (262) they were with respect to their own lives. The following passage states his position directly (636):

> If I should sell my forenoons and afternoons to society,
> as most appear to do, I am sure that for me there would
> be nothing left worth living for... I wish to suggest that a
> man may be very industrious, and yet not spend his time
> well. There is no more fatal blunderer than he who
> consumes the greater part of his life getting his living.

But Thoreau saw his townsfolk labouring under this very mistake. 'It is a fool's life,' he asserted bluntly, 'as they will find when they get to the end of it, if not before' (261). It was the English poet, William Wordsworth, who penned the lines, 'Getting and spending, we lay waste our powers', and one can imagine Thoreau being wholly sympathetic to that critical sentiment.

It appeared to Thoreau as if his fellow citizens were falling into the consumerist mode of living not because they preferred it to any other, but because they honestly thought there was no choice left. 'So thoroughly and sincerely are we compelled to live, reverencing our life, and denying the possibility of change. This is the only way, we say' (266).

Thoreau, however, was not convinced. He was of the view that 'there are as many ways [to live] as there are radii from one center' (266), and a consumerist existence was only one of the options available, and by no means the wisest choice. 'Even the life which [people] praise and regard as successful is but one kind', and 'why should we exaggerate any one kind at the expense of others?' (274). Forever the thoughtful non-conformist, Thoreau tended to believe that '[w]hat old people say you cannot do you try and find that you can' (264), and on that basis he boldly proposed that there should be '[o]ld deeds for old people, and new deeds for new' (264). Surely, he thought, there were better ways to live.

It was time for Thoreau to begin his living experiment out in the woods, near the shores of Walden Pond.

The Walden Experiment

In the second chapter of *Walden*, entitled 'Where I Lived, and What I Lived For', Thoreau offers us a direct explanation for his exit from conventional society. 'I went to the woods because I wished to live deliberately, to front only the essential facts of life and see if I could not learn what they had to teach, and not, when I came to die, discover that I have not lived' (343). Elsewhere he said that his purpose in going to Walden Pond was to 'transact some private business with the fewest obstacles' (275). In one sense this 'private business' was simply to write in solitude, close to nature, and away from modern distractions. In another sense, though closely related to the first, his motivation was to solve, or at least better understand, the economics of living well. What is the proper relationship one should have with money, possessions, and other forms of material wealth? How much is enough? What is an economy *for*? How best to earn a living? Perhaps, Thoreau had decided, the best path was to reduce his material needs and desires and to live a simple life. Simplicity of living was to be his means to the elevation of meaning and purpose, his path to genuine freedom.

Thoreau had come to suspect that, 'If your trade is with the Celestial Empire' (275) – by which he meant, if your concerns are 'higher' than merely getting and spending – then very little is actually needed to live well and to be free, provided life is approached with the right attitude. 'Simplify, simplify' (344) was to be his refrain. One should not need an impressive house, fancy clothes, exotic foods, or extravagant possessions to live well. Those things are not the stuff of true satisfaction, but often merely distractions. By minimising our consumption, Thoreau argued, we will find ourselves with more freedom to pluck the finer fruits of life, in ways that are not always obvious.

This, in essence, exemplifies the economics of sufficiency Thoreau put to the test at Walden Pond, by living simply and largely rejecting the division of labour. As far as possible he grew his own food, and mostly drank water from the pond. He cut down some trees and built himself a cabin with but one small room, and made some furniture. It was not much, but it was enough. And just enough was plenty. Thoreau did not wish to be chained to the economy, so he practised self-reliance; he did not wish to be slave to artificial material desires, so he practised self-discipline; and he did not wish to live what was not life, so he avoided wasting his precious time working to acquire more than he needed.

In order to live a full life, Thoreau felt that one must begin by thinking seriously about what really are the necessaries of life, 'for not till we have secured these are we prepared to entertain the true problems of life with freedom and prospect of success' (267-8). This passage is important because Thoreau is seeking to avoid a misunderstanding that might arise, and sometimes does, from his celebration of material simplicity. Simplicity is not material destitution, he is saying. We all have basic physical needs that have to be met (though they may be fewer than we commonly think). But once those basic needs are met, we are not obligated to dedicate our lives to the pursuit of more. Thoreau proposed that when we have obtained those things necessary to life, 'there is another alternative than to obtain superfluities; and that is, to adventure on life now, [our] vacation from humbler toil having commenced' (270-1).

Thoreau is warning us not to assume that material wealth will always contribute positively to our lives, for often, in insidious ways, it will not. It is not that there is anything inherently evil about money or material things; it is just that each moment we spend pursuing such things beyond what is necessary is a moment we could have spent on some free, non-materialistic good – such as talking with friends, walking through the woods, meeting our civic duties, being creative, or just relaxing. Sometimes trading our time for money and things will be a good trade, no doubt. But sometimes such a trade will ultimately cost more than it is worth, making us not richer but poorer, and thus be a bad trade.

With respect to clothing, Thoreau expresses his simplicity by reflecting on his own modest attire: 'if my jacket and trousers, my hat and shoes, are fit to worship God in, they will do will they not?' (278). It is an interesting question to consider, if not in relation to the worship of God, necessarily, then more generally in relation to the living of a passionate life. Old clothes will do, will they not? Thoreau proposed that they will do just fine. His argument is not that one cannot live a happy and meaningful life in fine clothing, so much as fine clothing is not necessary for a happy and meaningful life. If so, he would suggest that we do not waste our freedom labouring to purchase fine clothing. If our goals are 'higher' than crude materialism, we should recognise the limited need for money and possessions in our lives. '[M]y greatest skill has been to want but little,' he proclaimed (324).

Thoreau makes essentially the same point with respect to shelter. An average house in his neighbourhood cost about eight hundred dollars (at the time) and Thoreau noted that to lay up this sum would take from ten to fifteen years of the labourer's life; add the farm and one would have to spend twenty, thirty, or forty years toiling – more than half of one's life is easily spent. Would the American Indians have been wise to give up their modest but functional tepees on these terms? Thoreau had his doubts, suggesting that 'when the farmer has got his house, he may not be the richer but the poorer for it, and it be the house that has got him' (288).

Thoreau wanted to show at what sacrifice our more 'advanced' dwellings were obtained, and to suggest that, by living more simply, we may secure all the advantage without suffering any of the disadvantage. With this in mind, he went to Walden Pond with an axe, cut down some trees, and in about three unrushed months had built himself a modest but sturdy cabin. Again exemplifying his alternative mode of economic analysis, Thoreau declared that, 'I intend to build me a house which will surpass any on the main street in Concord in grandeur and luxury, as soon as it pleases me as much and will cost me no more [in terms of life] than the present one' (304).

It appears, then, that Thoreau was perfectly content with his shelter, modest though it was. Did this not make him richer than a king who is dissatisfied with his palace? With a little more wit we could *all* be richer than kings, Thoreau implied; but, unfortunately, 'Most [people] appear never to have considered what a house is, and are actually though needlessly poor all their lives because they think that they must have such a one as their neighbors have' (290).

Despite being a formidable defender of the simple life, Thoreau also saw 'how easily and insensibly we fall into a particular route, and make a beaten track for ourselves' (562); how easily we fall into the 'deep ruts of tradition and conformity' (562). This troubled Thoreau, for he thought that if we do not live our lives deliberately – if we only get out of bed because of 'the mechanical nudgings of some servitor' (342) – then we are just sleep-walking through life, injuring eternity by killing time, to paraphrase Thoreau (263). 'Little is to be expected of that day, if it can be called a day, to which we are not awakened by our Genius' (342). Thoreau is speaking not so much to geniuses here, as to the genius (or poet) in us all. Take yourself and your life seriously, he is saying. Do not let yourself be swept along. Claim your freedom and exercise your capacity to create your own fate. Compose yourself! WAKE UP!

Thoreau's essential position is neatly summed up in the following passage: 'I am convinced, both by faith and experience, that to maintain one's self on this earth is not a hardship but a pastime, if we will live simply and wisely' (325). This is perhaps the most important lesson that he learned while living in the woods, and it was a lesson that stayed with him for the rest of his life.

We might not have a pond nearby to conduct a living experiment as Thoreau did, and we might not want to live alone in the woods. But Thoreau's writings nevertheless offer us profound lessons in simplicity that remain applicable to our own contexts, our own lives, if only we dare to think for ourselves. We must each find our *own* way' (325), Thoreau properly insisted.

Conclusion

By the time he died in 1862, Thoreau had attained a certain recognised position as a writer, although the amount of money he earned from his writing and lecturing over his entire life was minimal. Nevertheless, the fact that his books, essays, and poems, barely sold was of little consequence. He had woven literary baskets of a delicate texture, and although he had not made it worth anyone's while to buy them, he felt that it had nonetheless been worth his while to weave them. We should all be grateful that he did.

Thoreau's life is a reminder that dedicated individuals can establish a simpler, freer, way of life for themselves, simply by adopting a new frame of mind and acting upon it with creativity and conviction. Doing so may not be easy, of course, since it will involve moving in the opposite direction to where most of humankind is marching. But as Thoreau would say, 'If a man does not keep pace with his companions, perhaps it is because he hears a different drummer. Let him step to the music which he hears, however measured or far away' (564-5). Thoreau would also advise us not to wait for our politicians or peers to attain enlightenment before we begin our journey toward simplicity, for it might be a long time before they wake up. Those who have the courage to go forward alone, however, can start today.

References

Bode, C. ed. 1982. *The Portable Thoreau*. New York: Penguin.

Vanenbroeck, G. ed. 1991. *Less is More: The Art of Voluntary Poverty*. Rochester: Inner Traditions.

Further Reading

Cafaro, P. 2006. *Thoreau's Living Ethics:* Walden *and the Pursuit of Virtue*. Athens, Georgia: University of Georgia Press.

Krutch, J. 1974. *Henry David Thoreau*. New York: William Morrow & Co.

Neufeldt, L. 1989. *The Economist: Henry Thoreau and Enterprise*. Oxford: Oxford University Press.

Stoller, L. *After Walden: Thoreau's Changing Views on Economic Man*. Stanford: Stanford University Press.

PIONEERS OF THE DEEP FUTURE

CHAPTER ELEVEN

JOHN RUSKIN

DAVID CRAIG

John Ruskin (1819-1900) was the leading art critic in Victorian Britain. His early interest in how to read the beauty of art and architecture expanded into the question of how consumers read the value of the products they bought. Ruskin pursued his initial studies of nature's beauty and Gothic architecture into a practical interest in the social conditions for excellent work and good consumption. Finding industrial capitalism antithetical to both aspirations, he developed one of the most trenchant critiques of classical economics. He took his arguments to the public in a series of lectures and essays collected in such books as *The Political Economy of Art* (1857), *The Two Paths* (1858), *Unto this Last* (1860), and *The Crown of Wild Olive* (1866).

Ruskin's voluminous writings and diverse interests confound any simplistic idea of simple living. Studies of natural history, Greek mythology, literary criticism, and drawing mix with arguments for a living wage, unemployment insurance, and national parks. The breadth of Ruskin's corpus is reflected in two very different trajectories of his historical influence. On the one hand, his global apostles included Mohandas Gandhi, who advocated one of the more austere approaches to simple living in the twentieth century. Inspired by reading *Unto this Last*, Gandhi established his Phoenix settlement in 1904 as an experiment in simplifying needs and sharing equally in all types of labour (Hanley, 2013). On the other hand, the first Members of

93

Parliament elected from the British Labour Party in 1906 cited Ruskin as their greatest influence. The Labour Party would become the architect of Britain's welfare state, an expansionist economic program in tension with Gandhian *Swadeshi*, or local self-sufficiency (Harris, 1999).

Ruskin's complex legacy results from his being both an engaged practical critic and a visionary social theorist. The practical wellspring of his criticism was his searching inquiry into the virtues, or excellences, that people cultivate in 'practices' (Craig, 2006: 11-14). Human virtues, whether moral, aesthetic, intellectual, or manual, are acquired and exercised through devotion to a practice. Gardening, animal husbandry, artisan trades, cottage industries, and other crafts are all practices alongside the refined arts of landscape painting and stone carving that first captivated Ruskin. A sketcher and a painter himself, Ruskin honed his observational skills through lifelong studies of geology, botany, and ornithology. Common to these crafts, arts, and sciences is their capacity to hitch participants' passions to the larger purposes, the mastery of techniques, and the integrity of materials that make for excellence in a practice. Such formative pursuits also generate soulful delights easily shared among the practitioners.

'The Nature of Gothic', the keystone chapter of Ruskin's *Stones of Venice*, celebrates the dignity and creativity of practical labour. William Morris had this chapter printed for the 1854 inauguration of the Working Men's College of London (Boris, 1986: ch. 1), later declaring it to be 'one of the very few necessary and inevitable utterances of the century' (Ruskin, 1904: lix). For Ruskin, the soaring spirit of Gothic cathedrals testifies to the intrinsic value of work fed by gifts of tradition and ingenuity and serving an array of purposes too complex to fashion by oneself. By contrast, he condemned the repetitive machine production and manufactured tastes of his day. These economic conditions and cultural aspirations were too confining to make the workers, products, or consumers well. Building on the medieval guild model, Ruskin undertook a series of largely quixotic reforms in the 1860s and 1870s through the St. George's Guild, while also investing more successfully in the housing reformer Octavia Hill's early work (Harris, 1999).

Ruskin's most evocative and complete statement of simple living is his 1858 lecture on 'The Work of Iron, in Nature, Art, and Policy'. Delivered in the spa town of Tunbridge Wells, Ruskin must have shocked his audience with his countercultural declaration that iron's chief 'virtue' is to rust. Fixated on the riches produced by iron machinery, his prosperous listeners heedlessly ignored the 'saffron stain' on the town's fountains, vibrant evidence of iron's more healthful operation in the mineral baths that made the town famous. In an imaginative *tour de force*, Ruskin canvassed the myriad ends served by iron's material virtues. Starting with its rusted oxidised forms, iron colours the landscape in the purplish and reddish hues of slate and brick. Its decomposition in the soil is essential to the earth's productivity. Its proclivity to grab hold of oxygen draws these 'circles of vitality' into our own lifeblood (Ruskin, 1985: 115-117). What explains the careless disregard for iron's primary value in natural beauty and ecological systems? According to Ruskin, his contemporaries' desires are disordered. They love monetary riches, manufactured excess, and the accumulation of commodities devoid of human creativity and spiritual meaning. Lost are the shared abundance and more lasting satisfactions of nature's splendour and the earth's fertility.

Proceeding to art and policy, Ruskin's portrait of a good life turns from iron's virtues to human virtues. Artistically, iron's virtues of ductility and tenacity fit it for the intricacies of wrought iron fences of twisted vines and cut flower petals. The workers hammer out their virtues of artistic vision, natural piety, and tactile agility with every new design they strike. The purchasers endeavour to surround themselves in the justice of a society that sustains healthful and creative work. This wise consumption invites passers-by to stop and delight in the gifts of human effort and nature's bounty, extending gratitude across the usual economic divisions. Instead, Ruskin charges, the Victorian taste for iron fences of rails and spikes bristles around every affluent house. Such consumer desires testify to the vices stoked by the social scorn of the rich and inflicted through stultifying toil.

Iron's role in policy speaks to both sides of Ruskin's Tory radicalism. On the one hand, his gendering of the plough and the needle reveals the conservative Tory cast of his ideal of a society joined in organic harmony. Men's natural virtues stem from disciplined provision, women's from nurturing domesticity. The policy implements of the sword and fetter, he insisted, elevate an honourable obedience to law over the mere liberty of individual interests. On the other hand, Ruskin's radicalism put his beliefs in people's natural inequalities to remarkably egalitarian purposes. In part he argued for *noblesse oblige* in assigning the rich and the powerful the duties of ensuring just wages, quality goods, healthy work, basic education, and economic security for the lower classes. The sharp edge of Ruskin's social criticism reflected, however, his keen eye for the wealthy's systematic abuse of power to exploit their social and economic advantages. Citing Proverbs, he excoriated his peers for setting their eyes not simply 'away' from but 'against' the poor. Championing the principle of universal bread labour, he decried the 'only one way of taking our hands off the Plough-handle' – namely, 'binding another's upon it' (Ruskin, 1985: 131, 133).

Ruskin's practicality and moralism drove his theoretical arguments in *Unto this Last*. A decade before William Stanley Jevons' reorientation of economics toward consumer judgments of marginal utility, Ruskin placed consumers at the centre of economic life. Charging consumers with deciding what their economy is for, he memorably affirmed, *'There is no wealth but life*. Life, including all of its powers of joy, of love, and of admiration.... That country is richest which nourishes the greatest number of happy and noble human beings' (Ruskin, 1985: 222). Simply put, economic value (wealth) depends on human virtue (nobility). As a result, measuring economic welfare in terms of Gross Domestic Product or subjective wellbeing is insufficient. Economic welfare cannot be reduced to average income for purchasing economic goods or reported satisfaction of current preferences. Questions of social justice matter, too. Is income distributed equitably enough for people to afford life's necessities and participate in society? Do people have secure access to the health, education, and culture needed to know their actual preferences? Simply having personal income and personal preferences cannot ensure wellbeing, for as Ruskin put it, 'wealth, instead of depending merely on a "have", [depends] on a can' (Ruskin, 1985: 210). By 'can' he meant a person's developed capacities. Ruskin's linkage of economic welfare to human development anticipates, in large part, Nobel Laureate in economics Amartya Sen's capabilities approach. For Ruskin, developing well-made people who produce and enjoy well-made things is the crux of economic prosperity.

How can we practise such complex theoretical ideas in living simply? As Ruskin advised his contemporaries about their iron fences, it is:

> in your power to turn all your police force of iron bars into drawing masters, and natural historians. Not, of course, without some trouble and expense....The main question is only – what is worth doing and having (Ruskin, 1985: 126).

Notice the word order. The choice of activities (doing) precedes the choice of possessions (having). The cardinal rule of ethical consumption is to support activities that foster human virtues and shared goods. Crafted fences of natural designs are excellent purchases for the workers who forged them. For homeowners and neighbours, their delight in nature's boundless surprise and people's creative imagination only increases with the sharing. Two virtues are vital to the wise consumption of simple living. Natural piety acknowledges the world's many gifts in sustaining our lives and stirring a sense of awe and wonder. Social justice demands paying just prices and supporting practices that develop people's capabilities. For Ruskin, the difficulties of justly pricing and acknowledging the worth of other people's labour favour more local economies. For example, a farmer's market can be a small commonwealth, a meeting place of good work, fair pay, healthful food, and sustainable agriculture, mutually affirmed by all the participants (cf. McKibben, 2007: esp. chap. 2). Consuming well also requires the preservation of such shared wealth as land preserves (Walton, 1995) and cultural heritage (Chitty, 1995).

Ruskin's social vision has sometimes been written off as nostalgia for a face-to-face society where everyone knows his or her place. His hierarchical appeals to masters and servants and his gendered divisions between the plough and the needle are critical elements that I reject for democratic reasons. His ethics of consumption might be rejected as impractical, too. How can today's consumers possibly answer his three basic questions: How well does a product use the natural world? How does its production make workers' lives good or ill? What kind of society and culture are thereby purchased?

Ruskin transcends both objections in his account of the idolatry of money which, in my judgement, excels Karl Marx's analysis of commodity fetishism (see: Craig, 2006 chaps. 4 & 7). As money enters our economic transactions, its distancing effects unsettle the fixity of traditional roles. At the same time, Ruskin argued, if consumers fail to exercise their moral imagination across the distances of monetary spending, then money's own value, and thus its purchasing power, will decline. The 2008 global financial collapse is a case study of how the frenzied imagination of economic value can mask the reality of human and social deficits. In the United States, poorly-constructed houses were erected in fabricated neighbourhoods and sold to people whose work did not afford the necessary credit. Mortgages were bundled and split into derivatives and sold to global speculators with no purchase whatsoever on the wealth – or to borrow Ruskin's apt phrase, the 'illth' – behind their investment. Once the gap between value and virtue came to light, money's value crashed along with the economy.

Ruskin himself was no ascetic, and he encouraged his contemporaries to spend money actively but wisely. As a conduit of imagination, money affords consumers the idolatrous power of projecting their desires onto every purchase and dominating other people's labour. As a social power, money hoarded can hold people in idolatrous thrall to the rich. Instead money is made to circulate; it is literally a sign of interdependence. This interdependence can consist in nothing more than what Ruskin called a 'mutual covetousness' to take advantage of one another. Wise consumers will, however, strive to base their inter-dependence on a deliberate consensus about what an economy is for and how best to ensure that everyone takes turns at ethical consumption. Advocates of simple living have sometimes eschewed the money economy. Ruskin's singular challenge is to spend abundantly on wise purchases of human excellence and common goods.

References

Boris, Eileen, 1986. *Art and Labor: Ruskin, Morris, and the Craftsman Ideal in America*. Philadelphia: Temple University Press.

Chitty, Gill, 1995. '"A Great Entail": The Historic Environment.' In *Ruskin and Environment: The Storm-Cloud of the Nineteenth Century*, ed. Michael Wheeler, pp. 102-122. Manchester: Manchester University Press.

Craig, David M, 2006. *John Ruskin and the Ethics of Consumption*. Charlottesville: Virginia University Press.

Hanley, Keith, 2013. 'The Ruskin Diaspora.' In *Persistent Ruskin: Studies in Influence, Assimilation and Effect*, eds. Keith Hanley and Brian Maidment, pp. 179-195. Farnham, Ashgate.

Harris, Jose, 1999. 'Ruskin and Social Reform.' In *Ruskin and the Dawn of the Modern*, ed. Dinah Birch, pp. 7-33. Oxford: Oxford University Press.

McKibben, Bill, 2007. *Deep Economy: The Wealth of Communities and the Durable Future*. New York: Henry Holt.

Ruskin, John, 1904. *The Works of John Ruskin*. Eds. E.T.

Cook and Alexander Wedderburn. London: George Allen.

Ruskin, John, 1985. *Unto this Last and Other Writings*. Ed. Clive Wilmer. London: Penguin Classics.

Walton, John K, 1995. 'The National Trust: Preservation or Provision?' In *Ruskin and Environment*, ed. Wheeler, pp. 144-164.

CHAPTER TWELVE

WILLIAM MORRIS

SARA WILLS

When William Morris died in London in 1896 at the age of 62, his doctor stated that the cause was 'simply being William Morris, and having done more work than most ten men' (Mackail, 1899, 2: 336). At one time or another (and often concurrently), he was a prolific poet and novelist; a designer and manufacturer of furniture and interior decorations; an accomplished weaver and reviver of the art of vegetable dyeing; a calligrapher and translator of Icelandic sagas; a pioneering preservationist; an active socialist, speaker and campaigner; a typographer, printer and publisher; and also a caring father, stoic husband and stalwart friend. Thus the broad field of 'Morris studies' has given us 'Morris the artist', 'Morris the poet', 'Morris the craftsman', 'Morris the businessman', 'Morris the preservationist', 'Morris the utopian', 'Morris the red' and, most recently, 'Morris the green' (Wills, 2006). With such breadth of activity (and interpretation), one could be forgiven for thinking that Morris would have little to offer those interested in simple living.

But Morris is arguably the person who produced the most compelling vision of a simpler life in the nineteenth century: a vision articulated in hundreds of lectures delivered the length and breadth of Britain in the 1880s and in the passionate earthiness of the utopian *News from Nowhere* (1889). It is a vision that emerges from a life that both lived and fought the contradictions of the rapidly industrialising Victorian age, and from a mind that developed a politics and aesthetics that has been characterised as making the transformation 'from romantic to revolutionary'. In the decade in which middle-class England 're-discovered' the problem of poverty, Morris assimilated and transformed Marx, and developed a position that incorporated a more pronounced concern for the nature of work and for the human figure in the landscape.

As a result, Morris's is the voice most urgently and honestly raised against all that defied just, fair and simple living in the Victoria era – whether in the realm of art, work or politics. Determined to 'kick against the pricks' – 'first because I cannot help it, and secondly because I am encouraged ... that something will come of it' – (Morris 1984-96, 2: 52), Morris's distinctive contribution to simple living lies in his analysis of what he termed the 'grim net' of life under conditions of industrial capitalism, and particularly in his effort to imagine, inform and educate our desire for 'pleasurable labour' and 'fellowship' 'in 'decent sur-roundings'.

Useful work versus useless toil

'How can men gain hope and pleasure in their daily work?' (Morris, 1910-15, 22: 202). This was 'the great question' Morris claimed that 'all ought to ask'. A dominant theme throughout his writings on socialism, in lectures such as 'Useful Work versus Useless Toil' Morris argued that labour could and should be useful, personally meaningful work, and that it should carry within it 'the hope of pleasure in the rest, the hope of the pleasure in our using what it makes, and the hope of pleasure in our daily creative skill' (Morris, 1910-15, 23: 100). This vision of a world of pleasurable work makes Morris's socialism distinct. Whereas Marx spoke of the disappearance of 'natural necessity' and the 'abolition of labour', Morris held that human joy lay precisely in the natural necessities of life.

Morris's socialistic vision focused particularly on the character of work, which he defined as a 'transition between works of Nature and Art' (Morris, 1910-15, 22: 428).

Reflecting his thorough grounding in the thought of Ruskin, he argued that '[i]t is the province of art to set the true ideal of a full and reasonable life ... a life to which the perception and creation of beauty ... shall be felt to be as necessary to man as his daily bread' (Morris, 1910-15, 23: 279). This is where Morris takes hold of Ruskin and adds Marx, and out of both of their ideas makes something new. For Morris, 'man' was not just *Homo faber* but *Homo artis*. He believed that the task, the joy of work – in Marxian terms, of 'completing' nature – was essential to life. Art and all signs of 'external beauty', he argued, are 'above all the token of what chiefly makes life good and not evil, of joy in labour' (Morris, 1969, 52).

The exploration and re-invention of work is a central focus of *News from Nowhere*, which provides a vision of an England reclaimed from the ravages of industrial capitalism. *News from Nowhere* is a tale structured on many different levels, but the internal organisation of the story concerns a journey from the capitalist, urban, industrial London of the late nineteenth century to a small, communal, rural village on the Upper Thames in the early twenty-second century. We encounter this landscape and society through the eyes of nineteenth-century narrator and protagonist, William Guest, who finds an England that has been socially, economically, politically and aesthetically transformed. The tale is a journey of discovery in which Guest observes that many social institutions have been overturned to create new and simpler relationships between people, and between people and the rest of the natural world, principally through new modes of work.

Specifically, Morris emphasises that the people of Nowhere enjoy 'the absence of artificial coercion and the freedom for every man to do what he can do best, joined to the knowledge of what productions of labour we really want' (Morris, 1910-15, 16: 92). The result of these circumstances is that goods are produced 'because they are needed: men make for their neighbours' use ... not for a vague market of which they know nothing, and over which they have no control'. As a consequence, one inhabitant of Nowhere explains to Guest: 'we are not driven to make a vast quantity of useless things,

[and] we have time and resources enough to consider our pleasure in making them' (97-98). Workers in Nowhere enjoy freedom from the clock, factory whistles and bells, and Guest is told that there is no longer a 'desire' not to work because '*all* work is now pleasurable', and 'the reward of labour is *life*' (91). In Nowhere, art 'has no name amongst us now, because it has become a necessary part of the labour of every man who produces' (134).

This emphasis on the sensual pleasure of work is a constant theme in Morris's vision of a better world. In lectures such as 'How We Might Live' and 'Art Under Plutocracy', as well as *News From Nowhere,* Morris emphasises that this requires a critique of the use of technology and 'mechanical power' in the workplace. If an item could be made well and pleasurably by hand, Morris reasoned, why use a machine? He never tired of emphasising that he believed the phrase 'labour-saving machine' to be elliptical: that what it really meant was machinery that saves the cost of labour (Morris, 1910-15, 23: 180). While he recognised that some machines could free us from arduous work, he did not believe they could produce items that testified to human pleasure in their creation. In Nowhere, '[a]ll work which would be irksome to do by hand is done by immensely improved machinery; and in all work which it is a pleasure to do by hand machinery is done without' (Morris, 1910-15, 16: 94, 97).

This 'pleasurable' work includes direct interaction with nature, reflecting Morris's belief that 'there are few men ... who would not wish to spend part of their lives in the most necessary and pleasantest of all work – cultivating the earth' (Morris, 1910-15, 23: 112). The description of haymaking in Nowhere is certainly romanticised. Guest sees a 'long line of haymakers' all 'gaily' dressed and '[t]he meadow looked like a gigantic tulip-bed because of them'. '[A]ll hands were working deliberately but well and steadily, though they were as noisy with merry talk as a grove of autumn starlings' (Morris, 1910-15, 16: 154). While viewed by many as simplistic, Morris's key point is that this vision represented 'friends working for friends on land which was theirs, as many as were needed, with leisure and hope ahead of them

instead of hopeless toil and anxiety' (Morris, 1936, 2: 212-13)
– in other words, a vision of alienation overcome. For the
inhabitants of this transformed England, the 'necessity' of
work operates not as a limitation or constriction of desire; it
is precisely how they feel and experience desire – the very
system through which they express their 'love [of] the earth,
and the seasons, and weather, and all things that deal with it,
and all that grows out of it' (Morris, 1910-15, 16: 201-2).

The fairness of the earth

Human livelihood within and love for 'the earth, and the
seasons, and weather' is a constant throughout all of Morris's
writing, and is perhaps what appeals most today. The
'fairness of the earth' becomes an emphatic refrain in
Morris's later work, particularly from the 1880s onwards as
he looked with increasing dismay at his society's incapacity to
produce 'joy in labour' and 'wield the forces of Nature' to
produce work-as-art. As he visited Britain's industrial centres
to make the case for a better way of life, he emphasised that
human interaction with nature had become 'wasteful,
misdirected and unrewarding for the majority' (Morris, 1910-
15, 23: 217), and that most work tends to 'shame her and
befoul her, and turn her rest and order and beauty into
feverish ragged squalor' (Morris, 1969: 69). 'What kind of
account shall we be able to give to those who come after us of
our dealings with the earth?', he asks his audience during
these years (Morris, 1910-15, 23: 165).

First expressed as an exhortation to art and its patrons
and protagonists to 'do their best to give us back the fairness
of the Earth', it soon came to be expressed more emphatically
as a 'fairness' that was 'just' as well as 'beautiful'. In February
1880, for example, he challenged an audience in Birmingham
to '[h]ave nothing in your houses that you do not know to be
useful, or believe to be beautiful' – certainly a motto for a
kind of simple life (Morris, 1910-15, 22: 76). By early 1881,
however, such pleas to opt for 'white-washed walls, and the
green trees and flowery meads', rather than 'a grimy palace
amid the smoke with a regiment of housemaids always

working to smear the dirt together', were linked to calls to reject the luxury that 'choke[s] both demand and supply of Mechanical Toil' (Morris, 1910-15, 22: 149-50).

Nevertheless, Morris never stopped his condemnation of damage done to the 'fairness of the earth'. An audience at Oxford in 1883 received this Ruskinian blast:

> Not only are London and our other great commercial cities mere masses of sordidness, filth, and squalor, embroidered with patches of pompous and vulgar hideousness, no less revolting to the eye and the mind when one knows what it means: not only have whole counties of England, and the heavens that hang over them, disappeared beneath a crust of unutterable grime, but the disease, which ... would seem to be a love of dirt and ugliness for its own sake, spreads all over the country, and every little market-town seizes the opportunity to imitate, as far as it can, the majesty of the hell of London and Manchester (Morris, 1910-15, 23: 170).

As a socialist, Morris ultimately blamed capitalism for the accumulation of such a 'crust', but he reserved special venom for the Victorian industrial city and its voracious appetite for nature as resource, dumping ground, and above all 'profit':

> It is profit which draws men into enormous un-manageable aggregations called towns ... which crowds them up when they are there into quarters without gardens or open spaces, profit which won't take the most ordinary precautions against wrapping a whole district in a cloud of sulphurous smoke; which turns beautiful rivers into filthy sewers... (Morris, 1910-15, 23: 22).

Thus in Nowhere he emphasises a simpler vision where it is no longer necessary for workers to come together to use mechanical power. 'The big murky places which were once ... the centres of manufacture ... have ... disappeared', and natural resources are collected and distributed 'with as little possible of dirt [and] confusion' (Morris, 1910-15, 16: 68-69).

For Morris, life in such conditions was ultimately a form of 'slavery'. An inhabitant of Nowhere describes this 'mistaken' way of living to Guest as 'bred' of a 'life which was always looking upon everything, except mankind, animate and inanimate – 'nature', as people used to call it – as one thing, and mankind as another'. 'It was natural to people thinking in this way, that they should try to make "nature" their slave', Guest is told, 'since they thought "nature" was something outside them (Morris, 1910-15, 16: 179). In a lecture delivered the same year he was writing *News From Nowhere*, Morris insisted:

> We shall not be happy unless we live like good animals, unless we enjoy the exercise of the ordinary functions of life: eating sleeping loving walking running swimming riding sailing we must be free to enjoy all those exercises of the body without any sense of shame; without any suspicion that our mental powers are so remarkable and godlike that we are rather above such common things (Morris, 1971: 12).

Eating, sleeping, loving...

Thus Morris also provides us with a vision of living that extends beyond the organisation of government, economy and labour, and extends right into our daily and personal lives. His writings reflect upon, for example, the artificiality of intimate human relationships in nineteenth-century England and works like *News From Nowhere* provide a world where the 'artificial perversion' of sexual relationships under private property has been dissolved. Echoing aspects of radical romantic writing on love, sex and marriage, but also an awakening in the latter half of the nineteenth century to the links between human sexuality and the productive vitality of nature, the inhabitants of Nowhere regard sexual desire as a 'natural' force that will not, and should not, be thwarted; relationships are started and continued on the basis of free will, and are grounded in emotional attachment rather than proprietorial constraint.

This represents in fictional form Morris's views set out in a letter of 1886. Responding to a friend's inquiries regarding sexual relations under socialism, Morris explained that he considered '[c]opulation ... worse than beastly unless it takes place as the outcome of natural desires and kindliness on both sides'. '[D]ecent animalism plus human kindliness', Morris asserted, are 'infinitely better than the present system of venal prostitution which is the meaning of our marriage system'. 'In short', he argued, 'artificial bolstering up of natural human relations is what I object to' (Morris, 1984-96, 2: 584).

In this respect, it is worth noting that Morris's views on alternative personal relations and less artificial modes of living were also informed by a number of contemporary 'simple lifers'. In 1883, for example, he met Edward Carpenter, who had a market garden business in Chesterfield and whose *Towards Democracy* had just been published. This called upon all men and women 'to come close to the Earth itself and those that live in direct contact with it' (Carpenter, 1915: 28), and for the formation of self-sufficient communities of limited wants and needs. Though Morris was wary of the 'faddist' element among some 'back to nature' enthusiasts, he confessed to a close friend that Carpenter's was perhaps 'the real way to enjoy life':

> I went to Chesterfield and saw Carpenter ... and found him very sympathetic and sensible... I listened with longing heart to his account of his patch of ground, seven acres: he says that he and his fellow can almost live on it: they grow their own wheat, and send flowers and fruit to Chesterfield and Sheffield markets: all that sounds very agreeable to me (Morris, 1984-96, 2: 353).

The visit caused Morris to reflect that all life's 'necessary ordinary details' should be a source of pleasure, and that one of the most serious indictments of 'modern civilisation' was that it 'huddles them out of the way, has them done in a venal and slovenly manner till they become real drudgery which people can't help trying to avoid' (Morris, 1984-96, 2: 353). Moved by Carpenter's adherence to a simple lifestyle and land ethic, Morris drew on his practical example. In 'The Society of the Future', Morris held out a vision of 'a society conscious of a wish to keep life simple, to forgo some of the power over nature won by past ages in order to be more human and less mechanical, and willing to sacrifice something to this end' (Morris 1936, 2: 466).

But Morris was also conscious of his difference from the 'simple lifers' of the late nineteenth century. During his visit to Chesterfield, Carpenter lent Morris his copy of Thoreau's *Walden*. Morris wrote back to Carpenter:

> I have read a good bit of Walden, & find it (of course) very interesting – only it seems to me that he looks on human life as a spectator only. That's a convenient and pleasant position to take up; but quite apart from the question of whether one ought to do so or not, very few people can... I don't object to a one-sided way of looking at matters so long as we understand that it *is* one-sided. And I know from experience what a comfortable life one might lead if one could be careful not to concern oneself with *persons* but with *things*; or persons in the light of things. But nature won't allow it, it seems... (Morris 1984-96, 2: 430).

Here Morris underlines the differences between Thoreau, Carpenter and himself. Morris felt life could not be lived simply under the conditions of industrial capitalism, and that he could not turn his back on wider 'fellowship'. 'Fellowship is heaven, and lack of fellowship is hell: fellowship is life, and lack of fellowship is death', he emphasised in *A Dream of John Ball* (Morris 1910-15, 16: 230); and while he provided one of the best-known visions of a rural utopia, he never left his base in 'the hell of London'.

Yet in works like *A Dream of John Ball* and *News From Nowhere*, he produced an alternative vision of fellowship with and within nature that has remained compelling. When Morris died in 1896, Carpenter wrote in the anarchist newspaper *Freedom* that Morris's 'great contribution' was 'the impulse of growth' and that it had 'been one of the most potent, most generous and humanly beautiful, of all the many impulses ... of modern Socialism' (Faulkner, 1973:

400). From this side of the twentieth century, Morris's analysis of life under industrial capitalism stands out as frank and fearless, but so does his revolutionary vision that affirms our duty to imagine something better. And in our own struggle between necessity and desire, the 'fairness' of Morris's vision resonates most with those concerned about relations of nature and livelihood. In his efforts to 'teach desire to desire, to desire better, to desire more, and above all to desire in a different way' (Thompson, 1976: 790), Morris has provided us with a key distinction between 'useful work and useless toil', affirmed the value of 'fellowship' and a kind of society that emphasises 'a reasonable share in the beauty of the earth' for all.

References

Carpenter, Edward. 1915 (1883). *Towards Democracy*. London: GeorgeAllen & Unwin.

Faulkner, Peter, ed. 1973. *William Morris: The Critical Heritage*. London: Routledge & Kegan Paul.

Mackail, J.W. 1899. *The Life of William Morris*. 2 vols. London: Longmans, Green & Co., London.

Morris, William. 1910-15. *The Collected Works of William Morris*. 24 vols. Edited by May Morris. London: Longmans, Green & Co.

Morris, William. 1984-96. *The Collected Letters of William Morris*. 4 vols. Edited by Norman Kelvin. Princeton University Press, Princeton.

Morris, William. 1936. *William Morris: Artist, Writer, Socialist*. 2 vols. Edited by May Morris. Oxford: Basil Blackwell.

Morris, William. 1969. *The Unpublished Lectures of William Morris*. Edited by Eugene D. LeMire. Detroit: Wayne State University Press.

Morris, William. 1971. 'An Unpublished Lecture of William Morris'. Edited by Paul Meier. *International Review of Social History* 16 (2): 7–15.

Thompson, E.P. 1976 (1955). *William Morris: Romantic to Revolutionary*. Revised edition. New York: Pantheon Books.

Wills, Sara. 2006. *The Greening of William Morris*. Melbourne: Circa.

CHAPTER THIRTEEN

GANDHI

WHITNEY SANFORD

Mohandas Karamchand Gandhi has become an iconic figure for simple living, or voluntary simplicity, and today, the phrase 'live simply so that others may simply live' is widely (and probably erroneously) attributed to him. Also known by his honorific title Mahatma (the great-souled one), Gandhi wove the thread of simple living throughout his campaign for political, social, and economic justice for India's poor, and the image of a dhoti-clad Gandhi sitting in his ashram beside his spinning wheel, popularised by *Life Magazine*'s Margaret Bourke White, illustrated his personal practice of simple living. For Gandhi, simple living was an integral aspect of independence or freedom. Although Gandhi is best known for his campaign for Indian independence, Gandhi argued for independence (*swaraj*) at the personal, village, and national levels.[1] Simple living, Gandhi thought, helped individuals (including women and lower castes) cultivate self-discipline and offered personal autonomy. On a larger scale, simple living reduced consumer desires that Gandhi feared would

---

[1] This summary is necessarily brief and highlights those elements most relevant for environmental and agricultural issues. Readers interested in a more comprehensive discussion are directed to M. K. Gandhi, *An Autobiography or My Experiments with Truth*, translated by Mahadev Desai, (Ahmedabad: Navajivan Publishing House, 1927); Gandhi, *Village Swaraj*; Hardiman, *Gandhi In His Time and Ours*, 2003; and Rudrangshu Mukherjee, ed., *The Penguin Gandhi Reader*, (Delhi: Penguin Books, 1993).

enslave Indians, both rich and poor, as consumer goods became the driving force of society (Mukherjee, 1993: 16-18). Simple living became a cornerstone of both Gandhi's personal practice and his social and political activism.

Mohandas Gandhi grew up in a Vaishnava, merchant family in the western state of Gujarat, India and was heavily influenced by his devoutly religious mother from whom he absorbed the importance of fasting. (Vaishnavas are those Hindus who worship Vishnu and his descents, such as Rama and Krishna.) In developing his moral philosophy, Gandhi drew both on the Hindu and Jain traditions. Gandhi's home state of Gujarat, while predominantly Hindu, housed significant populations of Jains, from whom he imbibed an ethos that emphasised non-violence and non-possessiveness. In 1888, Gandhi travelled to London to pursue legal studies and, for the first time, read the *Bhagavad-Gita* (The Song of the Lord), a Hindu text that provided the religious framework for understanding his views on voluntary simplicity, duty, and non-violence. For Gandhi, the *Bhagavad-Gita's* teachings regarding selflessness and reducing ego attachments complemented Jain values such as non-possessiveness and non-violence.

In 1893, after completing his legal training, Gandhi accepted a position in Natal, South Africa where he lived for 21 years. During this period, Gandhi became attuned to social and economic injustices faced by both Africans and Indians and began cultivating his practice of simple living. In the early 1900s, Gandhi corresponded with Russian author Leo Tolstoy from whom he adopted the concept of 'bread labour'. The Russian author Leo Tolstoy argued that everyone should perform some 'bread labour', or physical work, to support their own existence, whether growing food, building shelter, or making clothes, rather than simply living off the labour of others. Performing bread labour insures that we recognise the work that produces our food, homes, and clothing and inculcates humility, the concept that none are above essential, and often denigrated, chores.

Later Gandhi adopted this concept in his campaign for Indian Independence and the freedom and dignity of Indian peasants. He founded the Tolstoy and Phoenix Ashrams in

South Africa, and these utopian farm-ashrams have emphasised the dignity of human labour and promoted 'bread labour', that each person should contribute their own labour for goods consumed (Sanford, 2013: 70). Gandhi demanded that all ashram residents share in the labour of cleaning the latrines, causing tensions with high caste Hindus who typically avoided work deemed polluting. Although Gandhi borrowed the concept of bread labour from Tolstoy, he stated that the third chapter of the *Bhagavad-Gita,* a central Hindu text, reflects the principle that food eaten without sacrifice, or bread labour, is stolen (Gandhi, 1962: 43). Gandhi returned to India in 1914 and became a leader in the home-rule movement and encouraged nonviolent resistance to British colonial rule. He established Sabarmati Ashram in Ahmadabad, Gujarat in 1917 and Sevagram in Wardha, Maharashtra in 1936.

Ashrams are long-established elements in the Hindu and Indian landscapes. Historically, ashrams provided residents for ascetics or others seeking religious retreat. Ashram life included austerities, such as physical hardship and limited food, to help practitioners stifle desire and direct focus inward, away from the body and the physical. These austerities increased *tapas*, or spiritual heat, that led to spiritual purification. Traditionally, Hindu ashrams focused on the spiritual and had little to do with social, political, and economic activity. Simple living was a *sine qua non* at ashrams, but the goals were spiritual, not related to broader social change.

While Gandhi's ashrams certainly held a spiritual dimension and addressed personal transformation, these ashrams also functioned as laboratories for broader social change. Gandhi founded his ashrams, in part, to explore patterns of eating, living, and thinking that would lead to social and economic equity, and these ashrams could be considered religious only in the broadest terms. His ashrams functioned, in part, as test labs for social change, and his ashrams emphasised simple living so that nothing would distinguish him from the poorest Indian. Gandhi was not interested in ideology or philosophy; instead, Gandhi was pragmatic and experimented with his practices. Sharing tasks equitably meant that no jobs were relegated to a specific caste or gender. Gandhi himself referred to his work as a series of experiments and rejected the term 'Gandhism', a term that would imply a particular ideology, although many continue to use the term (Tendulkar, 1960: 4).

Gandhi emphasised bread labour, in part, to demonstrate the difficulty and dignity of all labour and hoped to eradicate the caste hierarchies that divided Indian society. Many residents of Gandhi's ashrams came from wealthy and high caste backgrounds and were accustomed to a household of servants cooking meals, cleaning, and making tea. Gandhi insisted that all residents help clean latrines, a policy that proved especially divisive because this polluting task had been restricted to those at the bottom of the social order. Arun Gandhi recounted how Gandhi (his grandfather) insisted that Shriman Narayan, the then Governor of Gujarat, clean the ashram's latrines, inculcating a sense of humility (Gandhi, 2003: 92-3). For Gandhi simple living and equitable sharing of tasks erase existing hierarchies and, in particular, a path to eradicate the stigma of untouchability.

Many images of Gandhi, such as Margaret Bourke-White's photographs for *Life Magazine*, portray him with his spinning wheel. For Gandhi, spinning was a dense and critical symbol that encapsulated his views on the multiple facets of independence, self-sufficiency, and self-discipline. Gandhi believed home-based work such as spinning offered women unprecedented autonomy over their economic lives. As a political symbol, the spinning wheel, or *charkha*, represented freedom from Great Britain's cotton industry that had blocked India's attempts to develop their own manufacturing base. Wearing home-spun clothes, or *khadi*, became for Gandhi and many Indians means to demonstrate their allegiance to the incipient Indian state and to related Gandhian ideals such as local economies. Even today, virtually every village in India holds a Khadi Emporium that sells cloths and other village-produced items.

For Gandhi and contemporary spinners, spinning functioned as a means of self-transformation and mindfulness, a means to develop the inner transformation necessary for changed practices, and the work of taming self-indulgence with self-control (Sykes, 2006: 184). Gandhi considered personal transformation necessary for meaningful social change, and his emphasis on self-discipline provided a counterforce to consumerism. This disciplined self is able to control desires that lead to greed and violence and places service over one's self. As people adopted the discipline and practice of spinning, reciprocally, their identities changed, and this practice changed their ideas of what constituted appropriate clothing – from British to local homespun.

Gandhi's practice of simple living and spinning reflected more than a personal philosophy. Instead, these practices reflected a form of regional development that would lift India's masses out of poverty. Simple living gave Indians control over their lives and economies; for example, he argued that villages must be able to grow their own food and produce materials for their basic needs (e.g. food, clothing, and shelter). Short-term gains in productivity, he claimed, would result in depleted soils, and he recognised the need to maintain soil quality and for equitable access to water and seed (Gandhi, 1962: 31).

Gandhi wanted to loosen the colonial stranglehold on India's natural resources and the production of food and clothing. Gandhi argued that freedom lay in democratic and broad access to the means of production and survival, and he fiercely resisted the centralised control of resources. If colonial, corporate, or centralised governmental structures control access to resources such as water or seeds, citizens are enslaved to those structures.

Gandhi called for *swadeshi* – localised economics – arguing that villages should be self-sufficient and self-reliant and only exchange commodities that are not locally producible. He was concerned that large-scale industrialism and centralised control of resources would not help the bulk of India's population, 75 percent of whom were agriculturalists and lived in villages. The point is not that villages should remain isolated or never import external goods, but that villages should first look locally to supply basic needs; to first focus on local economies. It is one's duty to first look to one's neighbours to supply goods and services rather than simply seeking the cheapest commodity.

Gandhi advocated programs and what we now think of as appropriate technologies (the term 'appropriate technology' was coined by E. F. Schumacher, in *Small is Beautiful*) that would enhance agricultural productivity and return the benefits to village populations, rather than cities or foreign markets (Gandhi, 1962: 26-7). Gandhi thought that placing control of resources in the hands of village assemblies would ensure a more democratic allocation of these resources. For example, instead of massive dams, he encouraged small-scale and local irrigation schemes that could be developed and maintained at the village level to address local needs. Again, Gandhi's emphasis on local economies was not intended to create a series of isolated villages, but rather to provide villagers a path to self-sufficiency and freedom from the power and violence of centralised authority.

Gandhi's comprehensive thought and practices – and his emphasis on local economies, voluntary simplicity, non-violence, and appropriate technologies – have proven particularly inspirational for leaders and participants in worldwide social movements. In the United States, Martin Luther King, Jr., nonviolence activist A. J. Muste, and Peter Maurin, co-founder with Dorothy Day of the Catholic Workers Movement, drew upon Gandhi's thought and practice. Peace activist and community land trust pioneer Bob Swann enacted Gandhian thought on nonviolence, simple living, and local economies in the US through his work on land trusts and community economics (Mills, 2010). The comprehensiveness of Gandhi's social thought combined with his pragmatism and attitude of experimentation resonated profoundly with the civil rights movement and the peace and justice movements of the 1960s and now with individuals and communities focused on voluntary simplicity and social justice.

Over time, Gandhi's words and practices have been condensed into the pithy and engaging 'Be the change you wish to see in the world' that has become a guiding principle for many seeking social change. Although it is probable that Gandhi never said those actual words, the phrase communicates a critical idea: that it is not enough to simply condemn or criticise the world we live in; instead, we must create and inhabit the world we desire. Gandhi's thought and practice has inspired thinkers and practitioners who advocate simple living. Gandhi's practice of voluntary simplicity and appropriate technologies provide a model for environmental sustainability, and his statement 'the earth provides enough to satisfy every man's need but not enough for every man's greed' points towards simple living (Weber, 2004: 227). However Gandhi's demonstration and practice of simple living reflects his conviction that, to effect social change, we must first change ourselves, both in thought and deed, and live those changes.

References

Cosgrove, Ben, 2014. 'Gandhi and His Spinning Wheel: the Story Behind an Iconic Photo | LIFE.com.' Life.Time.com. Accessed May 5, 2014. http://life.time.com/history/gandhi-and-his-spinning-wheel-story-behind-famous-photo/.

Gandhi, Arun, 2003. *Legacy of Love: My Education on the Path of Non-Violence*, North Bay books.

Gandhi, Mahatma, and Rudrangshu Mukherjee, 1993. *The Penguin Gandhi Reader*, Penguin Books India.

Mahatma, Gandhi, 1962. *Village Swaraj*. Edited by H M Vyas, Ahmedabad, Navajivan Publishing House.

Mills, Stephanie, 2010. *On Gandhi's Path*. Gabriola Island, BC: New Society Publishers.

Sanford, A Whitney, 2013. 'Gandhi's Agrarian Legacy: Practicing Food, Justice, and Sustainability in India.' *Journal of the Society of Religion, Nature, and Culture* (2013): 65–87. Doi:10.1558/jsrnc.v7i1.65.

Sykes, Marjorie, 2006. *Moved by Love: the Memoirs of*

Vinoba Bhave. Translated by Marjorie Sykes, Wardha: Gram-Seva Mandal.

Tendulkar, Dinesh G, 1960. *Mahatma*. Vol. 4. 2nd ed., Ahmedabad, Navajivan Publishing House.

Weber, Thomas, 2004. *Gandhi as Disciple and Mentor*, Cambridge; New York: Cambridge University Press.

CHAPTER FOURTEEN

DITCHLING VILLAGE

WILLIAM FAHEY

> I was working, perhaps kneeling as I worked, on the land that lay round my cloistered home at Hawkesyard in the rich Trent valley. Suddenly, I saw the town that man made, and the land that God made. But I saw that the town as man made: it was not only unproductive, but essentially based on wasted material and wasted time. Then something began to say and indeed sing, within me, 'When we come back to the earth as God made it, and as God made it for us, we need never waste an ounce of material or a moment of time.' (Valentine 1955, 146-147)

With this vision, the Domincan Friar Vincent McNabb became aware that he longed to see Catholic social teaching incarnated in the land, not merely propagated in Papal Encyclicals. In the years before the First World War, McNabb had been hard at work attempting to find a compelling way to present Pope Leo XIII's critique of modern society to the British. In particular, he desired to communicate the Pope's indictment of the economic conditions that had destroyed the traditional communitarian life of Europeans, leaving people who had formerly possessed the dignity of artisans as now mere workers, ground up between the ideological gears of liberal capitalism and a nascent communism. The community that arose at Ditchling, to which McNabb would be an intellectual and spiritual participant, allowed him to ensure that such a vision would take flesh.

At roughly the same time, Arthur Eric Rowton Gill – soon simply to be known as Eric Gill – was struggling with his self-proclaimed vocation as heir to John Ruskin's and William Morris's politicised Arts and Crafts movement. Gill was inspired by the Movement's turn towards the richness of medieval tradition. He admired the communal life of the various revival guilds that it generated. He and his young wife embraced the *avant garde* sexual openness typically associated with its practitioners. Ultimately, however, Gill felt the Arts and Crafts movement was affected and financially unstable, catering to the whims of an aesthetically sensitive upper class.

On a deeper level, the movement offered no real program for integrating a vision of beauty and a way of life; spirit and matter remained divorced. Similarly, the Fabian Socialism of Gill's early years did not satisfy his desire for an integrated life. The complex theories of its intellectual champions offered no vision and no hope for breaking the shackles of the Industrial order. Despite the sales of H.G. Well's fantasies and similar Fabian works, the movement was incapable, he felt, of bringing about change – if in fact it ever aimed at meaningful social change. Increasingly, the intense desire to live simply and to communicate beauty consumed Gill. He did not believe, however, that this desire for a simple, but richly beautiful life was his individual desire. For Gill it was a universal desire, a desire that wed normal domesticity with a mystical yearning for the transcendent.

Arts and Crafts and Socialism made for a strange alliance which, Gill would later observe, was 'hardly more than an attempt to re-order the distribution of factory products and factory profits' (Keeble, 2009: 55-56). In what became a parting lecture to his socialist friends, Gill would share his vision – one far more radical than the Fabians and bourgeoise artists dared articulate: 'There will be no artist craftsmen because all men will be artist craftsmen, and no one will talk about it. It will be quite the thing for chairs, bridges, tea pots and butterfly nets to be beautiful' (MacCarthy, 1989: 70).

In 1907 Gill retreated to the Sussex countryside, to a place called Ditchling, a small village where, with a handful of like-minded craftsmen and friends, he began to live out this vision of a life which could rejuvenate the traditional arts of metalwork, sculpture, weaving, letter carving, and carpentry. The restrained simplicity of their craft would mirror – indeed, would be nourished by – an equally restrained form of family life: life on the land, old songs around the hearth, clean and simple pursuits, homespun clothing, fresh bread, and beer from the village. All of these things were being lost or threatened, Gill and his craftsmen believed, by the homogenising progress of industry and commerce.

McNabb and Gill were both very British in their inner turmoil. For a century, a deep part of the English political, intellectual, and artistic tradition focused on what to do with the past, which was increasingly understood as the Catholic past. Arguably, with the formal defeat of the last Catholic claimant to the British throne on the field of Culloden in 1745, British culture became increasingly transfixed by such a past. The grandfather of self-sufficiency, William Cobbett, whose *Cottage Economy* (1822) and *Rural Rides* (1822-26) remain canonical texts for those pursuing the simple life, penned what would become the mournful paean to the passing of English Catholic culture, *A History of the Protestant Reformation* (1827). Cobbett's *History* provided detailed statistical analysis of the richness of the earlier, simpler peasant life. His conclusion to the *History* set forth a new battle cry to restore what was lost. Cobbett was Anglican, but he argued that only by conscious reflection and the revival of traditional customs, would men and women be able to turn back 'that misery, that beggary, that nakedness, that hunger, that everlasting wrangling and spite, which now stare us in the face and stun our ears at every turn, and which the 'Reformation' has given us in exchange for the ease and happiness and harmony and Christian charity enjoyed so abundantly, and for so many ages, by our Catholic forefathers' (Cobbett 1897: 2-3 and again at 373).

Such works as these set the trajectory for various resistance movements to industrialisation and provided a charter for the defence of British village traditions. Cobbett, the Tractarian movement, the pre-Raphaelites, the revived Anglo-Catholicism of the Universities and British society, were all so many sallies against the classical liberalism of Malthus and Mill. Britain was under a kind of civil war, the battle lines of which never mapped on consistently to any political party. The fight, as McNabb would sketch it, was between the spirit of Metropolis and the spirit of the Village, between an anti-culture of machine-made tokens and a true culture of home-made things, between wage slavery and freedom.

Several years after Gill and McNabb met, the Guild of St. Joseph and St. Dominic was established. The Guild was the heart of the Ditchling 'moment'. Son of a non-conformist minister, Gill converted to Roman Catholicism with his wife in 1913. He would remain a Catholic his whole life, and despite his jarring infidelities he and Mary Gill remained married. With his friends and fellow craftsmen Edward Johnston and Hilary Pepler, Gill had been living and articulating a new kind of Guild. Vincent McNabb would become the spiritual architect for the community at Ditchling. Although he never lived in the Village, he frequently wrote and visited, and had a quasi-authoritative role in the founding years of the community (Valentine, 1955: 140-149; Corrin, 1981: 94-99). McNabb's Thomism and deep knowledge of the emerging Catholic social teaching shaped the conversation and the form of the Guild. The Ditchling craftsmen also had their imaginations set ablaze by Distributism, the new political movement formed around the ideas of Hilaire Belloc, G.K. Chesterton, and later McNabb.

At the core of Distributism was the belief in a decentralised political structure, where economic power remained in the hands of free families and small associations of craftsmen and labourers. Distributism was generally localist or communitarian in its focus. It favoured hand-crafts, small boroughs, the rural life, and traditional domestic arts as symbols of freedom, but also as essential elements for self-sufficiency against both the State and large-scale business. Distributists viewed themselves as foes of both communism and *laissez-faire* capitalism (McNabb, 2003: 12-20). The Guild at Ditchling would be an example to the modern world that dignified work could yet support a family and that simple living was not only bearable, but even preferable to the stress and dissension of the industrial and consumer age.

The Guild, and the life of the guildsmen and their families at Ditchling, was more than just another artist colony or quasi-monastic workshop. Family life was central to the Guild, and a common education was provided for the members' children at the Guild school at Ditchling. The original buildings were arranged so that families were nearby, and religious life – praying the 'hours' from the medieval *Office of the Blessed Virgin Mary*, or Mass – was a daily and communal event. The chapel at Ditchling also eventually opened for non-guild families. The Constitution of the Guild set forth the rules of a society in which members wished to have faith unify 'not only their life but . . . their workmanship and to that end live and work in association in order that mutual aid may strengthen individual effort' (Cribb, 2007: 27-28). Work was related back to worship. Mammon was the enemy. Craftsmanship was strictly undertaken out of a love of God and neighbour – executed with an eye towards beauty, but also to the 'absolute standard of usefulness'. Private ownership of tools and workshops was balanced by collective use of buildings, gardens, orchards, fields, a school, and a chapel. The 'good of the work and the freedom of the workman' were 'the test of [the Guilds] methods, tools, and appliances'. Originally, members had to be Catholics and lay members of the Domincan Order. Under Fr. McNabb's suggestion the latter requirement was eventually dropped. There was a clear constitution on election, offices, duties, prayer life, and principles of private and communal ownership and finances.

Over the 60 years of the Guild's and Ditchling's existence, as many as 40 craftsmen and their families lived in Ditchling Village or deeper in the countryside at Ditchling Common, where the Guild property was located. Initially, stone-carving (Gill's favoured occupation) was the best-known activity at Ditchling, but very quickly St. Dominic's Press, overseen by Hilary Pepler, became almost synonymous with Ditchling. Using a hand-operated Stanhope Press, lettering designed by Gill or David Jones, and art produced by various Ditchling craftsmen, the St. Dominic's Press issued hundreds of works in the areas of art, poetry, political pamphlets, and philosophy. Some of the first English translations of Jacques Maritain were executed by St. Dominic's Press. Silversmithing, weaving, etching, engraving, and woodworking were all added. Furthermore, others moved to Ditchling to participate in its life and support it, like former submarine commander Herbert William Shove, who took up silversmithing, distilling, and beekeeping, in addition to small-scale farming.

Surrounded by controversy, Eric Gill left the community in 1924, less than a decade after Ditchling's and the Guild's founding. His own life manifested a pattern of exuberance and retreat, which may be tied to the outrageously libertine sexual life he led, while publically speaking in favour of Catholic moral teachings. Gill claimed his departure was over Hilary Pepler's leadership style, misallocation of funds, and the increasing popularity of Ditchling as a destination for admirers. Yet despite the usual drama over leadership and the graver disruption of the Second World War, Ditchling and the Guild continued with little modification to its way of life until recent years. Some limited use of electrical tools was permitted. Female members were admitted in the early 1970s. Many of the craftsmen successfully handed down their skill to family members who continued the tradition. The last member, the Calligrapher Ewan Clayton, was admitted in 1982, seven years before the formal closure of the Guild and the intentional destruction of the Guild property.

While Gill's own internal turmoil wounded the founding of Ditchling, it did not destroy it. Whether full members of the Guild or not, the men and women associated with Ditchling – such as Edward Johston, Joseph Cribb, David Jones, George Maxwell, Valentine and Jenny KilBride, Philip Hagreen, Dunstand and Winefride Pruden, Edgar Hollaway and others – were of the highest calibre, as the recently-established Ditchling Museum of Art and Craft is making apparent.

Even more credit will need to be shown in the future to Ditchling for its impact on social and political movements of the twentieth century. While the ideas of McNabb, Belloc, and Chesterton may have encouraged the craftsmen at

Ditchling in the years before World War I, Ditchling inspired the Distributist writers to argue for a program of renewal, possible and reproducible, rather than a merely theoretical critique of consumerism and collectivism. Throughout the 1930s and '40s, dozens of regional and national land association movements rose up, attempting to pattern themselves on Ditchling and its Distributist principles: the Catholic Land Associations (with publications like *The Cross and the Plough*); the various Distributist Leagues and branch groups in the British Isles, Canada, Australia, and America; the Council for Church and Countryside; the Soil Association; the Rural Reconstruction Association; the Apostolic Farming project of Madonna House (Canada); the original Catholic Worker farms. All these took their inspiration from Ditchling.

Without exaggeration, it can be argued that hundreds of thousands of farming families embraced the simple life of traditional craftsmanship and agriculture due to the example of Ditchling. Ditchling was also part of the critical reconsideration of industrial methods of modern farming. The work of H. J. Massingham and Viscount Lymington, both Distributists and admirers of Ditchling, along with their colleague Lord Northbourne, provided the foundational works on organic farming and biodynamic self-sufficiency widely admired today. Finally, the influential economists E.F. Schumacher and Wilhelm Röpke were both deeply influenced by the integrated vision of a simple, decentralised community of labourers, artisans, and farmers, which they viewed as providing the essential anchor of a human economy. Though still little-known, Ditchling continues to offer those who desire models of the simple life an inspiring example.

References and Further Reading

Corrin, Jay P. 1981. *G.K. Chesterton & Hilaire Belloc: The Battle Against Modernity*. Athens and London: Ohio University Press.

Corrin, Jay P. 2002. *Catholic Intellectuals and the Challenge of Democracy*. Notre Dame, Indiana: University of Notre Dame Press.

Cribb, Ruth & Joe. 2007. 'The Guild of St. Joseph and St. Dominic (1920-1989),' *Eric Gill and Ditchling: The Workshop Tradition* (Ditchling: The Ditchling Museum).

Distributist Perspectives: Essays on the Economics of Justice and Charity, (no editor listed). Vol. I (2004) and Vol. II (2008). Norfolk, Virginia: IHS Press.

Keeble, Brian. 2009. *God & Work: Aspects of Art and Tradition*. Bloomington, Indiana: World Wisdom

MacCarthy, Fiona. 1989. *Eric Gill: A Lover's Quest for Art and God*. New York: E.P.Dutton.

McNabb, Vincent. 2003. *The Church and the Land*. Norfolk, Virginia: IHS Press; Original edition, London: Burns, Oates and Washbourne, 1925.

McQuillan, John, et al. 2003. *Flee to the Fields: The Founding Papers of the Catholic Land Movement*. Norfolk, Virginia: IHS Press; Original edition, London: Heath Cranton, 1934.

Valentine, Ferdinand. 1955. *Father Vincent McNabb, O.P.: Portrait of a Great Dominican*. Westminster, Maryland: The Newman Press.

CHAPTER FIFTEEN

THE AGRARIANS

ALLAN CARLSON

Twentieth-century America witnessed the blossoming of Agrarianism as an intellectual and cultural movement. Its roots lay within the mythos of the early American Republic, which cast the self-sufficient yeoman farm family as the foundation of ordered liberty. As Thomas Jefferson wrote in 1785:

> Cultivators of the earth are the most valuable citizens. They are the most vigorous, the most independent, the most virtuous, and they are tied to their country and wedded to its liberty by the most lasting bonds (Jefferson, 2009: 41).

Similar early celebrations of Agrarianism came from Jean Hector St. John de Crevecoeur (*Letters from an American Farmer*, 1782) and John Taylor of Caroline (*Arator*, 1813). Such paeans to the largely self-sufficient family farm reflected certain realities of that era. In the fateful year of 1776, about 90 percent of all Americans resided on farms and plantations. Despite the rapid growth of factories and cities in the next century, the number of farms and persons on farms continued to grow, reaching peaks – respectively – of 6 million and 31 million in 1917.

By this time, however, there were also signs of stress within rural American life: a surge in bankruptcies followed by growing tenancy and sharecropping; challenges posed by new technologies and machines and their displacement of human labour; and a new commercialism, spurred on by advertising, that undercut the quest for self-sufficiency. Modern Agrarianism emerged as a reaction seeking to justify, reconfigure, and promote the family farm as a way-of-life still suitable – even necessary – to the preservation of true democracy in the twentieth century. These 'new' agrarians included: Liberty Hyde Bailey, Dean of the College of Agriculture at Cornell University and author of *The Training of Farmers* (1909), *The Country-Life Movement in the United States* (1911), and *The Holy Earth* (1916); Carle Zimmerman and Pitirim Sorokin, co-founders of the new discipline of rural sociology through their tome *Principles of Rural-Urban Sociology* (1929); and Louis Bromfield, author of the autobiographical novel *The Farm* (1933) and the non-fiction *Pleasant Valley* (1944).

The most representative early twentieth century American volume, though, was *I'll Take My Stand,* by the 'Twelve Southerners' loosely affiliated with Tennessee's Vanderbilt University. While their essays were not entirely consistent in argument, all twelve of the contributors agreed on 'A Statement of Principles' which opened the book. Notably, they yearned for simplicity, casting themselves as a community 'opposed to industrialism and wanting a much simpler economy'. Vital to this would be the protection of labour as 'one of the happy functions of human life', since too little work and too much consumption led to 'satiety and aimlessness'. The Statement denounced modern advertising and 'its twin, personal salesmanship' as aspects of 'the great effort of a false economy of life to approve itself'. While acknowledging the sure need 'for industries, for professional vocations, for scholars and artists, and for the life of cities', their Agrarianism would situate agriculture as 'the leading vocation, whether for wealth, for pleasure, or for prestige', a 'model' that other professions should emulate ('Twelve Southerners', 1977 [1930], xxxix-xlvii).

The theme of simplicity found its strongest application in the delightful chapter, 'The Hind Tit', by Andrew Lytle. He described the life patterns still to be found among the 'plain people' on small farms in the Upland South. In such homes, a quilting rack continued to hang from the ceiling, 'ready to be lowered to the laps of the womenfolk when the occasion demands'. Household activity focused on the kitchen, where an iron range had replaced the old open fireplace. 'This much machinery has added to the order of the establishment's life without disrupting it.' Here occurred 'the canning and preserving necessary to sustain the family during the winter', alongside the preparation of three bountiful meals each day. 'The abundance of nature, its heaping dishes, it bulging-breasted fowls, deep-yellow butter and creamy milk, fat beans and juicy corn, and its potatoes flavored like pecans' filled the homestead with satisfaction, for the farm family did not yet look upon its produce 'at so many cents a pound'. Rather, each dish consumed by the family bore a special meaning, for family members had as a body raised and created it.

Lytle also stressed how the Southern hill people held to a different sense of time. If wild game was in abundance or the fish were biting, 'the boys might knock off a day and go fishing, or hunting'. Since their father did not yet keep a ledger, 'their time is their own'. Naps followed the midday meal, while the evenings featured 'play parties', the sharing of 'ballets' on guitar or fiddle, a 'Sacred Harp' hymn sing, or a square dance (with its 'very fine balance between group and individual action').

Lytle vividly described as well the threats to this agrarian order. 'Good roads' opened the rural economy up to salesmen from the asphalt, oil, and automobile companies. The farmer traded in his horses for a truck and a tractor, both with notes bearing interest at the bank, forgetting that – unlike livestock – the machines could not reproduce themselves. The tractor also supplanted the tasks once done by the boys: 'Thus begins the home-breaking. Time is money now, not property, and the boys can't hang around the place.' Electrification had a related impact: 'If his daughters had not already moved away, he would have to send them, for [the] Delco [generator] has taken their place in the rural economy.' Meanwhile, the farm wife now became 'a drudge.... She has changed from being a creator in a fixed culture to an assistant to the machines', and she grew restless.

In response, Lytle urged Southerners 'to return to our looms, our handcrafts, our reproducing stocks'. At the level of culture, 'throw out the radio and take down the fiddle from the wall. Forsake the movies for the play-parties and the square dances' ('Twelve Southerners,' 1977 [1930], 208-244).

A different agrarian accent marked the contemporaneous work of Ralph Borsodi. Where Lytle wrote in the melodic cadence of the rural South, Borsodi used the direct language of New York City, which he called home. He had begun his career as a consulting economist on Madison Avenue, working for leading corporations and trade associations. His early books dissected 'The New Advertising' and the 'Distribution Age'. However, his commentary grew sharply critical. Borsodi finally condemned modern advertising for creating artificial necessities in people's lives that had 'no economic or moral basis in fact'. He denounced laws governing joint-stock corporations for granting legal privileges (limits on liability, perpetual life, and the ability to issue stock and debt instruments to raise capital) that were denied to families and individuals. Borsodi also emphasised the artificial nature of large industry in the twentieth century, calling the massive factory 'a steam-age relic rendered obsolete by the electrical age', yet sustained by political favours.

On a related point, he rejected the modern assumption – shared by capitalists, communists, and fascists alike – 'that mass production is the most efficient' method of securing goods and services. Using appropriate modern small tools, families could produce two-thirds of the things they needed. And he indicted industrialism as the source of family turmoil:

> Against the family... the factory wages a ruthless war of extermination.... Industrialism seeks to root out individual devotion to the family and the homestead and to replace it with loyalty to the factory.

The same process had turned children into 'economic catastrophes' for a household; a decent standard of living could be maintained 'only on condition that we... sterilize ourselves' (Borsodi, 1928: 416-417).

Borsodi's alternative was to break ties with the artificial complexities of the industrial order, in favour of a revivified domestic economy. As he explained:

> Family production is a program for folk who aim at virtue and happiness, and for whom the good life is represented by home and hearth, by friends and by children, by lawns and flowers (Borsodi, 1938, 5).

The home must cease to be a mere consumption unit; once again, 'it must be made into an economically creative institution'. A family on a specialised, industrial farm should 'cut down its farming to its own needs'. Meanwhile, 'the non-farming family should farm enough to supply itself with the essentials of life'. Unlike Andrew Lytle, who dreaded the effects of electrification, Borsodi welcomed the advent of small-scale electrical and internal combustion engines; these, he argued, negated most productive advantages of the centralised factory and created ways to heal the breach between home and work.

This also made possible a liberation of human life from the crushing rigour of the clock: 'Time is not money at all. Time is life itself.' In a renewed home economy, 'young and old, strong and weak, can *all* contribute *time* to the creation of what the home needs and desires'. They could rediscover, as well, authentic means of celebration and re-creation: songs inherited from ancestors and the special rituals of dance. Such family activity, broadly defined, was 'absolutely essential to the preservation of individual economic independence and freedom' (Borsodi, 1928: 272, 283, 351-352).

And yet, this quest for a simplified economic life actually ran into a paradox at that level of the individual. Whatever its complexities in the realms of organisation and exchange, industrialism did mandate an extreme simplification among factory workers. As Adam Smith had explained, economic gain came as workers ceased to be generalists doing many tasks tolerably well, becoming instead specialists ideally doing only one thing very quickly and very well. Managerial organisation and a complex system of distribution would then satisfy human needs. By the 1920s, several generations of industrial workers had come and gone without gaining the old knowledge of how to live in independence and family-centred security. As a result, modern city dwellers – even if provided 'with all the tools and implements which the Swiss Family Robinson providentially found' – would during an emergency 'die of exposure, of sickness, and of hunger', so complete and 'pathetic' was their dependence on factory-made goods.

In response, Borsodi resolved in 1933 to create The School of Living, a place that would retrain men and women in the skills of independent living. Built at the foot of the Ramapo Mountains north of New York City, this school operated through several departments. The Homemaking Division focused on cooking, food preservation, and laundering. The cultivation of vegetable gardens and the care of poultry and dairy animals came under the Agricultural Division. The Craft Division taught furniture making and home spinning and weaving (using the advanced 'Borsodi Loom') while the Building Division provided training in home construction. Another department studied and taught methods for launching and maintaining a small home business. 'Young couples planning for homes of their own are good prospects for entrance', Borsodi wrote, and hundreds of 'Borsodi Homesteads' could actually be found on the American landscape by decade's end.

World War II put an end to most mid-century agrarian dreams of a simplified, home-centred economic order. Promising developments during the 1920s and '30s were swept aside by the greatest centralising, industrialising, and complex event in human history. Standing almost alone as a national voice for Agrarianism after 1960 was the novelist, poet, essayist, and Kentucky farmer Wendell Berry.

He paid homage to Thomas Jefferson for advancing the ideal 'that as many as possible should share in the ownership of the land' and so be bound to it 'by the investment of love and work' and by family bonds, memory, and tradition. As had Andrew Lytle, Berry yearned 'with a kind of homesickness' for the 'naturalness of a highly-diversified, multi-purpose landscape, democratically divided' and 'hospitable to the wild lives of plants and animals and to the wild play of human children'. Along with Ralph Borsodi, Berry shared enthusiasm for the recovery of self-sufficient farming. 'Commercial farming must never be separated from subsistence farming', he maintained. '[T]he farm family should live from the farm' (Berry, 1987: 103-106, 124-125; Berry, 1977: 13-14).

Berry did not normally use the language of simplicity, actually preferring sterner words. Writing in the essay *What Are People For?*, he summarised: 'We must achieve the character and acquire the skills to live *much poorer* than we do.' A proper economy 'exists by the willingness to be anonymous, humble, and unrewarded' (Berry, 1990: 200).

His critique of the complexities of the industrial order reached deep and included challenges to the foundational realm of science. He rejected, for example, attempts at biological categorisation, arguing that lives – including those of animals – cannot be adequately explained by quantified generalisations. Indeed, science was a distraction: 'We are learning to know precisely the location of our genes, but significant numbers of us don't know the whereabouts of our children.' In place of the abstractions of science, Berry urged a return to pictures, stories, songs, and dances, through which the lives of creatures and people might find meaning. Wendell Berry underscored the authentic power of community, a company of neighbours and friends with shared experiences who gave pleasure and meaning to private lives. The true community transcended individual lives. As one of Berry's fictional characters explained:

> He has heard the tread of his own people dancing in the ring, the fiddle measuring time to them, a voice calling them, through the steps of change and absence, home again, the dancers unaware of their steps, with only the music, older than memory, remembered.

As with earlier agrarians, Wendell Berry linked human happiness and destiny to a revitalised home economy. As he explained in his poem 'The Farm':

But don't neglect your garden.
Household economy
Makes family and land
An independent state.
Never buy at a store
What you can grow or find
At home – this is the rule
Of liberty....

The act of creating this simple economy actually brought an inner peace:

In time of hate and waste,
Wars and rumors of wars,
Rich armies and poor peace
Your blessed economy,
Beloved sufficiency
Upon a dear, small place,
Sings with the morning stars.

Berry also focused on a distinct notion of time. He held that being fully human required submission to the rhythms of nature. The farmer found his place in 'the Dear Opening between what was and is to be', as he submitted to the natural flow and special conditions of his farm. In this way, '[h]e became the man it asked him to be..... [H]e'd become the farm's belonging, necessary to it.'

Living simply and well through the self-sufficiency of the home economy, finding meaning and identity in family and community as expressed through song and dance, and joyfully submitting to the cadences of nature: these were the common attributes of the American Agrarians.

References

Berry, Wendell. 1987. *Home Economics*. Berkeley, CA: North Point Press.

Berry, Wendell. 1977. *The Unsettling of America: Culture and Agriculture*. New York: Avon.

Berry, Wendell. 1990. *What Are People For?* San Francisco: North Point Press.

Borsodi, Ralph. 1938. *Prosperity and Security.* New York: Harper and Brothers.

Borsodi, Ralph. 1928. *This Ugly Civilization.* New York: Simon and Shuster.

Jefferson, T. 2009. *Thomas Jefferson: Thoughts on War and Revolution: Annotated Correspondence.* Edited by Brett F. Woods. New York: Algora Publishing.

'Twelve Southerners.' 1977 [1930]. *I'll Take My Stand: The South and the Agrarian Tradition.* Baton Rouge and London: Louisiana State University Press.

PIONEERS OF THE DEEP FUTURE

CHAPTER SIXTEEN

THE NEARINGS

AMANDA MCLEOD

> We left city living, with its civilized polish and its murky poverty, and launched out into a simpler, more self-sufficient, life in the country (Nearing, 1979: 391).

Simple living on the land has long been pursued by those seeking to escape the perils of city life. Disillusioned, yet relatively affluent, city dwellers across the western world, have experimented with homesteading, self-sufficiency and neo-pioneering with various levels of commitment, energy and success. For some simple living practitioners, going 'back-to-the-land' to provide for themselves, offers personal freedom and gives meaning to daily life that can be missing or impossible in the city. For some, it has an even wider application; it could be the panacea to the ills of modern capitalism.

It was in the aftermath of the First World War, at the height of the Great Depression, that Helen and Scott Nearing, who were to become the godparents of the modern homesteading movement, began their own simple living experiment. Leaving New York City in 1932 to settle in rural Vermont, the Nearings set out with a well-formulated plan to live their version of the 'simple life', one they believed could be replicated by those seeking to free themselves from the exploitation.

The Nearings' successful homesteading experience, conducted over half a century in rural North America, showed that a planned home economy could remove one from the exploitation usually associated with modern industrial life. Freedom and prosperity was tenuous in Depression-ravaged cities. Homesteading, living on and from the land, could provide nearly all of one's basic needs – both materially and spiritually. Cities, as the War and the Great Depression had shown, could not.

For the American Progressive economist and political activist Scott Nearing (1883-1983), industrial civilisation had more than failed to live up to its promises. Rather than elevating people out of poverty, city living relied on class divides by locking workers into unequal and exploitative relationships with employers. Before the First World War, Nearing actively campaigned against the use of child labour in Pennsylvania and taught and wrote numerous books and pamphlets advocating that 'new economics' could be used to solve various social problems. During this time of immense political, social and economic upheaval, he lost various academic positions due to his radical beliefs about income and wealth distribution, pacifism and commitment to socialism. Scott Nearing met Helen Knothe (1904-1995), a trained musician, life-long vegetarian and writer in 1928. Despite their privileged urban upbringings, that they found themselves in rural Vermont in 1932 was no accident of timing.

Ultimately, Scott's radicalism saw him unable to negotiate the conservative interests at the institutions where he had previously held various research and teaching positions. His continued commitment to exposing the in-justices of capitalism, the rising cost of living and income distribution ultimately made Scott Nearing unemployable. Driven by the need to keep body and soul together and, most importantly, to live ethically, the Nearings devised a way of life that was both economically and socially 'good'.

The Nearings' story and their contribution to the history of simple living is very much the product of the time and place in which it developed. The Nearings rejected American industrialisation and the social structures that were, from their point of view, based on 'a social order activated by greed and functioning through exploitation acquisition and accumulation' (Nearing, 1954: 13). However, despite Scott's ties to the Communist Party and belief in socialism, the Nearings did not seek to move overseas to a place where their politics may have found a more favourable reception. While they remained firmly committed to living the 'good life' in the United States as United States' citizens, their philosophies did not centre on reforming the existing social and economic orders. Rather, their planned homesteading economy was to be an entirely new economic model.

Many of Scott Nearing's writings, prior to going back-to-the-land, had centred on the failings of capitalism and militarism. Much of the population had fallen victim to the exploitation that was an integral part of modern capitalism or had been slaughtered, in their thousands, during the Great War. The Great Depression was evidence that most people were vulnerable to the flaws inherent in capitalist economics. The Nearings rejected modern capitalism's growth model and its directive to buy all one's needs, giving citizens little control over the origin and manufacture of products. They were strongly committed to healthy living and ethical production and consumption. The Nearings chose to provide for themselves and to grow their own organically produced wholefood instead of buying fruit and vegetables that were loaded with poisonous sprays and dusts and processed food with little nutritional value (Nearing, 1954: 152-3). 'We are opposed to the theories of a competitive, acquisitive, aggressive, war-making social order', they wrote,

> which butchers for food and murders for sport and for power. The closer we have to come to this social order the more completely are we a part of it. Since we reject it in theory, we should, as far as possible, reject it also in practice. On no other basis can theory and practice be unified. At the same time, and to the utmost extent, we should live as decently, kindly, justly, orderly and efficiently as possible (Nearing, 1954: 192).

It is not my intention here to describe, in detail, the daily homesteading life of Helen and Scott Nearing. Their memoirs, *The Good Life* (1954) and *Continuing the Good Life* (1979), part homesteading how-to, part autobiography, provide a richer insight into their subsistence life than any summary here could hope to convey. It is, however, important to note that their success rested on their unrelenting commitment to the demands of the lifestyle and also on the highly organised design for living, what they described as their 'four-four-four' formula:

> four hours of bread labor; four hours of professional activity; and four hours dedicated to fulfilling our obligations and responsibilities as members of the human race and as participants in various local, regional, national and world civic activities (Nearing, 1979: 388).

Daily life was primarily structured around subsistence living and such demands required careful planning and hard, physical work. But the Nearings' 'good life' was not merely consumed by daily toil. It also brought with it the personal satisfaction of providing for oneself and of living an ethical life. Most importantly, it provided freedom:

> Our general aim was to set up a use economy for ourselves independent of the established market economy and for the most part under our own control, thereby freeing ourselves from undue dependence on the Establishment (Nearing, 1979: 391).

Limiting their engagement with the cash economy was central to the Nearings' simple living economy, describing it as a desire to make a 'livelihood' rather than to accumulate wealth. Conventional capitalist economics was all about the getting and keeping of money, pursuits that were, for the Nearings, highly problematic, undesirable and unethical. Some money, of course, would always be necessary. By cash-cropping, they were able to generate a meagre, but vital, income from both their properties: harvesting sugar maple in Vermont and blueberries in Maine, in order to pay taxes and other necessities such as fuel for transport and cement for stonework. Rather than building their business of cash crops, the Nearings intentionally chose to cease production when they had earned 'enough' to cover their annual expenses.

While the Nearings' homesteading lifestyle was driven by a desire to separate themselves from the exploitative cycle of modern production and consumption, they were also driven by the necessity to provide for themselves due to the physical constraints of isolation. Rural life in Vermont and Maine was very different to the life they had experienced in New York City. Careful planning was a necessary part of the home-steading lifestyle:

> Dwellers in a remote valley cannot send or phone to the corner grocery an hour before supper. They must plan and prepare during the previous season. If radishes are to be ready for the table on the first of June, they must be planted not later than the first week in May. If seeds are to yield the best results, the soil must be prepared before the planting day. Soil preparation with us, necessitated compost. Compost piles, to be available in the Spring, had to be set up by mid-summer of the previous year. To enjoy fresh radishes on June 1, we began to get ready ten or twelve months in advance (Nearing, 1954: 156).

And that was just for radishes!

The Nearings' vision of the good life was based on a tripartite desire to be protected economically, hygienically and ethically. Homesteading provided economic depression-free living and through physical work and predominantly raw organic food it maximised human health. Equally import-antly, homesteading was driven by a strong social and ethical objective not to harm the environment or any living creature. Although Helen had always been vegetarian, Scott also consciously chose not to eat meat. Unlike other self-providers, who saw animals as central to the fertility and productivity of the home economy, the Nearings also kept no animals on their farms. This decision fulfilled their objective not to enslave any being and also not be enslaved themselves by the unrelenting daily demands of animal husbandry.

The day to day life of the Nearings, during their half a century 'experiment' in simple living, outlined a well thought-out prescription for simplicity – an economic, planned and organised 'good' life. Necessarily austere, restricted and controlled, the Nearings gained both physical and intellectual satisfaction from their life on, and connection to, the land.

Yet the Nearings did not merely 'drop out' of society and cut themselves off from the rest of the United States. Despite having been ostracised by the Academy and the Establishment, they maintained a strong and vocal interest in social, economic and political life. Scott maintained a regular schedule of speaking engagements and writing assignments and they played host to an enormous number of visitors, which began as a trickle during their early years in Vermont. As the development of a nearby ski resort encroached on their farm, the increasing numbers of visitors precipitated their desire to move to regain their privacy, routine and isolation. They simply wanted to get on with their business of living. As Scott approached his seventieth year, the Nearings moved from Pikes Falls, Vermont to Harborside, Maine, to start their homesteading experiment over again. Despite their isolation and desire for privacy the visitor numbers increased exponentially:

> Before we moved from Vermont to Maine, the trickle of visitors had become a stream. During the next years in Maine it became a flood. By the 1970's the number of visitors by head count has ranged between 2000 and 2500 in the course of a year. It often reached dozens in a day (Nearing, 1979: 361).

In assessing the success or failure of the Nearings' homesteading experience, one should not be surprised to discover that the number of couples or families living self-sufficiently has remained small. Despite the perfect storm that occurred during 1960s and 1970s that saw large numbers of young people seek alternative lifestyles, many of the resulting homesteading adventures had neither the longevity of the Nearings' experience nor the social justice activism of their lived experience.

The Nearings concluded that their own lifestyle had, from a health and happiness point of view, been an overwhelming success. From their own point of view, their homesteading experiment had been less successful as a social experiment. In what they saw as a disintegrating society, it had been difficult to attract likeminded individuals – with sufficient energy, commitment or skills – to join in their projects. Despite the vast numbers who came to see and talk to them, the Nearings had found the lifestyle wanting for a diversity of ideas or a community population large enough to make large-scale building projects more economical (Nearing, 1979: 199).

The thousands of visitors that travelled to Vermont and then to Maine to view homesteading in action, and to see the 'native homesteaders' in their natural habitat, were all interested in freedom but they were not interested in collective action for the social, ethical and economic cause. Despite the increasing interest that the Nearings' home-steading lifestyle generated, along with the popularity of their writings, the socialist beliefs underpinning it did not hold the same appeal for those who found their way to Vermont and Maine in the post-WWII period. The Nearings found most of their young visitors to be 'apolitical, impatient of restraints – especially when government imposed' (Nearing, 1979: 328). They were dismayed to find that the majority were,

> wanderers and seekers, feeling their way toward an escape from orthodoxy and superficiality, with the nervous dissatisfaction that characterizes people who do not have home base in any real sense. Perhaps they can best be described as unsettled. Never before in our lives have we met so many unattached, uncommitted, insecure, uncertain human beings (Nearing, 1979: 358-9).

The Nearings were more than willing to share their land with other likeminded and equally committed individuals. Yet, only a handful of those who met the Nearings were serious about the (homesteading) cause. The Nearings sold parcels of their land to a couple of young people, leaving them with a more manageable 26 acres (from about 100). To their disappointment, homesteading had done little to breakdown the class divide. Most, if not all, of their visitors were from white affluent middle class families: 'We do not remember having one black youngster come, or one daughter or son of a coal miner, nor do we recall young people whose parents worked in textiles factories or steel mills' (Nearing, 1979: 360). It seemed that the Nearings' homesteading lifestyle had not reached the groups they had thought most at risk of exploitation by modern capitalism.

But the Nearings' greatest success was living a long and healthy life that was not dependent on the Establishment. As they explained in 1954, they were doing little to support mass consumerism:

> As a means of providing a subsistence household with the cash necessary to buy out the market, to shop from one end of a mail order catalog to another or to provide the family with endless comforts, conveniences, labor-saving gadgets, trinkets and habit-forming drugs, our project was a dismal failure (Nearing, 1954: 195).

Despite contributing nothing to the American Dream, the Nearing's subsistence lifestyle was a real success as 'a venture in economic self-containment and an experiment in economy, frugality, self-discipline and day-to-day training for a new way of life' (Nearing, 1954: 195).

Despite the climatic challenges associated with subsistence farming in extreme temperatures, the disruptions caused by the increasing number of visitors to their routine, speaking commitments and advancing years, the Nearings kept working on their daily tasks and using their four-four-four formula. What is striking about the Nearings' description of their day to day life, building in stone and harvesting and splitting wood for construction and fuel, gardening, canning and of meal preparation, is that there is no sense that the Nearings found their life monotonous or boring. Stonework, for example, and the Nearings built numerous dwellings and other buildings in stone, was described as 'interesting, productive, creative and collective' (Nearing, 1979: 328). That they chose to start over again in Maine in 1952, when others of Scott's age would have been slowing down and thinking about a quiet retirement, is testament to the Nearings' belief in, and commitment to, homesteading as a valid and worthy pursuit.

The Nearings' portrait of homesteading was not one of a romanticised rural life, describing it rather as 'simple and austere; some would say hard and comfortless' (Nearing,

1954: 198). Yet they were healthy and happy, 'living sane in an insane world' (Nearing, 1979: 391).

> Personally, we in our entire homesteading venture have endeavoured to keep our social as well as physical muscles in shape. We tried, as a couple, and insofar as we could in groups, to set up and continue a life a pattern to maintain health and sanity in a period of social insecurity, conflict, disruption and disintegration (Nearing: 1979: 390-1).

The Nearings' legacy shows that simple living can be desirable, enjoyable and rewarding even when it is necessary. The 'good life' as they lived it was not solely based on homesteading for food and shelter; it was a whole life prescription for 'productive and creative endeavor' (Nearing, 1979: 392). Overwhelmingly, it demonstrates that, despite capitalism's domination, there remains a viable alternative for those who seek a better, more ethical way of life.

References

Nearing, Helen and Scott. 1954. *Living the Good Life: How to Live Sanely and Simply in a Troubled World*, reprinted in Helen and Scott Nearing. 1989. *The Good Life:* New York: Schocken Books.

Nearing, Helen and Scott. 1979. *Continuing the Good Life: Half a Century of Homesteading*, reprinted in Helen and Scott Nearing. 1989. *The Good Life*, New York: Schocken Books.

Nearing, Scott. 1972. *The Making of a Radical: A Political Autobiography*, New York: Harper and Row.

Further Reading

Saltmarsh, John A. 1991. *Scott Nearing: An Intellectual Biography*. Philadelphia: Temple University Press.

CHAPTER SEVENTEEN

IVAN ILLICH

MARIUS DE GEUS

When analysing the ideas of Austrian social philosopher Ivan Illich (1926-2002), attention is mainly focused on his educational, social, developmental and medical insights. Often it is overlooked that in the seventies, eighties and nineties of the last century, he was a highly engaged environmentalist publishing extensively about ecological issues and how they related to high consumptive lifestyles. In fact, Illich has been one of the most imaginative thinkers who have written about the necessity of sufficiency and simplification of lifestyles.

In this Chapter I shall first explore the way in which Illich approached modern problems of resource scarcity and environmental degradation. What was his general perspective on our modern day industrial society? How did he envision a future society in which the inhabitants of the world could live comfortably and well, without exceeding the ecological limits of the earth?

According to Illich, it was critical to reject the dominant high-energy conceptions of 'the good life'. However, what would such a simpler and less consumption-oriented lifestyle look like? And to what extent would a simplified lifestyle lead to a different structure of consuming and producing?

Particularly in his *Celebration of Awareness: A Call for Institutional Revolution* (1971), *Tools for Conviviality* (1973) and *Energy and Equity* (1974), Illich presented valuable ideas about the interrelationship between society, ecology, and human lifestyles. So what, then, was his general perspective on our modern day industrial society?

Illich stresses our current society is based on a number of flawed assumptions. In *Tools for Conviviality* he explains that nowadays it is believed unlimited economic growth is the highest goal, and only high energy use can produce welfare and happiness among the citizens. However, as Illich argues, for environmental and social reasons ecological limits will have to be issued to curb excessive energy consumption.

High energy consumption will inevitably cause scarcity of natural resources and will produce addiction to luxurious lifestyles. When ignoring strict ecological limitations, energy demand growth will have a corrupting effect on society and increase social injustice within and across countries. In Illich's analysis, wealthier sections of society profit disproportionately from an increase in energy consumption (Illich, 1973: 26-29).

Another assumption of modern industrial society relates to the increase of motorised speed. Ever faster modes of transport imply that more energy is spent on mobility, and seduces people to travel more frequently and over longer distances. A comprehensive mobility industry has evolved (transport by buses, trams, subways, trains and airplanes) which has created new modes of behaviour. Many modern citizens no longer accept mobility by foot or bicycle, and only want to be transported by motorised and speedy transport. As a consequence, citizens have started to believe that freedom of mobility equals an unrestricted right to transportation.

Illich argued that higher speed transport would be to the detriment of social justice, free time and personal autonomy. Particularly the rich and privileged would be able to afford these high speed forms of transport. Consequently, their considerably higher energy consumption would lead to a reduction of social justice. In addition to this, higher transportation speeds go at the cost of one's leisure time. Illich calculated that the average American spent 1,600 hours per year to earn the money to purchase the car, drive in the car, stand in traffic jams, and maintain their car, just to travel some 10,000 km.

This means that modern citizens are only achieving an average speed of around 6 kilometres per hour: hardly more than the speed of someone who is walking, and by far not as fast as a person who opted for the elegant simplicity of bicycle riding. Hence, people are forced to work long hours in order to afford their 'speedy mobility' by car, which greatly impacts on their leisure time and personal autonomy (Illich, 1974: 27-32).

Another basic assumption of our modern society is that industrially produced products such as mobility by car or motorcycle, are more valuable than self-produced activities like walking or bicycling. Overall, society is systematically and constantly prioritising high speed above 'just going' which causes numerous detrimental environmental effects.

As a result, our transportation system is dominated by an immense mobility industry which has achieved a monopoly in the field of satisfying consumer preferences for transportation. This transportation industry is providing for preferences and needs which can only be satisfied by this elaborate system. The transportation industry influences the wants of consumers, and through this is making itself indispensable. The upshot has been that nowadays social life is dominated by the transportation industry, which largely determines the speed of travelling and the level of energy consumption (Illich, 1973: 49-62).

Illich explained that for at least four reasons the industrial system has lost its balance. In the first place, its stability has been harmed by many forms of expansion in different fields of society. Excessive population growth made humankind more dependent on scarce resources, and increasing material consumption had led to much higher energy use. The application of inappropriate, large-scale technologies had produced inefficient ways of dealing with the remaining sources of energy (Illich, 1971: 159-175; Illich, 1973: 20-46).

Secondly, the instability of our social and technological industrial system had been furthered by a growing polarisation of power. Illich concluded there was a growing divide between powerless citizens on the one hand and powerful elites on the other hand. In his analysis, a small group of managers were in total control of the industrial 'Mega-machine', whereas the large group of employees were getting less involved in policy making. Successively, production processes became centralised: the top ruling over the bottom.

Comprehensive multinational corporations are in control of the main tools of society, and are deliberately looking for new opportunities for achieving production and consumption growth (see also, Borgman, 1984: Chapter 2). Unfortunately, liberal democratic states are unable to effectively counter-balance the massive power of these multinational 'Mega-machines'.

Thirdly, instability of the social and industrial system was augmented by purposely built-in obsolescence of consumer goods. It was in the interest of big corporations to ensure their products would age prematurely and soon be replaced by new ones. Older models of a product diminished in value fast, and when spare parts are no longer produced consumers are obliged to purchase the latest model. According to Illich a core problem of modern industrial society is the assumption that what is new, will be better:

> ... new models constantly renovate poverty. The consumer feels the lag between what he has and what he ought to get. He believes that products can be made measurably more valuable and allows himself to be constantly re-educated for their consumption. The 'better' replaces the 'good' as the fundamental normative concept (Illich, 1973: 75).

Today, this view has become the norm and is now a quintessential part of the dominant industrial-capitalist ideology.

Fourthly, instability of the social and productive system was enlarged by deep frustrations and the addictive consumption of goods and services. The expansion of the economy made people addicted to consumption. Addicts of any sort are prepared to spend larger sums leading to constantly diminishing satisfaction. In the end, a systematic end to economic expansion will be needed, in order to eradicate the socially undermining addiction to growth of production and consumption (Illich, 1973: 107-8).

As noted, Illich criticised the obsession with economic growth in today's consumer society. He was among the first social thinkers to argue for limits to economic growth and a moderation of individual consumption levels. His ideal was to ensure that by means of an open and democratic process, society would decide which level of welfare would be sufficient for an ecologically sustainable existence (See also: Alexander, 2013; De Geus, 1999).

For Illich, society should voluntarily limit economic growth in order to repair the equilibrium between human wants and the biosphere. In this context, he was referring to the vitality of realising a 'stationary state' in the production of goods. In line with his contemporaries like Herman Daly, Lester Brown and Dennis Meadows, he pleaded for a 'steady-state economy'. This is an economy which did not exceed the basic carrying capacity of the earth and which is fundamentally in harmony with nature (Illich, 1973: 48-52).

Another central theme in his work was to develop the boundaries which have to be applied to the tools and technologies of society. Illich sketched the contours of a so-called 'convivial society':

> A convivial society is the result of social arrangements that guarantee for each member the most ample and free access to the tools of the community, and limit this freedom in favor of the equal liberty of another member's freedom (Illich, 1973: 12).

In a convivial society the tools are adapted to human scale, and machines would no longer 'enslave' humans. In our current society, capital-intensive, complex, and centrally ruled techniques are prevailing, producing a highly specialised division of labour. With respect to ecological values, applying this type of tool is nothing but disastrous (See also, Weston, 1989: 171-182). In contrast, Illich preferred environmentally friendly, 'convivial' tools which provide for freedom to make those things we need in order to survive.

> Convivial tools are those which give each person who uses them the greatest opportunity to enrich the environment with the fruits of his or her vision. Industrial tools deny this possibility to those who use them and they allow their designers to determine the meaning and expectations of others. Most tools today cannot be used in a convivial fashion (Illich, 1973: 21)

The critical point to note here is that Illich favoured relatively simple and decentralised techniques, which implied a limited division of labour. He argued for simple forms of education, and preventing workers and citizens from becoming dependent on experts. This change to convivial tools would necessitate opting for a socialist model of society in which capitalist institutions have been radically altered, and 'socialist justice' has become paramount (Illich, 1973: 17-8).

An integral part of his convivial society was to reduce speed and hurry. Against energy consuming transport by cars, he argued for simple and environmentally benign ways of travelling by foot or bicycle, convivial tools *par excellence*. Illich attacked the high pace which caused people to get stressed, whereas the quality of life was to a large extent determined by the chance to calm down, to relax and develop oneself (See also, De Geus, 1999: chapter 12).

Part of his vision was that limitations were put on the pace of the enforced change and renewal of goods. Hence, products must become extremely durable, must be tested for reparability as well as recyclability. He emphasised goods should be manufactured from sturdy materials and always be repairable, in order to prevent waste of materials and dumping (Illich, 1973: 73-76).

Illich noted that a vital element of realising a simplified lifestyle was to create plenty of room for citizen participation. All citizens should have a direct say in the social, political and economic spheres. A lack of political involvement of ordinary workers and citizens was interpreted as a serious danger to society. The prevention of concentrations of power in society was taken as a necessary condition to liberate humanity from the spiral of economic expansion.

Illich notes that a vital element of realising a simplified lifestyle is to create plenty of room for citizen participation. All citizens should have a direct say in the social, political and economic spheres. A lack of political involvement of ordinary workers and citizens is interpreted as a serious danger to society. The prevention of concentrations of power in society is taken as a necessary condition to liberate humanity from the spiral of economic expansion.

In addition, Illich argued that a more simple and self-sufficient lifestyle would require a halt to the many forms of overconsumption. He observed 'that in a consumer society there are inevitably two kinds of slaves: the prisoners of addiction and the prisoners of envy' (Illich, 1973: 82). Members of the social elite have gradually become accustomed to high standards of living, and are reluctant to give up this privilege, as it is thought that only high consumption will lead to satisfaction and happiness.

According to Illich, however, this argument is in-adequate. A moderate style of living was essential for liberating people from their addiction to economic welfare and superfluous luxuries. In order to live in a less stressful way, citizens can better opt for an attractive life of voluntary simplicity; a life which is well provided, while not excessive and wasteful. Only such a moderated lifestyle will provide us with the inner harmony and mental balance which are the backbone of a free and happy existence (Illich, 1973: 48-51).

The difficult part of this fundamental change will be to teach addicted citizens how to get rid of their addiction(s), and to start living within reasonable ecological limits. Indeed, he argued that people will have to restrain themselves from producing unlimited off-spring. In his view, people have to reduce overall consumption and general use of products. Only then humankind may have the realistic hope of preventing irreversible environmental dangers to our planet and securing a sustainable life on earth, as well as being able to live active and responsible lives (Illich 1973: 65-7).

Illich demonstrated that many Western consumptive needs and wants are generated by the capitalist production system, which tended to stimulate consumer demand and increase the supply of goods and services. In his analysis, the economy should focus on the production of high quality goods which are robust, repairable and recyclable. Illich explained that responsible members of society should avoid buying shoddy and unrepairable goods, which suffer from built-in obsolescence.

His personal preference for small scale and simple technological tools was founded upon the idea that these are understandable, transparent, and suitable to be managed by non-experts such as ordinary factory workers. By introducing adapted technologies in society, people could be empowered to participate actively in social and political decision-making, and local communities could regain power over their tools and technology.

By embracing a lifestyle of voluntary simplicity and self-sufficiency, citizens would be able to enjoy more free-time, become less anxious and stressed, and overcome their addiction to high levels of consumption. Illich did not advocate a life of scantiness, scarcity and poverty, but a high quality life that was simple in means but rich in ends.

Illich evoked an intriguing vision of what a green lifestyle based on voluntary simplicity might actually look like, and what the consequences were for our personal views on 'the art of life'. Illich invites us to look most critically at the modern world, and develop new conceptions of a low carbon, happy and fulfilling life. In the end, it will be crucial to renounce the dominant high-energy conceptions of 'the good life', and decide for a lifestyle of simplification, moderation, and self-restraint.

References

Alexander, S. 2013. *Entropia: Life Beyond Industrial Civilisation*, Simplicity Institute Publishing, Melbourne.

Borgman, A. 1984. *Technology and the Character of Contemporary Life*, University of Chicago Press.

De Geus, M. 1999. *Ecological utopias: Envisioning the Sustainable Society*, International Publishers, Utrecht.

De Geus, M. 2003. *The End of Over-consumption; Towards a Lifestyle of Moderation and Self-restraint*, International Publishers, Utrecht.

Illich, I. 1971. *Celebration of Awareness: a call for institutional revolution*, published by Doubleday Anchor, New York.

Illich, I., 1974. *Energy and Equity*, edition used is published by Marion Boyars, New York / London.

Illich, I. 1973. *Tools for Conviviality*, edition used was published by Marion Boyars, New York / London.

Weston, A. 1989. 'Ivan Illich and the Radical Critique of Tools', in *Research in Philosophy and Technology*, no. 9, Jai Press, London

CHAPTER EIGHTEEN

JOHN SEYMOUR

AMANDA MCLEOD

In his 1976 foreword to John Seymour's *Complete Book of Self-Sufficiency*, E.F. Schumacher described the shift from self-reliance to dependence on the mainstream economy. Never before, Schumacher lamented, had people been so dependent and less able to do things for themselves. There were serious consequences for being too dependent: 'What if there is a hold-up, a breakdown, a strike, or unemployment?'. He accepted that the State could no longer be relied upon to provide a safety net; even if it existed people could fall through the cracks. 'Why can't they help themselves?,' Schumacher asked. For him the answer was all too obvious: 'they would not know how to; they have never done it before and would not even know where to begin (in Seymour, 1976: 6). For Schumacher, economist and author of the highly influential *Small is Beautiful: A Study of Economics as if People Mattered* (1973), some of the answers lay in Seymour's how-to manual: *The Complete Book of Self-Sufficiency* (1976). The book was to sell over a million copies and become the bible of the self-sufficiency movement.

> Here we all sit, Sally my wife, Jane who is five and a half, Ann who is two and a half, and Kate who is seven (days), a mile from a hard road, with no electricity, no gas, no deliveries of anything at all excepting coal, provided that we take at least a ton. ... And we are self-supporting for every kind of food excepting tea, coffee, flour, sugar and

159

salt. We have no car – we drive about with a pony and cart (Seymour, 1961: 9).

If there is one name that is synonymous with self-sufficiency in Britain it has to be John Seymour. Like many of those who had sought a simple rural life before him, Seymour (1914-2004), from whom the above quote is drawn, came to self-sufficiency through an intense dissatisfaction with modern city life. Seymour's version of self-sufficiency was one in which life was centred on rural small-holdings where families lived close to nature and became part of existing farming communities. The authentic and ethical philosophy of self-sufficiency, based on the belief that 'real' living lay in consuming what you have produced yourself, found resonance with thousands of disaffected urbanites throughout the second half of the twentieth century and into the twenty-first. John Seymour's style of self-sufficiency always had a strong ethical element; by owning the means of production, self-providers would do no harm to workers, animals and the land. And by also controlling the means of consumption they would limit their involvement with the external economy and limit their impact on the environment.

Seymour, author of more than forty books on travel, the natural environment and, of course, self-sufficiency, was strongly influenced by his experiences living and working with Indigenous farming communities in India and Africa during the 1930s and '40s, and later across England, Ireland and Wales. Despite his privileged middle-class upbringing, Seymour chose not to enter his step-father's manufacturing business. He instead removed himself from the world of society parties, private schools, business and finance, and pursued an agricultural career, built-up a large body of written work and lived a practical life on the land (Peacock, 2005). Seymour, along with others drawn to self-sufficiency, grew to believe that a real, more authentic life lay in traditional crafts, skills, and culture, and a strong attachment to the land, rather than in modern office buildings and factories that made up city life.

Despite Seymour's early affection for the land which was developed during his time living and working in India and

Africa, during his war service and extensive travels, self-sufficiency was not part of his personal experience until he settled down on a rural small-holding with his family in the late 1950s. Seymour and his wife Sally (Medworth), an accomplished potter and artist, lived self-sufficiently first in Suffolk, England and later, Pembrokeshire, West Wales. Although John Seymour has largely been given the credit for being the 'father of self-sufficiency', one should not under-estimate the significant contribution made by his wife Sally whom he married in 1954. Indeed, self-sufficiency was not a part of John's day-to-day life until he 'settled down' to raise a family. Sally illustrated many of his books on self-sufficiency bringing their lifestyle to life (see for example, Seymour, 1983). Through her evocative illustrations and relentless day-to-day work on the farm, she made the lifestyle work in practice while John worked away or wrote his many accounts of self-reliant living.

Regardless of where John found himself, it was always the countryside and its people that defined and fulfilled him. Modern city life simply held no appeal:

> It just seems very silly to work for eight hours a day in an office (and I can't stand air-conditioning) to get the money to pay for things that we can produce so much better and more pleasantly ourselves (Seymour, 1973a: 243).

But Seymour's distain was more than a personal dissatisfaction. Industrialisation and commercialisation were responsible for a whole raft of societal ills including the unethical treatment of people, animals and the environment:

> Just as we cannot, for ever, go on keeping hens in wire cages, or pigs in total darkness, or suppressing every species of life on the land except one money-making crop, so we cannot go on for ever ourselves living in human battery cages and more and more distorting our environment (Seymour, 1973a: 246).

For Seymour, of course, the solution lay with the land, what he referred to as 'our only real and abiding asset' and self-sufficiency would provide the means by which the problem of modern life would be solved. By living on the land, by providing sustenance from it and feeling the earth beneath his feet, Seymour believed that not only he and his family but the rest of humanity would be happiest and most fulfilled.

Self-sufficiency as described and lived by the Seymours was about living independently and producing as much of one's food and other needs as possible. Most importantly, for those who sought self-reliance, the solution to the problem of mainstream of consumerism was also universal. In order to achieve satisfaction and reward for effort one needed to do productive work, most often hard physical labour. While some during this period saw the answer to society's woes lying in communities and communes, and many of these arrangements had self-sufficiency in the form of food production as one of their goals, the majority of people actively seeking post-industrial self-sufficiency were doing so as part of nuclear families in sole households not attached to communities. Despite the obvious economic advantages, and although the idea appealed to John, Sally was less than enthusiastic: 'Oh no – we don't want to start some bloody community!' (Seymour, 1974: 167). And so, the Seymour's expression of self-sufficiency remained a family affair.

Proponents of self-sufficiency argued that they were living out the innate desire to provide for their families. By removing themselves from the mainstream, self-providers needed to produce the necessities of life: food, shelter, clothing etc. But most lived less frugally than the austere lifestyle of Thoreau at Walden Pond, or the Nearings (1989), who lived on a vegetarian diet limited by very short growing seasons and the (self-imposed) restriction of four hours of 'bread labour' per day. Thoreau, Seymour mocked:

> didn't work very hard at all. He spent a very large part of his time there wondering around in the woods, peering into the depths of his pool, thinking and dreaming and meditating. I think he was a very sensible and enviable young man indeed. But he didn't have a wife and a family to bring up. Personally, I would not be prepared to live ... on beans. Sally certainly wouldn't either, and we would be very hard put to make the children do it (Seymour, 1973a: 12-13).

Seymour's sustained commitment to traditional farming and the preservation of traditional crafts and skills had, by the 1970s, taken on a political dimension. What he called 'post-industrial self-sufficiency' was about creating a new, and better, way of life. But it was not just city life that had changed during the post-war period; rural life was becoming increasingly industrialised with farming being conducted by fewer people with bigger machines. Seymour lamented the breakdown of community and the loss of traditional skills. The answer to modern life's ills lay with a version of self-sufficiency that was very much a product of the post-war period's mass production, mass consumption and over-consumption. Ultimately, self-sufficiency was about abundant produce of the highest quality, and freedom and independence: all important post-war consumer values that resonated with those who wanted to step back from the consumer market and do-it-themselves by being self-providers. Seymour summed up the self-sufficient philosophy:

> Now self-sufficiency is not 'going back' to some idealized past in which people grubbed for their food with primitive implements and burned each other with witchcraft. It is going *forward* to a new and better sort of life, a life which is more fun than the over-specialized round of office or factory, a life that brings challenge and the use of daily initiative back to work, and variety, and occasional great success and occasional abysmal failure. It means the acceptance of complete responsibility for what you do or what you do not do and one of its greatest rewards is the joy that comes from seeing each job right through – from sowing your own wheat to eating your own bread, from planting a field of pig food to slicing a side of bacon (Seymour, 1976: 7).

One could easily get caught up in a debate about whether the lifestyle lived by John and Sally Seymour was truly self-sufficient, given that John spent long periods writing or working away from home making documentaries for the BBC. For John, however, spreading the self-sufficiency message was just as important as its private pursuit on the land. But

John was no slouch. As John himself was at pains to point out, self-sufficiency was a practical, not just theoretical, philosophy. It was a plan of action; a call to arms. Linking self-sufficiency's philosophical underpinnings to its practical application on the land, Seymour issued an ultimatum to time (and land) wasters:

> everyone who owns a piece of land should husband that land as wisely, knowledgeably, and intensively as possible. The so-called 'self-supporter' sitting among a riot of docks and thistles talking philosophy ought to go back to town. He is not doing any good at all, and is occupying land which should be occupied by somebody who can really use it (Seymour, 1976: 7).

As had been the case with many back-to-the-land philosophies, John Seymour also believed his version would improve the lives of working people. Self-sufficiency, however, remained predominantly a middle-class pursuit. Much to his disappointment, John found that his farming counterparts in Ireland and Wales were quickly (and willingly) adopting industrial farming techniques in order to give up manual labour and rely more heavily on the mass consumer market for their own domestic needs.

While self-sufficiency on a rural small-holding was a logical progression for John Seymour, after his war experiences and extensive travels which drew him closer to the land and nature, its resonance with the public in the 1970s was driven by a different cause. The sense of urgency that had grown during the latter part of the 1960s and early 1970s, about the developing environmental emergency, industrial pollution in cities and the looming oil crisis, created a perfect storm which increased self-sufficiency and self-reliance's public appeal. Seymour, too, saw the writing on the wall; mainstream society was bankrupt:

> It's all going to collapse. Either the oil will run out, or the grub, or the uranium-235, or the power of Man to withstand the unutterable *boredom* of it all, and Mankind will have to find a different way of life (Seymour, 1973a: 246).

Regardless of Seymour's affection for working people and his desire to preserve their traditional skills and way of life, he found his greatest supporters and greatest successes amongst those who had 'gone through the big-city-industrial way of life and [had] advanced beyond it and want[ed] to go on to something better' (Seymour, 1973b: 9). It was not those who had toiled on the land for generations that turned to or remained committed to self-sufficiency. Rather it attracted the younger middle classes who voluntarily chose to adopt such a lifestyle (and who also had enough capital to finance it). Seymour's most successful book *The Complete Book of Self-Sufficiency* (1976) was published at a time of heightened consumerism and social and economic change. The connection between self-sufficiency and the rejection of mass-consumption by a certain section of the middle-class should not be over-looked.

Seymour's political activity increased as the years progressed. His personal dissatisfaction grew at the ineffectual attempts to solve global environmental issues, the development of genetic modification, battery and other forms of factory and industrial farming. Like many of his contemporaries, Seymour saw the nuclear power and oil crises of the 1970s as an opportune moment for widespread change. Either by being willingly adopted by those seeking a better way of life, or as a necessary response to declining oil stocks, self-sufficiency was the way forward. Seymour personally shared and eloquently expressed the fears of many during this period; it was only a matter of time before oil became scarce, forcing people to provide for themselves. The answer, he argued, was self-sufficiency. In husbanding the land carefully, and as 'wisely, knowledgeably, and intensively as possible', Seymour wrote: 'We will one day have to derive our sustenance from what the land, unaided by oil-derived chemicals, can produce' (Seymour, 1976: 7).

It is important to note that the characteristics of the Seymours' expression of self-sufficiency were very different to the homesteading life of Helen and Scott Nearing, the other key back-to-the-landers of the twentieth century. Animal husbandry, for example, played a fundamental part in the daily life of self-sufficiency as envisioned by Seymour yet they were notably absent from the Nearings' farm life. Central to the self-sufficient small holding's fertility, animals provided not only sustenance but also manure and labour. However, by incorporating animals into the lifestyle self-sufficiency became an ever-expanding project (as many self-providers have themselves found and the Nearings had warned). For Seymour it was the 'cow' that was central to the self-sufficient small-holding. But cows were labour intensive – they had to be fed and they also needed to be milked, sometimes twice a day. Large quantities of milk, then, required all the paraphernalia associated with processing milk into cheese, yoghurt and butter. But the work did not simply end there; cows produced too much milk for one family to use, so pigs were brought in to make use of the excess milk and by-products of dairy production. Pigs had their own special set of needs and requirements. And on it went. The type of self-sufficiency carefully described by John and beautifully illustrated by Sally required constant problem solving, maintenance, and commitment.

It is also worth noting that Seymour's work carries a contradictory message about self-sufficiency and one for which the lifestyle is oft criticised. While he and Sally had experienced most of the things he wrote about, he could not claim or advocate complete self-sufficiency for individuals or couples. But for Seymour, such a life was neither desirable nor possible. Instead, he argued for a community set-up of households living within a few miles of each other, dividing up the workload, specialising in particular skills and then sharing the proceeds. While Sally did not aspire to communal life, Seymour saw its advantages. One family, for example, could take the responsibility of dairy production by owning a cow etc., another pigs and yet another family, the garden (Seymour, 1973a). 'We have been very *nearly* self-supporting. ... the tax-eaters have not done very well out of us', wrote John Seymour (1973a: 13). 'We have not contributed much to the development of the atom bomb', he continued, 'nor to the building of *Concorde*'.

Ultimately, while it was complicated and 'extremely hard work', life on a self-sufficient small-holding was unlike office or factory work – it was fun. For John Seymour it was never boring; it was full of life and good-cheer (Peacock, 2005; Seymour, 1980: 9). It was 'real life' – a life of substance and meaning and one that was physically and spiritually independent as well as fulfilling. While both were rurally isolated, the Seymours were far less segregated from the wider community than the Nearings when it came to politics, entertainment and outside employment. John had far greater financial expectations and expenditure, and was far less frugal with money (Peacock, 2005).

The difference in approaches by the Nearings and the Seymours can, in part, be explained by the timing of their experiment during the relative affluence of the post-war period, rather than at the height of the Great Depression. But the similarities are more important than the differences. Both groups wanted a higher and healthier standard of living in which they had full control over their production and consumption processes. The Seymour's adoption of self-sufficiency was not initially driven by the sense of personal urgency that drove the Nearings. Yet the Nearing's adoption of homesteading, of course, was the product of a very different time and place.

When *The Complete Book of Self-Sufficiency* was published in 1976 Seymour announced that circumstances were such that self-sufficiency was not only attractive but likely. With the threat posed by nuclear power, environmental destruction and the oil crisis it was likely that it would become a necessity for the majority. One can only wonder what Seymour would think of city life and industrial farming today. All the things he feared have advanced: global warming and climate change no longer hover on the horizon; peak oil looms; genetically modified organisms are far from limited to fringe or experimental farming, etc. On one level, of course, the Seymours' adoption of self-sufficiency was a personal choice by relatively privileged individuals. On another, however, their commitment, dedication and longevity of their experiment, suggests something far more than a lifestyle novelty. John Seymour's books resonated with would-be self-providers across the developed world and self-sufficiency remains the ideal for many. Self-sufficiency, described and worked by the Seymours, provides a working model for an alternative to modern capitalism, one that they maintained is more authentic and abundant than its adversary.

References

Seymour, John. 1976. *The Complete Book of Self-Sufficiency*, London: Corgi.

Seymour, John. 1980. *Getting It Together: A Guide for New Settlers*, London: Michael Joseph.

Seymour, John. 1961. *The Fat of the Land*, London: Faber and Faber.

Seymour, John. 1983. *The Smallholder*, London: Sidgwick and Jackson.

Seymour, John and Sally. 1973a. *Farming for Self-Sufficiency: Independence on a 5-acre Farm*, New York: Schocken.

Seymour, John and Sally. 1973b. *Self-Sufficiency: The Science and Art of Producing and Preserving your own food*, London: Faber & Faber.

Further reading

Paul Peacock. 2005. *A Good Life: John Seymour His Self-Sufficiency Legacy*, Preston (UK): Farming Books and Videos Ltd.

CHAPTER NINETEEN

VOLUNTARY SIMPLICITY

MARY GRIGSBY

People adopting voluntary simplicity express concern about environmental degradation and dissatisfaction with the quality of life, social relations, and health and wellbeing of people and the planet that is fostered by the dominant consumerist culture. Participants in the voluntary simplicity movement are critical of conspicuous consumption and careerism, viewing them as co-constructing driving forces that propel people toward overconsumption and over-work which is destructive of their own wellbeing, social integration and community life, as well as the global environment. Advocates maintain that happiness, fulfilment, time to participate in community life and creative endeavours, increased time for relationships with others, and reduced pressures on environmental resources, may be derived from simplifying life so that one has 'enough'. This involves avoiding the work-and-spend cycle that sees material goods and services as a primary life goal. People who live simply generally maintain that consumerism ultimately does not meet the deepest of human needs for connection to nature, to other human beings and to their creative capacities. They suggest that individuals need to decide for themselves how much is 'enough' for them to live a full and dignified life, and to earn what they need to have that lifestyle, rather than buying into the idea that more and constant consumption is desirable.

The contemporary voluntary simplicity movement, which originated in the United States, jelled as a contemporary cultural movement in the late 1980s and early 1990s, emerging in Seattle and diffusing through books, workshops, and small support groups (Grigsby, 2004). The ideas and practices resonated mostly with white, educated city dwellers in developed regions. There is an abundance of literature aimed at helping people adopt voluntary simplicity, but I will outline several core key texts of the contemporary movement which stand out as foundational. The first is Duane Elgin's *Voluntary Simplicity: Toward a Way of Life that is Outwardly Simple, Inwardly Rich* ([1981] 1993). Elgin brought together a range of cultural ideas, many with roots in the 1960s and 1970s counter culture, particularly the 'ecological simplicity movement' that emerged in those decades.

The counterculture of the 1960s and 1970s questioned the status quo in gender relations, sexual mores, racial segregation, and the environmental and social impacts of industrialisation, including regimented work and consumerism. The civil rights, women's liberation, gay and lesbian rights, environmental, and anti-Vietnam war movements came together in this era. The generation coming of age at the time envisioned a different American dream from the 1950s orthodoxy and demanded a less violent, more environmentally conscious, and more egalitarian society. The voluntary simplicity movement drew especially on the environmentalist threads and the questions about the impacts of industrialisation, overwork, and consumerism. David Shi (1985) also provides an interpretation of the historical context of the voluntary simplicity movement, tracing the ideas of the movement back to the founding of the United States. Elgin, on the other hand, emphasises an integration and interpretation of Eastern and Western intellectual and spiritual traditions. His core thesis is that a trend toward voluntary simplicity was emerging within a predominantly white, middle class, with more females than males as the early adopters.

Elgin was the first to apply the term 'voluntary simplicity' to the emerging contemporary movement. He borrowed the term from the work of Richard Gregg. Gregg, who was a Quaker and student of Ghandi, is credited with coining the term in his 1936 work *The Value of Voluntary Simplicity*. Elgin maintained that human choice would determine future evolutionary change and that an apocalyptic future could be avoided if human beings would shift toward sufficiency. Elgin viewed voluntary simplicity as a shift away from the 'industrial era' and toward an emerging 'ecological era' (1993: 163-65). Initially published in 1981, Elgin's book is foundational as the ideological bedrock of the contemporary movement. It brings together a diverse range of cultural ideas, interpreting and linking them in a way that is distinctly that of the contemporary voluntary simplicity cultural movement. While many of the ideas were circulating in the wider society, the interpretation Elgin brought to them, and his claim that a broad cultural shift toward simplicity was underway, was new.

A survey questionnaire included in *Co-Evolution Quarterly* in the summer of 1977 provided the data for the analysis of the movement in Elgin's book. While the data from these findings was based on responses from people reading *Co-Evolution Quarterly*, and might therefore be questioned in terms of the implications for social change theorised, this work captured and elaborated the unique shape of the emerging movement. It brought together ideas to support an alternative way of living that was less consumerist and competitive and at the same time advocated being fully engaged in community and self-fulfilment.

Joe Dominguez and Vicki Robin's *Your Money or Your Life: Transforming Your Relationship with Money and Achieving Financial Independence* was drawn from the content of self-help seminars they gave. First published in 1992, the book provides a nine-step plan for achieving financial security, reducing or eliminating the need to engage in waged work, reducing conspicuous consumption, and living in accordance with your values. The approach involves tracking expenditures to analyse the use of money as a form of life energy that aims to help the simplifier reduce consumption to free up life energy for more highly valued activities. Spending is reduced and investment is increased with the goal of creating a crossover point where investment income meets the costs of living comfortably. The book, a core reading in many simplicity circles, was marketed to and became popular beyond those in the voluntary simplicity movement.

In 1997, Cecile Andrews' book *The Circle of Simplicity: Return to the Good Life*, was published and also quickly became important in the diffusion of the movement. Andrews was a central figure in the voluntary simplicity movement in Seattle where she gave workshops and organised the first 'simplicity circles'. The book involves a seven step approach using support groups (simplicity circles) to assist people in simplifying and maintaining commitment to the voluntary simplicity lifestyle.

The problems and solutions posed by voluntary simplicity proponents focus overwhelmingly on solving environmental and social problems. They are associated with an economy and culture that generate overconsumption, waste, greed, unfulfilling working conditions and stress for people like them. The looming environmental collapse can be mitigated by choosing a lower consumption lifestyle, disposing of excess possessions that are not useful or treasured, and obtaining only what is needed to be sufficient. They target themselves and others who are members of the global high-consumer class.

As a cultural movement the voluntary simplicity movement is not formally organised, centralised or hierarchical. Instead, it uses a grassroots, voluntary, self-help form of support for change (Grigsby, 2004). Elgin's grand evolutionary theory of human responsibility for the precarious environmental situation holds that human beings are faced with the choice of changing and adopting sustainable ways of living or being responsible for the collapse of the eco-system. He forecasts a cultural shift toward simple living that will make human beings happier and more fulfilled and avert ecological disaster. The works of Dominguez and Robin (1992) and Andrews (1997) operationalised the mode of transition from industrial-era to post-industrial civilisations theorised by Elgin in the form of multi-step self-help books for those in high-consuming regions of the world. The books they wrote could be used in groups or individually and were frequently used in support groups of people trying to simplify. Both books focus on self-change because of personal discomfort linking changes that will lead to greater personal happiness and fulfilment to simultaneously having a positive impact on broader social change outcomes. This is consistent with the idea embraced across the movement's ideology that all things in the universe exist in interdependent relationship with each other. For instance, Dominguez and Robin (1992: 139) wrote 'the fact that we are literally made from the body of the earth means that all of life is one creation, unfolding everywhere all at once'. Andrews (1997: 9) links the personal anomie she sees around her to signs of ecological collapse, noting:

> as the outer world sickens, so does our inner world. Everything around us is dying. Global warming, the hole in the ozone layer, polluted air and water, depleted topsoil, deforestation: With the earth dying how could we feel alive? The sicknesses of people and the planet are linked.

For a detailed discussion of the literature see Grigsby (2004). Sympathetic critiques have noted that as an unbounded cultural movement, voluntary simplicity ideas have diffused widely and played a role in creating greater awareness in the wider society about issues associated with consumerism. But it lacks political teeth. Some have suggested the movement would hold greater promise of bringing about change in economic policy, energy sourcing and use, population growth, commitment to human rights, and laws and policies that are consistent with a post-consumerist consumption agenda mapped by the voluntary simplicity movement, if it were more organised and had a coherent political agenda. Yet the less structured more flexible quality of the movement appears to have contributed to fostering the diffusion of the ideas. Rather than having to adhere to a set script of positions, people can identify with the aspects of the movement that resonate with them. The loosely bounded quality of the movement allows for people with a wide range of interests, concerns and levels of commitment to identify with the simplicity movement.

In 2011 The Simplicity Institute launched an extensive (and ongoing) online survey of this emerging movement. Conducted and analysed by Samuel Alexander and Simon Ussher, the survey suggests that a movement of people 'choosing to move away from high consumption lifestyles and who are embracing lifestyles of reduced or restrained income and consumption', (Alexander and Ussher, 2012: 71) is fully underway. The reasons for simplifying identified in the early core literature of the voluntary simplicity movement is consistent with the motivations of respondents reported by Alexander and Ussher – with 'environmental concerns' topping the list. 'Being healthier' was the second most important motivation, followed by other motivations such as 'self-reliance/self-sufficiency' and 'decluttering life/ minimalism'. Saving money (while buying ecologically and locally); living more spiritually or mindfully; seeking more time for oneself or time for family; humanitarian and social justice concerns; and more time for community involvement; were also reported as motivations.

The power of this cultural movement endures in part because the movement's ability to simultaneously recognise and affirm unfulfilled needs or issues of similarly situated people; to offer the promise for change; and to be 'doable' for people. Voluntary simplicity aims to combine altruism and self-interest, and advocates practices that are open to a wide range of people, especially those in the more affluent regions of the world.

The deeply humanist individualist assumption that human agency and choice drives the fate of the world is consistent with the Enlightenment idea of progress. While questions about the political or collective social movement capacity of voluntary simplicity may remain, the diffusion of the ideas of the movement in culture have gained momentum and broader acceptance over the forty years since the contemporary movement emerged. Perhaps like Weber's classic argument in the *Puritan Ethic and the Spirit of Capitalism* – that ideas of appropriate actions aimed at spiritual salvation produced the emergence of the capitalist economic system – the simple living ethic is among the catalysts for the spread of beliefs and practices that will foster post-consumerist sustainability. The question of whether the voluntary simplicity movement is largely a movement of individuals seeking change to reduce the negative impacts of the current economic system in their lives (with the hope that their actions will have positive impacts more broadly), or whether there is a groundswell of change underway that will result in a collective more formally organised social movement with a political change agenda, remains. This question, however, may be less important than the mix of ideas that people who are part of this diverse cultural movement have already brought together, elaborated, and shared with the generalised culture.

References

Alexander, Samuel, and Simon Ussher. 2012. 'The Voluntary Simplicity Movement: A Multi-National Survey Analysis in Theoretical Context. *Journal of Consumer Culture* 12 (1): 66-86.

Andrews, Cecile. 1997. *The Circle of Simplicity: Return to the Good Life*. New York: Harper Collins.

Dominguez, Joe, and Vicki Robin. 1992. *Your Money or Your Life: Transforming Your Relationship With Money and Achieving Financial Independence*. New York: Penguin.

Elgin, Duane. [1981] 1993. *Voluntary Simplicity: Toward a Way of Life That Is Outwardly Simple, Inwardly Rich*. New York: William Morrow.

Gregg, Richard. 1936. *The Value of Voluntary Simplicity*. Wallingford, PA: Pendle Hill.

Grigsby, Mary. 2004. *Buying Time and Getting By: The Voluntary Simplicity Movement*. Albany, NY: State University of New York Press.

Shi, David. 1985. *The Simple Life: Plain Living and High Thinking in American Culture.* New York: Oxford University Press.

CHAPTER TWENTY

RADICAL HOMEMAKING

SHANNON HAYES

Long before we could pronounce Betty Friedan's last name, Americans from my generation felt her impact. Many of us born in the mid-1970s learned from our parents and our teachers that women no longer needed to stay home, that there were professional opportunities awaiting us. In my own school experience, homemaking, like farming, gained a reputation as a vocation for the scholastically impaired. Those of us with academic promise learned that we could do whatever we put our minds to, whether it was conquering the world or saving the world.

I was personally interested in saving the world. That path eventually led me to conclude that homemaking would play a major role toward achieving that goal.

My own farming background led me to pursue advanced degrees in the field of sustainable agriculture, with a powerful interest in the local food movement. By the time my Ph.D. was conferred, I was married, and I was in a state of confusion. The more I understood about the importance of small farms and the nutritional, ecological, and social value of local food, the more I questioned the value of a 9-to-5 job. If my husband and I both worked and had children, it appeared that our family's ecological impact would be considerable. We'd require two cars, professional wardrobes, convenience foods to make up for lost time in the kitchen – and we'd have to buy, rather than produce, harvest, and store, our own food.

The economics didn't work out either. When we crunched the numbers, our gross incomes from two careers would have been high, but the cost of living was also considerable, especially when day-care was figured into the calculation. Abandoning the job market, we re-joined my parents on our small grass-fed livestock farm and became homemakers. For over ten years now, we've been able to eat locally and organically, support local businesses, avoid big box stores, save money, and support a family of four on less than $45,000 per year.

Wondering if my family was a freaky aberration to the conventional American culture, I decided to post a notice on my webpage, looking to connect with other ecologically minded homemakers. My fingers trembled on the keyboard as I typed the notice. What, exactly, would be the repercussions for taking a pro-homemaker stand and seeking out others? Was encouraging a Radical Homemaking movement going to unravel all the social advancements that had been made in the last 40-plus years? Women, after all, have been the homemakers since the beginning of time. Or so I thought.

Upon further investigation, I learned that the household did not become the 'woman's sphere' until the Industrial Revolution. A search for the origin of the word housewife traces it back to the thirteenth century, as the feudal period was coming to an end in Europe and the first signs of a middle class were popping up. Historian Ruth Schwartz Cowan explains that housewives were wedded to husbands, whose name came from *hus*, an old spelling of house, and bonded. Husbands were bonded to houses, rather than to lords. Housewives and husbands were free people, who owned their own homes and lived off their land. While there was a division of labour among the sexes in these early households, there was also an equal distribution of domestic work. Once the Industrial Revolution happened, however, things changed. Men left the household to work for wages, which were then used to purchase goods and services that they were no longer home to provide. Indeed, the men were the first to lose their domestic skills as successive generations forgot how to butcher the family hog, how to sew leather, how to chop firewood.

As the Industrial Revolution forged on and crossed the ocean to America, men and women eventually stopped working together to provide for their household sustenance. They developed their separate spheres – man in the factory, woman in the home. The more a man worked outside the home, the more the household would have to buy in order to have needs met. Soon the factories were able to fabricate products to supplant the housewives' duties as well. The housewife's primary function ultimately became chauffeur and consumer. The household was no longer a unit of production. It was a unit of consumption.

The effect on the status of the American housewife was devastating. In 1963, Betty Friedan published *The Feminine Mystique*, documenting for the first time 'the problem that has no name', Housewife's Syndrome. Friedan described an America where girls grew up fantasising about finding their husbands, buying their dream homes and appliances, popping out babies, and living happily ever after. In truth, pointed out Friedan, the happily-ever-after never came. Countless women suffered from depression and nervous breakdowns as they faced the endless meaningless tasks of shopping and driving children hither and yon. They never had opportunities to fulfil their highest potential, to challenge themselves, to feel as though they were truly contributing to society beyond wielding the credit card to keep the consumer culture humming. Friedan's book motivated many women to enter the workforce. Corporate America seized upon a golden opportunity to secure this cheaper workforce and offer countless products to use up their pay cheques.

Before long, the second family income was no longer an option. In the minds of many, it was a necessity. Home-making, like eating organic foods, seemed a luxury to be enjoyed only by those wives whose husbands garnered substantial earnings, enabling them to drive their children to school rather than put them on a bus, enrol them in endless enrichment activities, oversee their educational careers, and prepare them for entry into elite colleges in order to win a 'leg-up' in a competitive workforce. At the other extreme, homemaking was seen as the realm of the ultra-religious, where women accepted the role of Biblical 'Help Meets' to their husbands. They cooked, cleaned, toiled, served and remained silent and powerless. My husband and I fell into neither category, and I suspected there were more like us.

I was right. I received hundreds of letters from rural, suburban, and city folks alike. Some ascribed to specific religious faiths, others did not. As long as the home showed no signs of domination or oppression, I was interested in learning more about them. I selected twenty households from my pile, plotted them on a map across the United States, and set about visiting each of them to see what homemaking could look like when men and women shared both power and responsibility. Curious to see if Radical Homemaking was a venture suited to more than just women in married couples, I visited with single parents, stay-at-home dads, widows, and divorcées. I spent time in families with and without children.

A glance into America's past suggests that homemaking could play a big part in addressing the ecological, economic and social crises of our present time. Homemakers have played a powerful role during several critical periods in our nation's history. By making use of locally available resources, they made the boycotts leading up to the American Revolution possible. They played a critical role in the foundational civic education required to launch a young democratic nation. They were driving forces behind both the abolition and suffrage movements.

Homemakers today could have a similar influence. The Radical Homemakers I interviewed had chosen to make family, community, social justice, and the health of the planet the governing principles of their lives. They aspired to reject any form of labour or the expenditure of any resource that did not honour these tenets. For about 5,000 years, our culture has been hostage to a form of organisation by domination that fails to honour our living systems, under which 'he who holds the gold makes the rules'. By contrast, the Radical Homemakers are using life skills and relationships as replacements for gold, on the premise that he or she who doesn't need the gold can change the rules. The greater one's domestic skills, be they to plant a garden, grow tomatoes on an apartment balcony, mend a shirt, repair an appliance, provide one's own entertainment, cook and preserve a local harvest, or care for children and loved ones, the less dependent one is on the gold.

By virtue of these skills, the Radical Homemakers I interviewed were building a great bridge from our existing extractive economy – where corporate wealth has been regarded as the foundation of economic health, where mining our Earth's resources and exploiting our international neighbours have been acceptable costs of doing business – to a life serving economy, where the goal is, in the words of David Korten, to generate a living for all, rather than a killing for a few; where our resources are sustained, our waters are kept clean, our air pure, and families can lead meaningful lives. In situations where one person was still required to work out of the home in the conventional extractive economy, homemakers were able to redirect the family's financial, social and temporal resources toward building the life-serving economy. In most cases, however, the homemakers' skills were so considerable that, while members of the household might hold jobs (more often than not they ran their own businesses), the financial needs of the family were so small that no one in the family was forced to accept any employment that did not honour the four tenets of family, community, social justice and ecological sustainability.

While all the families had some form of income that entered their lives, they were not a privileged group by any means. Most of the families I interviewed were living with a sense of abundance at about 200 percent of the federal poverty level. That's a little over $40,000 for a family of four, about 37 percent below the national median family income, and 45 percent below the median income for married couple families. Some lived on considerably less, few had appreciably more. Not surprisingly, those with the lowest incomes had mastered the most domestic skills and had developed the most innovative approaches to living.

The Radical Homemakers were skilled at the mental exercise of rethinking the 'givens' of our society and coming to counter-cultural conclusions, such as: nobody (who matters) cares what (or if) you drive; it is okay to let go of the perceived ideal of independence and strive instead for interdependence; child care is not a fixed cost; education can be acquired for free; each and every home can be the centre for social change, the starting point from which a better life can ripple out for everyone.

As for domestic skills, the range of talents held by these households was as varied as the day is long. Many kept gardens, but not all. Some gardened on city rooftops, some on country acres, some in suburban yards. Some were wizards at car and appliance repairs. Others could sew. Some could build and fix houses; some kept livestock. Others crafted furniture, played music, or wrote. All could cook. None of them could do everything. No one was completely self-sufficient, an independent island separate from the rest of the world. Thus the universal skills that they all possessed were far more complex than simply knowing how to can green beans or build a root cellar. In order to make it as homemakers, these people had to be wizards at nurturing relationships and working with family and community. They needed an intimate understanding of the life-serving economy, where a pay cheque is not always exchanged for all services rendered. They needed to be their own teachers – to pursue their educations throughout life, forever learning new ways to do more, create more, give more.

In addition, the happiest among them were successful at setting realistic expectations for themselves. They did not live in impeccably clean houses on manicured estates. They saw their homes as living systems and accepted the flux, flow, dirt, and chaos that are a natural part of that. They were masters at redefining pleasure not as something that should be bought in the consumer marketplace, but as something that could be created, no matter how much or how little money they had in their pockets. And above all, they were fearless. They did not let themselves be bullied by the conventional ideals regarding money, status, or material possessions. These families did not see their homes as a refuge from the world. Rather, each home was the centre for social change, the starting point from which a better life would ripple out for everyone.

Home is where the great change will begin. It is not where it ends. Once we feel sufficiently proficient with our domestic skills, few of us will be content to simply practise them to the end of our days. Many of us will strive for more, to bring more beauty to the world, to bring about greater social change, to make life better for our neighbours, to contribute our creative powers to the building of a new, brighter, more sustainable, and happier future. That is precisely the great work we should all be tackling. If we start by focusing our energies on our domestic lives, we will do more than reduce our ecological impact and help create a living for all. We will craft a safe, nurturing place from which this great creative work can happen.[1]

Further reading

Hayes, Shannon. 2010. *Radical Homemakers: Reclaiming Domesticity from a Consumer Culture*. Richmondville, NY: Left to Write Press.

Hetzel, Rhonda. 2012. *Down to Earth: A Guide to Simple Living*. Camberwell: Penguin (Australia).

---

[1] A version of this chapter first appeared in *Yes! Magazine* (Feb, 2010).

.

CHAPTER TWENTY-ONE

INTENTIONAL COMMUNITIES

BILL METCALF

'Intentional community' is an umbrella term used to include communes, cohousing communities, ecovillages, and religious and political 'utopias'. The phrase emphasises people's *intention* to create a better, if not an ideal or utopian, society. Members imagine, or visualise, better ways of living, then consciously go about trying to bring these into reality.

While there is a wide range of *intentions*, most people interested in intentional communities have elements of 'simple-living' in mind, perhaps increasing their self-sufficiency by growing more of their food, providing more of their energy needs, being part of a close-knit, supportive community or pseudo-family, and having a smaller 'ecological footprint'. But do intentional communities have these desirable outcomes, and is life therein 'simpler'?

'Simple' living can be considered within social/cultural, economic, political/governance and environmental senses. On the social/cultural front, intentional community members face many people with whom to relate, opportunities for and expectations of closeness and trust beyond those found outside of conventional families, high expectations of on-going, inter-personal support, and expectations of tolerance and openness to people who might think rather differently. Just because everyone agrees to live within an intentional community does not mean that they will get along in the host of petty ways that bedevil such groups. Within small communal groups, challenges can be as 'simple' as who washes the dishes, where people drop their 'stuff', and table manners. In larger groups, such as ecovillages and cohousing groups, it can be who parks what vehicle where, what you think about me having a pet, and what your children do with the goats or my flowers. Socially and culturally, living in an intentional community is usually far from simple. Of course, for some people this lack of simplicity, seen as the rich tapestry of social life, is an attraction – but 'simple' it certainly is not. (Metcalf, 2004: 88-109; Christensen and Levinson, 2003: 685-90)

On the economic front, most intentional communities have *greater* self-sufficiency as one of their collective goals but rarely does this imply becoming isolated – in fact it usually entails far greater interaction with their local and regional community than would have applied had they depended more on macro markets. So simple it is not. On a personal economic level, some intentional communities offer simple solutions while others are the opposite. In groups that operate on a 'common-purse' principle, where all money is handled by the collective, one need not worry about personal income or expenses because everything will be shared. Of course other issues might arise such as guilt that one is not contributing as much, or taking more than others – or resentment that one is contributing more or receiving less than others. More commonly, intentional community members manage their own money while contributing a set amount, or set percentage of income, to support the collective. This is usually less than one would have had to contribute if living alone or in a conventional family at a similar standard – but one must still find the money. In cohousing groups, usually located in or near urban areas, paid work is often available, but in rural ecovillages work is often unavailable – or available only after a long commute to a nearby town or city. While commuting might solve the immediate financial problem, it creates other problems, wasting time and fuel. Intentional communities, more often than not, simplify economic matters but it is far from universal (Christensen and Levinson, 2003: 681-685).

Governance within intentional communities is rarely simple either. While people often assume that consensus is the norm, this is rarely the case. Within religiously-based groups, some form of modified theocracy is common and this can be quite simple – as long as members accept their leader's divinely-inspired decisions. Within most secular intentional communities, how the property is owned can dictate governance to some extent. For example, if the property is held as a private company (most common in Queensland) or as a co-operative (most common elsewhere in Australia) then legal requirements such as holding an AGM with a quorum, having a nominated Secretary, filing Annual Reports, etc., must be followed. Rarely, however, do members allow that to be the only form of governance, with many other decisions being made through modified forms of democracy, including elements of consensus and, occasionally, sociocracy. An example could be to discuss an issue and if agreement is not reached, to defer the matter to another meeting, discuss again, and then perhaps allow a decision to be made on a 75 percent, or even simple majority, vote. In some groups, everyone might have a right to veto new members, but decisions on buying new equipment might be by simple majority. In other groups, a single member can block a decision the first time it arises, but needs to find at least one or two others to support that block when the topic arises next time. None of these are simple. They can be time-consuming, emotionally-fraught, and frustrating when one thinks an issue is simple or obvious. For instance, most Australians might think that acquiring a pet cat or dog is a simple, personal choice but nothing could be further from the truth within most intentional communities (Christensen and Levinson, 2003: 693-697).

Intentional communities are often assumed to be part of a global solution to environmental problems, with images of low energy use, consumption of organic, home-grown food, creative waste-management, and a sustainable, non-consumerist approach to material goods. For example, Bruce Coldham (1995: 19) claimed that:

> cohousing's principle [sic] contribution to a
> sustainable society is that it offers another scale of
> social organisation – an intermediate scale between
> the single family and the town or municipality –
> thereby expanding the palette of technologies that can
> be applied.

Ian Lowe (in Meltzer, 2005: v) asserts that intentional communities, particularly cohousing, offer 'technical, social and environmental advantages … [using] resources and energy more efficiently, especially by sharing equipment that is only used a few times a month and making more economic use of living space'. Diana Leafe Christian (2007: 3) believes that intentional community members 'live on the planet with a smaller ecological footprint'. Likewise, Joshua Lockyer (2010: 197-198) argues that people in small-scale intentional communities 'voluntarily and deliberately change their lifestyles and reduce their carbon footprints'.

There is not a great deal of solid research to *unambiguously* support these claims. 'Ecological footprint', roughly based on energy use and material consumption, is commonly mentioned but is notoriously hard to measure because of the various forms of energy, measured in diverse units and ways, and complex issues of embedded energy in so-called 'energy-saving' products. For example, a new car will probably use less energy than the old car it replaced, but mining, shipping and refining the metals, making and transporting the plastic, fabric and electronic components, fabricating, assembling, shipping and retailing that new car, plus the energy needed to dispose of the old car, might result in so much embedded energy that it is less efficient, energy-wise, than what it replaced. And should we compare vehicle with vehicle, or compare according to how many people are served? And against whom/what should we compare? Should we compare the energy use of an intentional community member with what she/he consumed before joining, or with demographically similar, non-intentional community people? Should we compare per-person or per-household?

And what do we include/exclude in these calculations? Arguably, the simplest and most long-term way for an individual to dramatically reduce his/her ecological footprint is to not have children – yet none of the studies, above, even considered or attempted to estimate this. These problems have been briefly summarised by Stephen Tinsley and Heather George (2006: 33) who coyly admit to this being 'not an exact science'. Perhaps the best discussions of the issues surrounding ecological footprint can be found in the reports by Best *et al.* (2008), and Wiedmann and Barrett (2010).

Nevertheless, brave attempts have been made to quantify ecological footprint, comparing people living in intentional communities both to how they lived beforehand, and to non-intentional community folk in the same area.

One the best examples of this research is over 40 years old. Michael Corr and Dan MacLeod (1972) compared Americans living in urban communes with non-communards, and found that per-person energy consumption for communards was well under half the norm. Was this because the communards lived in relative poverty? Corr and MacLeod (1972, 3) point out '[t]his low rate of energy consumption was voluntary and was not considered by the people involved as lowering their standard of living'. Was the lower energy usage because of having less access to modern devices? Quite the opposite. Corr and MacLeod (1972: 4-5) found that:

> commune members are being served much better by their investment in appliances than are average occupants. Their per capita *access* to conveniences is almost equal to the average U.S. household member even though their per capita *consumption* is only 25 percent of the national average.

Graham Meltzer, during PhD research in the late 1990s, looked at energy use within cohousing groups and tried to compare to both their pre-intentional community patterns and to similar, non-intentional community members. Meltzer (2005: 15) worked on the hypothesis that cohousing's

> social ties and level of commitment enable residents to act as a single entity when implementing particular technologies ... centralised neighbourhood heating for

example. Such 'intermediate-scaled' energy and waste systems are likely to function more efficiently.

Meltzer (2005: 88) found that in Earthsong Cohousing, New Zealand, per-household energy consumption was less than half, and energy cost a quarter of the norm. In the same study (2005: 104) he found that in Cascade Cohousing, Tasmania, per-household electricity consumption was less than half that of similar sized houses, house floor space was about half that found in the larger community (2005: 121), and that increased sharing of appliances and equipment reduced consumption (2005: 138). Meltzer concluded (2005: 139), 'the consumerist imperative that seems endemic in the West is significantly diffused in cohousing'.

Samuelsson (2003) reported research showing Munksoegaard Ecovillage (Denmark) using two-thirds the water and three-quarters the energy, per-household, compared to other Danes, and through wood-pellet heating achieved CO_2 emissions about half the Danish norm.

Simon (2004) reports German research showing intentional community members emitting only a quarter of CO_2 compared to the national norm, and that residents 'used far less water, electricity, heating fuel, and fossil-fuel for heating'. Simon's study is one of the most comprehensive, but is not available in English.

The Findhorn Foundation, Scotland, one of the largest, oldest and best-known ecovillages, was studied by a group of environmental scientists from Stockholm Environment Institute. Tinsley and George (2006: 30) found that Findhorn's per-capita 'home and energy' consumption was about a quarter of the UK average, and general 'consumables' about half. They bravely sought to amalgamate a host of measures to determine the community's per-capita ecological footprint, and then to compare this to European standards. They found (2006: 31-2) intentional community members' per-person ecological footprint to be well under half that of UK, Scotland, and Inverness, their nearest city. While the researchers (2006: 33-4) admit to weaknesses in using this measure, their research certainly showed a difference which, even if inexact, is still highly significant.

These five studies, over 35 years, by different re-searchers, using different methodologies, in different countries, studying different types and sizes of intentional community, agree that people within intentional comm-unities have significantly lower ecological footprint (energy and resource demand) than non-community members. Unfortunately, we cannot be sure how much of those savings those people would have made whether or not they were living in an intentional community. Perhaps environ-mentally-minded people are more likely both to save energy *and to* live in intentional community, but the latter does not determine the former.

In conclusion, it is far from clear that intentional community automatically implies 'simple living'. Of course many people might join an intentional community precisely to avoid 'simple living' if, by that, they mean living alone and bored in a small flat. They might enjoy the complex web of daily social interactions within a culturally-diverse communal group; they might love the complex process of making decisions where so many voices need to be heard; and they might relish the finely-nuanced economic complexities of sharing income and assets. People can and do thrive in this environment – but it is far from 'simple'. While living in an intentional community usually results in people consuming less energy and having a smaller ecological footprint, it is not automatic.

Lockyer (2010: 212) sees intentional communities as 'living laboratories and demonstration centres for sustainable solutions to contemporary social, economic and ecological problems'. My own research concurs that for global survival it is important to have people willing to experiment with group living, reduced consumption, shared ownership, environ-mental stewardship, alternative governance and different family structures. Bottom-up social change complements, and might be more effective than, top-down initiatives to overcome environmental problems. (Forster and Metcalf: 2000).

But 'simple living'? Perhaps, but where intentional communities are concerned, nothing is very 'simple'.

References

Best, Aaron, et al. 2008. *Potential of the Ecological Footprint for Monitoring Environmental Impacts of Natural Resource Use*. Report to the European Commission. (*http://ec.europa.eu/environment/natres/studies.htm*)

Christensen, Karen and David Levinson. 2003. *Encyclopedia of Community: From the village to the virtual world*. Thousand Oaks: Sage.

Christian, Diana Leafe. 2007. *Finding Community: How to join an ecovillage or intentional community*. Gabriola Island: New Society Publishers.

Coldham, Bruce. 1995. 'The CoHousing Path to Sustainability'. *Co-Housing: Journal of the CoHousing Network* vol. 8, no. 3, pp: 19-21.

Corr, Michael and Dan MacLeod. 1972. 'Getting it Together'. *Environment* vol. 14, no. 9, pp: 2–9; 45.

Forster, Peter and Metcalf, William. 2000. 'Communal Groups: Social Laboratories or Places of Exile?', *Communal Societies* vol. 20, pp. 1-11.

Lockyer, Joshua. 2010. 'Intentional Community Carbon Reduction and Climate Change Action: from ecovillages to transition towns', in Michael Peters, Shane Fudge and Tim Jackson eds., *Low Carbon Communities: Imaginative Approaches to Combating Climate Change Locally*, Cheltenham: Edward Elgar Publishing, pp. 197-215.

Meltzer, Graham. 2005. *Sustainable Community: Learning from the cohousing model*. Victoria: Trafford.

Metcalf, Bill. 2004. *The Findhorn Book of Community Living*. Forres: Findhorn Press.

Samuelsson, Lone. 2003. 'Not Just Eco-Technology'. *Communities* no. 117, p.p. 43-4; 59.

Simon, Karl-Heinz. 2004. *Zusammenfassender Endbericht zum Vorhaben: Gemeinschaftliche Lebens – und Wirt – schaftsweisen und ihre Umweltrelevanz.* Kassel: Universität Kassel (http://www.usf.uni-kassel.de/glww/texte/ergebnisse/zusammenfassender bericht.pdf)

Tinsley, Stephen and Heather George. 2006. *Ecological Footprint of the Findhorn Foundation and Community.* Forres: Sustainable Development Research Centre. (http://www.ecovillagefindhorn.com/docs/FF%20Footp rint.pdf)

Wiedmann, Thomas, and John Barrett. 2010. 'A Review of the Ecological Footprint Indicator: Perceptions and Methods', *Sustainability* vol. 2, no. 6, pp. 1645–1693.

PIONEERS OF THE DEEP FUTURE

CHAPTER TWENTY-TWO

PERMACULTURE

ALBERT BATES

Permaculture is a philosophy of working with, rather than against nature; of protracted and thoughtful observation rather than protracted and thoughtless labor; and of looking at plants and animals in all their functions, rather than treating any area as a single product system (Mollison, 1991)

More than fifty years ago, the seminal ecologist, Howard T. Odum, warned that if complexity is added to a system without the resources and productive capacity to sustain it, the result is disorder, ultimately chaos (Odum, 1953; Odum and Odum, 2001). This is really all you need to know to explain the world as you experience it today.

We are entering an unprecedented era for humans as the clever but unwise keystone species in ecosystem Earth. Scientists are calling this the Anthropocene, the first 'man-made' geo-biological epoch of history. It is the result of, first, our capture of fire, then impudently breaking into a 500-million-year storehouse of fossil carbon, and finally, building a wasteful consumer society that ran through that one-off bonanza at breakneck speed, layering on ever more opaque and Rube Goldberg-like complexity as it did.

Our principal sin wasn't even the using of fossil carbon as much as deciding to burn it all at once, in a little more than a century. Or, to be more precise, we were undone by our *not deciding to stop* burning it once we learned of the damage we were doing to the delicate balances of Earth's natural systems.

The general recognition ('re-understanding') that we actually need natural systems to support our civilisation, even more than we needed that fire, was late in coming. Still, if there is a soft path to simplicity, it may have been mapped by a soft-spoken Australian game ranger about 40 years ago. That ranger's name is Bill Mollison and the trail he blazes still, as an octogenarian, is called permaculture. The word was originally coined by Mollison and his less folksy but more academically rigorous student, David Holmgren, during collaborations at the College of Advanced Education in Hobart, Tasmania in 1974-76.

Mollison and Holmgren were most directly influenced by the newly published *Limits to Growth* in 1972 (Meadows, 1972; Meadows, 2004; Bardi, 2011). Examining five variables of world population, industrialisation, pollution, food production and resource depletion, its authors explored the possibility of a sustainable feedback pattern that would be achieved by altering growth trends. That necessary work was met by such scorn and derision at the highest levels of government and society that Mollison and Holmgren grasped a fundamental reality – that the prospect for diverting humanity's collision course with natural resource limits would be unlikely to come from the top down. Still, they theorised, it might be achieved by a bottom-up social movement.

Permaculture was originally conceived to conjoin 'permanent' and 'agriculture', after the work of Joseph Russell Smith (Smith, 1929) but after considering the relationships of landscape architecture, patterns of human behaviour, energy, entropy, peak oil and climate change, the two founders came to better understand it as 'permanent culture'. Their seminal idea was that by mimicking the patterns that nature applied and how those coped with cyclical ebbs and flows, an idea later enlarged upon by Janine Benyus as 'biomimcry', clever and observant designers of the built environment could create human ecologies that self-mend, steadily enrich themselves, and deliver the basic necessities to their participants (Benyus, 1997).

Two of Holmgren's theoretical inspirations, Eugene and Howard Odum, foresaw before most the interconnected crises now widely apparent and the future energy descent. We are entering a time of de-industrialisation, de-globalisation, and de-complexification, not by choice (although some have wisely managed to get out in front of the wave), but rather by the immutable laws of physics. Greater simplicity is not optional. It is unavoidable (Odum and Odum, 2001).

While Mollison laboured to develop both a methodology for training designers and a movement of design activists, Holmgren concentrated on prototyping working examples, first in low-entropy food, shelter and energy systems for the homestead, and subsequently by designing larger models for broadscale production, towns and cities. By applying Keyline Management (a system of farm design developed by cattleman P.A. Yeomans) to the Fryer's Forest Ecovillage in Central Victoria, Holmgren demonstrated that human settlements could successfully weather long droughts (1994-2009) and peak rain events (early 2011) without flooding (Holmgren, 2006; Yeomans, 1973).

Permaculture as Mollison saw it was less important as a design science than as *a way of changing things*. Most of civilisation's problems are deeply imbedded, and defended fiercely by militaries, religions, cultural socialisation processes, and false prophets who have harnessed the power of contemporary mass media to point us in exactly the wrong direction.

For the few past decades, permaculture has laboured quietly in the shadows, at times lampooned for being New Age mumbo-jumbo, at times castigated for high-priced courses and expensive books. Although the most outspoken defenders of permaculture techniques – such as invasive weeds or 'mob grazing' as tools for ecological restoration – are university professors, their research has been assailed by critics as pseudoscience (Ferguson, 2013).

Permaculture is deeply subversive, and it is as relevant to the developing world as it is to the developed. Mollison called it 'a revolution disguised as organic gardening'. In consciously designing a future that might sustain some form of elegant human culture through the difficult Anthropocene period ahead, one must begin by jettisoning the baggage from the Holocene consumer civilisation. Yet, nobody enjoys watching their wardrobe being cast overboard.

If we think in terms of cultural DNA, what may be required, within the short space of one generation, is an epigenetic shift to a completely new expression. We have to deactivate the counter-survival tropes that are about to give us our Thelma and Louise moment, as we drive our Cadillac off the cliff. Once we are airborne, our options become severely limited. We have to activate (or, more precisely, *reactivate*), survival-oriented tropes for changed circumstances, and we have to do it sooner than the airborne, exhilarating, weightless experience.

In positing a new model for civilisation, Mollison and Holmgren set forward the three guiding ethics as:

- **Care of the Earth,** which includes all living and non-living things, such as animals, plants, land, water, and air;
- **Care of People,** to promote self-reliance and community responsibility; and
- **Share of Surplus,** to pass on anything not immediately useful to our needs (be that labour, food, information, or anything else) to better achieve the first two aims.

Implicit in these three is a **Life Ethic** – that all living organisms are not only means but ends. Apart from their instrumental value to humans and other living organisms, they have an intrinsic worth. Life on Earth is a family, and we must stop killing off whole species of our family members.

Permaculture is an ethical system, stressing positivism and cooperation. At the same time, its proponents do not hesitate to take a cudgel to prevailing inequities and atrocities. Holmgren put it succinctly in a 2013 paper:

> I believe that actively building parallel and largely non-monetary household and local community economies with as little as 10% of the population has the potential to function as a deep systemic boycott of the centralised systems as a whole, that could lead to more than 5% contraction in the centralised economies. Whether this

became the straw that broke the back of the global financial system or a tipping point, no one could ever say, even after the event (Holmgren, 2013: 22).

The challenge for designers is to tie elements together by waste and surplus streams (ultimately waste and surplus being synonymous), such that little or nothing would be allowed to become waste. In permaculture it is often said that there is no such thing as waste, because everything is food for something.

For complete use of any resource to occur, no element in the design can produce in greater abundance than there is a need for, and in turn must be able to supply its own needs within the available productive capacity of the community. If these criteria are not met, then unnecessary pollution and work result. Any system will become chaotic if it receives more resources than it can productively use. Work results when an element in the system does not aid another element and so intervention is needed to remove the excess and restore balance.

E.F. Schumacher once said:

> [T]he absolute bottom level of existence – where you don't have enough to even begin to keep body and soul together – should be called misery. The next level up – where people can reach the fullness of humanity but in a modest and frugal way with nothing really to spare – is actually what should be known as *poverty*. Then comes *sufficiency*. . . where you do have something to spare. This was the normal condition of Western Europe for centuries during the latter half of the Middle Ages when, as we know, great cathedrals were built and many advances were made in the arts and sciences. And finally, there is *surfeit*. . . which is limitless.
> ...
>
> I do not know which of these three increasingly insistent crises – human, environmental, or capital resource – is most likely to be the direct cause of our society's collapse. But I do know that a society which seeks fulfillment only in mindless material expansion does not

fit into this world for long. There simply is no place for
infinite growth on a finite planet (Schumacher, 1976)

In permaculture a resource can be defined as any energy
storage that assists yield. This may be obvious in a resource
such as coal, but may be less obvious for a resource such as
children, sunflower seeds or a wheelbarrow. Good design
takes advantage of common local forms of energy storage and
then tries to create sufficiency of them – both more of what is
found there (within the ability of the design to absorb yield)
and more different kinds of storage (tools, houses, water, soil,
etc.).

Between the source/resource and the end user or sink
(eventually returning to source in another form), lies a web of
interconnections that harvest and re-harvest the potentials,
using sunlight, gravity, and cycles of rainfall. Permaculture
looks to the patterns of ecosystems in modelling human
interactions within a cultivated bioregional ecology.

Diversity is related to stability. It is less about the
numbers of different elements than about numbers of
different working relationships that create this stability. The
role of permaculture master planning is to increase the
capacity of the system to support more connections. To avoid
the pitfalls of excessive organisational complexity, management is delegated to autonomous local cells. Lately,
permaculture has been drawing from the insights of Stafford
Beer and the system he developed called VSM (Viable
Systems Model) that mimics the functioning of an ecosystem
(although Beer himself, a steel mill manager in Yorkshire,
was not at all interested in ecology) to cohere autonomous
functioning parts. Beer observed that competition over
working hours, compensation, and resources can be most
easily be avoided by letting self-regulating autonomous
organisms/ organisations find ways to productively cooperate, and for that they need a good understanding of the
workings of the whole, adequate mechanisms for monitoring
and measuring productivity and waste, and quickly and easily
grasped feedback to permit self-regulation in their role.

As above, so below goes the Buddhist scripture. The
metastability of the whole is dependent on the stability of the

relationships amongst the parts. The effectiveness of self-regulation also depends on good mechanisms for coordination at the centre. Permaculturally designing stability at an appropriate complexity scale, whether one is considering business economy, financial commitments of members in the forms of dues or taxes, resolution of disputes, or building, electrical and sanitation codes, requires designing good information flows, transparency in decision-making, and as much levelling of inequalities (in power, wealth and social position) amongst community members as possible. Income-sharing communities have proven to be especially adept in these matters, and where they fail, it is most often from either external forces beyond their control or from the absence of open access to information equally by all members. The goal of the designer, therefore, is to build trust, harmony, and greater cooperation into the design for society.

If we can imagine a world that can sustain nature – a garden planet – with steady state energy flows embedded into its economy, can we design a path to take us from here to there with the least pain and suffering along the way? That is the grand project of permaculture (permanent culture). It does not entail doing without. It means knowing when is enough, and when is too much.

References

Bardi, U., 2011, *The Limits to Growth Revisited*. London: Springer.

Benyus, J., 1997, *Biomimicry: Innovation Inspired by Nature*. New York: William Morrow & Company.

Ferguson, R.S. and Lovell, S.T., 2013, Permaculture for agroecology: design, movement, practice, and worldview. A review, *Agron. Sustain. Dev.* INRA and Springer-Verlag France.

Holmgren, D., 2006, *David Holmgren: Collected Writings & Presentations 1978 – 2006* [eBook]. Hepburn, Victoria: Holmgren Design.

Holmgren, D., 2013, 'Crash on Demand: Welcome to the Brown Tech Future' *Simplicity Institute Report 13c*, 1-23.

Meadows, D.H., Meadows, D.L., Randers, J., and Behrens, W.W., 1972, *Limits to Growth*. Washington: Potomac Associates.

Meadows, D.H., Randers, J., and Meadows, D.L., 2004, *Limits to Growth: The 30-Year Update*. White River Junction VT: Chelsea Green and Earthscan.

Mollison, B., 1991, *Introduction to Permaculture*. Tasmania, Australia: Tagari.

Odum, H.T. and Odum E.C., 2001, *A Prosperous Way Down: Principles and Policies*. Boulder: University Press of Colorado.

Odum, H.T. and Odum E.P., 1953. *Fundamentals of Ecology* New York: W. B. Saunders.

Schumacher, E.F., 1976, Interview, *Mother Earth News, November/December 1976*

Smith, J.R., 1950, *Tree Crops: A Permanent Agriculture*. New York: Devin-Adair.

Yeomans, P. A., 1973, *Water for Every Farm: A practical irrigation plan for every Australian property*. Sydney: K.G. Murray Publishing Company.

CHAPTER TWENTY-THREE

TRANSITION TOWNS

SAMUEL ALEXANDER AND ESTHER ALLOUN

The 'Transition Towns' movement burst onto the scene in
Ireland, less than ten years ago, and yet already there are
more than one thousand Transition Towns around the world
(Hopkins, 2008; Hopkins, 2011). Given that some people are
saying this is one of the most promising and important social
movements on the planet at present, it is timely to ask
ourselves: what exactly is a Transition Town?

In order to understand the concept of Transition, one
first needs to understand that the Transition movement is a
response to a certain set of social, ecological, economic, and
political conditions. Over the last two centuries, industrial
societies have experienced unprecedented economic growth,
fuelled by a cheap and abundant supply of coal, gas, and most
importantly, oil. While this brought with it many benefits,
industrialisation also has an ominous dark side that today
threatens to overwhelm those benefits.

Most obviously, our planet's ecosystems are being fatally
degraded in the name of limitless growth, with the careless
overconsumption of fossil fuels contributing to climate
change with potentially dire consequences, some of which are
already unfolding. Furthermore, the flow of crude oil – the
world's most important source of non-renewable energy –
seems to have stagnated and will eventually decline, making
oil much more expensive. This dynamic is already well under
way, with the price of oil today almost four times as
expensive as it was only ten or fifteen years ago. What this
means is that oil-dependent societies in particular need to

begin preparing for a world where historic levels of oil production and consumption will be either unavailable or unaffordable (Heinberg, 2011).

What is most troubling of all, however, is that the high consumption lifestyles causing these problems often fail to fulfil their promise of a fulfilling and meaningful life (Alexander, 2012). In other words, many have worked hard to acquire the 'nice stuff', only to find themselves dissatisfied with a consumer-orientated existence. It seems that somewhere along the path of human development we took a disastrously wrong turn, and yet consumer capitalism marches steadfastly on.

If once we might have hoped that our national governments would honestly confront these great challenges and respond appropriately, everyday that hope withers further away. At the Rio+20 environmental conference in 2012, for example, the world's political leaders made a (non)commitment to try to solve the problems caused by growth by pursuing even more growth. This is but the latest sign that the world's governments either do not have a clue or are being wilfully blind.

It seems, then, that any solution to today's social, economic, and ecological problems will not be solved and probably only exacerbated at the highest governmental level. It follows that it is up to us – ordinary people, in ordinary communities – to step up and confront these problems ourselves, at the grassroots level. We can no longer conceive of ourselves as consumers merely. First and foremost, we must be citizens, with all the responsibility that this implies.

Against this backdrop, the Transition Town movement has emerged in cities, towns, and suburbs around the world, seemingly out of nowhere. Refusing to wait any longer for governments to act (or fail to act) on our behalf, groups of engaged citizens are taking things into their own hands, at the community and suburban levels. While this movement is brutally honest about the problems of climate change, peak oil, and economic instability, the movement is characterised more than anything else by its defiant positivity. Notably, crisis in the current system is presented not as a cause for despair but as a transformational opportunity, a change for the better that should be embraced rather than feared. The movement is showing by example that the transition to a new, post-carbon form of life is a process that can be extremely liberating and fulfilling, even if one must also accept that progress is often slow and uneven.

The Transition movement, according to its co-founder, Rob Hopkins, is based on four key assumptions (Hopkins, 2008: 134):

(1)   That life with dramatically lower energy consumption is inevitable, and that it's better to plan for it than to be taken by surprise;

(2)   That our settlements and communities presently lack the resilience to enable them to weather the sever energy [and economic] shocks that will accompany peak oil [and climate change];

(3)   That we have to act collectively, and we have to act now;

(4)   That by unleashing the collective genius of those around us to creatively and proactively design our energy descent, we can build ways of living that are more connected, more enriching, and that recognise the biological limits of our planet.

Two of the defining aims of a typical Transition Town (or 'Transition Initiative', as they are also known) are to decarbonise and relocalise the economy, in order to become less dependent on the globalised, oil-dependent economy (Heinberg and Lerch, 2010; De Young and Princen, 2012). This involves coming together as a community with the ambitious, long-term goal of using mostly local resources to meet local needs. For example, rather than relying on industrially produced food that is imported from all around the world, Transition Towns try to maximise local, organic food production, based on permaculture principles (Holmgren, 2002). Rather than relying on fossil fuel energy, Transition Towns take steps to radically reduce energy consumption while moving to renewable sources. Rather than mindlessly embracing consumerism, participants in Transition Towns are stepping off the consumerist treadmill, reimagining 'the good life', and discovering that community engagement provides great wealth to those brave enough to get involved. As Rob Hopkins claims, empowerment can flow from 'just doing stuff' (Hopkins, 2013).

As well as decarbonisation and relocalisation, another key concept in the Transition movement is 'resilience'. This refers to the ability of an individual or community to withstand societal or ecological shocks – shocks that can be expected in the future, sooner rather than later, if we continue down the path of growth without limits (Gilding, 2011). In order to become more resilient, communities need to relearn how to provide for themselves in ways that were commonplace not so long ago. This might involve sharing more of our assets with neighbours, rather than each individual having their own. Or it might involve 'reskilling' ourselves to acquire the lost arts of mending clothes, preserving food, or entertaining ourselves for free. Fortunately, this path to sustainability and resilience is filled with hidden joys and unexpected delights, in ways that perhaps need to be experienced to be fully understood.

As promising as the Transition Movement may be, there are crucial questions it needs to confront and reflect on if it wants to fully realise its potential for deep societal transformation (Alloun and Alexander, 2014). Firstly, some critics argue that the movement suffers, just as the broader Environmental Movement arguably suffers, from the inability to expand much beyond the usual middle-class, well-educated participants, who have the time and privilege to engage in social and environmental activism. While the Transition Movement is ostensibly 'inclusive', this self-image needs to be examined in order to assess whether it is as inclusive and as diverse as it claims to be, and what this might mean for the movement's prospects. That said, mobilising a community is never easy, so critics must not be too quick to blame the Transition *model*, as such, especially in the absence of providing a better alternative model for change. It is easy to be critical, but much harder to change the world!

Secondly, there is also the question of whether a grassroots, community-led movement can change the macro-economic and political structures of global capitalism 'from below', or whether the movement may need to engage in more conventional 'top down' political activity if it is to have any chance of achieving its ambitious goals. The orthodox left would argue that the Transition movement is being naive if it thinks it can be transformative without confronting state power and the structures entrenched by it. It is an important issue to consider, especially given that the Transition movement presents itself as very positive, fun, and non-confrontational. This raises the question: to what extent can the Transition movement avoid the pain, hardship, and conflict historically associated with significant social movements (e.g. Civil Rights, Women's Rights, Gay Rights, etc.)? After all, vested interests in the status quo are almost certainly going to try to maintain the status quo, suggesting that the ambitious goals of Transition (including decarbonisation and relocalisation) are probably going to confront hard political opposition from enormously powerful political and economic forces. For this reason, it may be that pain and conflict cannot be sidestepped on the path of transition.

At the same time, it should be acknowledged that activists and participants in such movements might well find the struggle meaningful and worthwhile, no matter how difficult the path turns out to be. A case can also be made that grassroots movements have the potential to be transformative, even in the absence of conventional political activity. In a neoliberal era, waiting for governments to do something may mean waiting a long time, so a case can be made that communities should do things themselves and lead by practical example using the resources they have at the local scale. Whatever the case, it is important that the movement is self-reflective about its strategies for change, because it hardly has energy, resources, or time to waste.

Finally, for present purposes, critics also raise questions about whether the movement is sufficiently radical in its vision (Trainer, 2010). Does it need to engage more critically with the broader paradigm of consumer capitalism, its growth imperative, and social norms and values? Is building local resilience within this paradigm an adequate strategy? And does the movement recognise that decarbonisation means moving away from affluent, consumer lifestyles? It is important that participants in the movement engage critically with these issues, for only by doing can they advance the debate around a movement that may indeed hold some of the keys to transitioning to a just and sustainable world.

Of course, these are early days, and the challenges that Transition Towns are facing are daunting, to say the least. To be sure, it will not be easy to build a new, simpler way of life from within industrial civilisation. Everything will conspire against the movement. But Transition provides a glimmer of hope in dark times, and at times that glimmer seems to be growing brighter. Could Transition be the movement we have been waiting for? While this young and promising movement is not without its critics, there are some who argue that if civilisation is to make it into the next half of the century without collapsing, it will be because the Transition Towns movement, or something like it, was able to drive transformative change from the grassroots up.

References

Alexander, S., 2012, 'The Optimal Material Threshold: Toward an Economics of Sufficiency' *Real-World Economics Review* 61: 2-21.

Alloun, E. and Alexander, S. 2014. 'The Transition Movement: Questions of Diversity, Power, and Affluence' *Simplicity Institute Report* 14g: 1-24.

De Young, R. and Princen, T. 2012. *The Localization Reader: Adapting to the Coming Downshift*. Massachusetts: MIT Press.

Gilding, P., 2011. *The Great Disruption: How the Climate Crisis will Transform the Global Economy*. London, Bloomsbury.

Heinberg, R. 2011. *The End of Growth: Adapting to our New Economic Reality*, New Society Publishers, Gabriola Island.

Heinberg, R. and Lerch, D. 2010. *The Post Carbon Reader: Managing the 21st Century's Sustainability Crises.* Healdsburg, CA: Watershed Media.

Holmgren, D., 2002. *Permaculture: Principles and Pathways beyond Sustainability.* Hepburn: Holmgren Design Services.

Hopkins, R. 2008. *The Transition Handbook: From Oil Dependency to Local Resilience.* White River Junction, Vt: Chelsea Green Publishing.

Hopkins, R. 2011. *The Transition Companion: Making your Community more Resilient in Uncertain Times.* White River Junction, Vt: Chelsea Green Publishing.

Hopkins, R. 2013. *The Power of Just Doing Stuff: How Local Action can Change the World.* Cambridge: UIT/Green Books.

Trainer, T. 2010. *The Transition to a Sustainable and Just World.* Sydney: Envirobook.

CHAPTER TWENTY-FOUR

DEGROWTH

SERGE LATOUCHE

Degrowth is a societal project of transforming industrial and market societies into socially and ecologically sustainable societies of frugal abundance. Its principle aim is to dismantle a widely shared belief in the productivist model of development – that is, the ideology of unlimited economic growth – and to reconstruct industrial societies according to the ideal of ecological democracy.

To say that degrowth is a societal project means it is both a politics and an ethics. For objectors to growth, including Aristotle, politics cannot be conceived without an ethics and vice versa, even though the two should not be confused. Politics as only ethics would be powerless or terrorist, but politics without ethics (which is currently the case, especially since the late '90s and the big neo-liberal leap backwards) leads to a triumph of the *banality of evil*. Consequently, degrowth cannot be reduced to an ethics, even an ethics of resistance, revolt and disobedience, as it is also an economic and social revolution leading to a different world. This other world is what we call a degrowth society. This is not merely a utopian future, no matter how desirable it may be, one that we will never know. This other world is also within the existing one. It is in us and we must attempt to live in it, here and now.

Degrowth is often associated with 'voluntary simplicity'. Indeed, a whole 'downshifting' movement has appeared in the last few decades, especially in Anglo-Saxon/English speaking countries (US, Canada, Australia). Downshifting means working, producing, spending and consuming less in reaction to mass consumerism.

Degrowth and voluntary simplicity share a long philosophical tradition that advocates limiting our needs to reach happiness. 'Those who are not content with little are not content with anything' Epicurus said. The absence of limits in consumer society can only lead to failure. The myth of the Danaïdes, those young women who were forced to fill bottomless jars in Tartarus because they had murdered their husbands on the first night of their weddings, illustrates this insatiability.

The American version of voluntary simplicity (simple living, downshifting, etc.) is greatly inspired by the philosophy of Henry David Thoreau. The European tradition follows on from Leo Tolstoy, but also Gandhi and his disciples such as Lanza del Vasto, who founded the Communities of the Ark.

Like voluntary simplicity, the *path* of degrowth is first and foremost a choice. When degrowth is *chosen*, it is not suffered. Yet degrowth cannot be summarised as an ethics of sobriety, which risks turning into a form of ascetic or mystic fundamentalism which is merely a reaction to the current model; this approach, however, is sometimes present amongst degrowth advocates. This attitude can only be part of the answer to the ecological challenge because it comes up against the rebound effect (Owen, 2012). Breaking away from the dominating consumerist culture is a heroic, even rational, choice, but it may not be enough to save the planet. Whatever name we give this desirable ethical stand (frugality, austerity, sobriety, simplicity, renouncing, etc.), it begs a number of questions that limit its reach. Calling for voluntary simplicity and frugal economy is all well and good, but it is likely to remain wishful thinking, given that we would need this unlikely behavioural shift to be extended to the whole of society. And it is here that we have to deal with the addiction to the drug of consumerism.

It is important to fully realise our toxico-dependence on growth. The devil of consumerism that we thought *we had driven out through the door* comes back even more strongly through the window. These are the objective and subjective traps of the rebound effect. We think we are saving the planet by moving to the countryside to eat organic food, but we end up using our cars even more for all sorts of seemingly good reasons (to go to town, for example). Moreover, what is reduced by Pierre is freed up for Paul, so in the end, the planet is still degraded. The conscientious degrowth advocate who really wants to reduce the human ecological footprint faces a real conundrum. The global logic is stronger than our personal voluntarism. This is why Murray Bookchin, who looked at voluntary simplicity and lifestyle change, developed a negative critique of it. Degrowth offers a real system change: getting out of consumer society to build *frugal abundance* or *prosperity without growth*; that is the ideal of an autonomous eco-socialist society. Consequently our references are to the likes of Murray Bookchin, Ivan Illich, Jacques Ellul, Cornelius Castoriadis, and André Gorz.

In *Tools for Conviviality*, Ivan Illich denounces the current human condition in which all technologies have become so invasive that we do not know how to find happiness, except in fasting from technology. He advocates 'the sober euphoria of life' (Illich, 1973: 222). For him, putting necessary limitations on consumption and production, and ending the exploitation of nature and the exploitation of labour by capital, does not mean going back to a life of privation and hard labour. On the contrary, by foregoing excessive material comfort, creativity can be unleashed, opening up the possibility of more worthwhile living. Indeed, a simple life has nothing to do with a commitment to masochistic frustration. It is a choice to live differently, to live better, and more in harmony with one's convictions, by replacing the race to material goods with the pursuit of more satisfying values. The rare families who choose to live without TV need not be pitied. They prefer other sources of satisfaction than the ones the *magic box* could offer: social or family life, reading, games, artistic activities, free time to dream or simply to enjoy life. The ethics of degrowth associates personal discipline with engaging the world for its betterment.

The elements of a complex economy like ours are interdependent. Producers, consumers, money, goods, and environment all interact. Nature hates a void, so what we save on one side creates a call for more spending on the other side. At the level of the individual lies two paths to degrowth: the first, consuming less, or sobriety; the second, self-production and trading based on the logic of giving. In any event, rather than merely consuming less, people would do more for degrowth by producing their own organic food or by using a short supply chain such as the [French] Association for Maintaining Peasant Agriculture (AMAP), which also exists in the US and elsewhere under the name Community Supported Agriculture (CSA). This type of short supply chain enables a strong relocalisation of production and consumption with positive ecological and social effects. There are no doubt other ways to reduce our dependence on the global logic. A degrowth politics should research how to find and promote them.

But can we, even then, escape all rebound effects? No, because the water that we saved, the air we did not pollute, the energy and petrol we did not consume, etc. are theoretically available for *others* who, following the growth narrative, want to produce even more so as to reap more profits and push people to consume even more. Until we put a bottom in the Danaides' barrels of consumerism, it will be impossible to tell if we are being effective at replenishing our world. However, this reduction of consumption is also a reduction in production. To the extent that virtuous circles have been triggered, and that an alternative sphere is flourishing, the systemic logic of productivism can only deploy itself within an ever-shrinking space. So without fully plugging all the holes, the leak can be kept under control. We will not have shut down the infernal 'machine', but we will have at least thrown a spanner in the works and thus fostered the planet's survival.

A deeper reflection on *ecological footprint* allows us to fully grasp the systemic nature of 'overconsumption' and the limits of voluntary simplicity. In 1961, the French ecological footprint was still one planet, in contrast to three today. Does this mean that French households used to eat three times less meat, drink three times less water and wine and burn three times less fuel or electricity? Obviously not. But the little strawberry yogurt that we ate back then did not yet incorporate the 8,000 km it does today! The beef steak consumed less chemical fertilisers, pesticides, imported soy beans, and fossil fuels. The suit that we wore did not require 50,000 km of transport. So it is not so much our current lifestyle itself that has become perverted, but the logic that enables it to exist.

The change in the social imaginary that would enable the success of a degrowth society cannot be decided on, as such, but results from multiple changes of outlooks that are partly prepared by education and example. We need fresh outlooks if the system is to change for the better. Getting out of the 'chicken or the egg' type of circular reasoning involves engaging in a virtuous dynamic. It also means drastically reducing working hours, internalising externalities, inciting the use of more convivial techniques, penalising harmful spending like advertising, etc. We can imagine that the sphere of the convivial society will end up absorbing and resorbing the sphere of productivist economy. Willem Hoogendijk, a objector to growth, presents a realistic scheme in which the GDP would decrease by 60 per cent, arguing that this would only translate into a 25 per cent decrease of useful consumption (Hoogendijk, 1991: 86).

Since there are no magic recipes or strategies, we can probably only start in modest ways, for example, according to one's own level. Voluntary simplicity constitutes a good way of preparing to face the chaos to come; a good way to initiate a degrowth scenario. It is a manner of living, a personal revolution, and a valuable exemplar at the same time.

However, it is important not to lose sight of the final and most ambitious goal. In the meantime, if people also choose degrowth because it is seen as a desirable path to live better, it is something at least for those who have embraced it. The Transition Town movement that was born in Ireland (Kinsale) and now flourishes in the UK and elsewhere, is probably the best example of building something that approximates an urban degrowth society from the bottom up (Hopkins, 2008). According to the network's charter, those towns aim to become energy self-sufficient in anticipation of the scarcity of fossil fuels and more generally they aim to become more resilient. The sustainable and 'post-carbon' cities in the US, the new municipalities, virtuous cities or slow cities in Italy, are going in the same direction.

To get a sense of proportion back, it is important to articulate an ethics of voluntary simplicity with a global political project of degrowth.

References

Hoogendijk, W. 1991. *The Economic Revolution: Towards a Sustainable Future by Freeing the Economy from Money-Making*. Utrecht: International Books.

Hopkins, R., 2008. *The Transition Handbook: From Oil Dependency to Local Resilience*. Totnes, Devon: Green Books.

Illich, I. 1973. *La Convivialité* [Tools for Conviviality]. Paris: Le Seuil.

Owen, D. 2012. *The Conundrum: How Scientific Innovation, Increased Efficiency, and Good Intentions Can Make Energy and Climate Problems Worse*. New York: Riverhead Books.

Further Reading

Latouche, S. 'Essays on Frugal Abundance: ' *Simplicity Institute Reports*, 14c, 14d, 14e and 14f. Available at: http://simplicityinstitute.org/publications [accessed 1 June, 2014].

CHAPTER TWENTY-FIVE

THE SIMPLER WAY

TED TRAINER

The core themes in the Simpler Way perspective on the global situation can be summarised as follows. Sustainability and justice problems are mostly due to the fact that far too much producing and consuming is taking place. The problems cannot be solved in or by a consumer-capitalist society. They can only be solved by transition to very different systems and lifestyles which allow us to live well on a small fraction of present resource use. An alternative Simpler Way is easily imagined and could be easily achieved − if enough of us wanted to do it − and a Simpler Way would liberate us to enjoy a far higher quality of life.

Since the 1960s various people have argued for this general position. My first statement, *Abandon Affluence* was published in 1985. My concern over subsequent years has been to elaborate the underlying 'limits to growth' critique of our present society and to work towards a more plausible, detailed and convincing vision of the alternative Simpler Way. If there is to be a transition it will only take place because large numbers of people have been persuaded that some kind of Simpler Way is needed, workable, and attractive.

My attempts to contribute to this goal take two forms. The first is in providing summary analyses detailing the Simpler Way perspective. These can be found at http://socialsciences.arts.unsw.edu.au/tsw/TSWmain.html, and have recently been integrated in my book, *The Transition to a Sustainable and Just World* (2010). The second is the

217

development of my bush homestead, Pigface Point as a site to introduce visitors to Simpler Way themes.

What follows is a brief outline of The Simpler Way vision for an alternative society.

It is crucial to begin with an understanding of how very unsustainable and unjust consumer-capitalist society is, because this shows that the reductions we must seek to make in resource use are huge. The common Ecological Footprint measure (WWF) shows that about 8 ha of productive land are needed to provide for one Australian. This is approximately *ten times* the per capita amount that will be available in the world by 2050. The multiples are much the same for most other resources. We in rich countries are living in ways that consume far more than all people could ever achieve. What matters here is the magnitude of the overshoot. We must get our use rates down to tiny fractions of their present values if we are to solve the many global problems being generated by resource scarcity and ecological impact. We in rich countries have our present rates because we are taking far more than our fair share of dwindling world resources, condemning billions of people to deprivation.

Despite this, the supreme and almost never questioned commitment in our society is to economic growth, to raising production, consumption 'living standards' and the GDP as far and as fast as possible.

It should be obvious from this that living standards and social systems enabling all to live well cannot possibly be achieved unless we work out ways of living on *far* lower per capita resource use rates, and create economies with zero growth in material and energy consumption. This is the context in which Simpler Way proposals have to be understood. Unless the magnitude of the overshoot and the required reductions are understood, Simper Way proposals will be seen as extreme and unnecessary.

The following key elements in an alternative way would allow us to make these big reductions.

A new overall economic system must include an economy with a GDP that is a very small fraction of the size of the present economy; that produces to meet genuine needs and not to maximise profits; that is not driven by market forces; and that has no growth in resource and energy consumption. There would be mostly small, highly self-sufficient local economies, largely independent of the remnant national and global economies, devoting local resources to meeting local needs, with little regional let alone international trade. As petroleum becomes scarce and materials become expensive there will be no choice about this.

Some other specific features within the general Simpler Way economic vision are:

- increased use of intermediate and basic technologies, especially craft and hand-tool production;
- building using earth, enabling all people to have very low-cost housing;
- extensive development of commons providing many free goods especially from 'edible landscapes';
- voluntary working bees developing and maintaining community facilities;
- many committees, for example: for agriculture, care of aged, care of youth, entertainment and leisure and cultural activities;
- large cashless, free goods, and gifting sectors;
- little need for transport, enabling bicycle access to work and conversion of most urban roads to commons;
- the need to work for a monetary income only one or two days a week at a relaxed pace, thus allowing intensive involvement in arts and crafts and community activities;
- town-owned banks;
- a local currency that does not involve interest;
- relatively low dependence on corporations, professionals, bureaucrats, high-tech ways or the global economy.

There would still be an important role for some more distant and centralised institutions, such as base hospitals, universities, steel works, railway systems and wind farms. Light industry would be located in the regions surrounding towns, small farms and factories, mostly producing goods for the region but providing some exports to 'pay for' imports from other regions and national sources such as steel works.

There need be *no* reduction in the level of highly sophisticated and socially useful scientific and professional expertise, such as within research institutes, universities and hospitals, although far fewer would be needed in most areas, notably law, IT and communications. Many entire industries will be no longer needed, such as advertising. There would actually be more socially beneficial high-tech R & D than at present, because resources presently being wasted in frivolous ventures could be transferred to it.

In my view most of the economy could take the form of small private firms operating within guidelines set by the community. Obviously the vision does not involve state control. States would have some but relatively few important functions, and should be under firm control by the citizen assemblies within all towns.

Secondly, there will be the need for more cooperative and participatory ways, enabling people in small communities to take collective control of their own functioning and development, to include and provide for all. In the coming era of scarcity it will be obvious that communities must cooperate to ensure that collective needs are met, no one is excluded, and that the available local productive capacity is very effectively geared to providing for all. This local self-government will involve commons such as community orchards, fish ponds and forests, committees, working bees, and town assemblies and referenda making the important decisions about local development and administration. Thus most governing will (have to) be carried out by citizens via highly participatory arrangements, partly because expensive centralised states will not be sustainable, but mainly because only the people who live within and have to maintain local economies are in a position to make and carry out the right decisions. The viability of the new systems will depend largely on the level of conscientiousness, community solidarity, empowerment and control, and experienced satisfaction. These crucial 'spiritual' qualities can only thrive in small, cooperative and largely self-governing communities in control of their own fate.

Thirdly, some very different values will be needed to make The Simpler Way function successfully. It would be impossible unless the predominant outlook involved values and ideas that are co-operative not competitive, much more collectivist and much less individualistic, and concerned with frugality, sufficiency and self-sufficiency rather than acquisitiveness and consuming and getting richer. In a viable zero growth economy there could be no concern with accumulation of wealth since that would quickly lead to breakdown as the strongest got hold of most of the zero-sum amount of production and property. High priority would have to be given to equity and the situation of the least advantaged, or again cohesion would quickly suffer. The basic orientation would have to be concern with giving, nurturing, helping others thrive, and with the public good and the welfare of the town. It would be obvious that your own individual welfare would depend on whether or not the town or suburb was thriving. The situation would *require* and *reward* cooperation, giving, responsibility, and good citizenship. Synergism would prevail; goodness, giving, helping, cooperating would generate and multiply further goodness. Thus the 'spiritual' benefits of The Simpler Way become evident. The conditions would provide incentives to enjoy living in and contributing to a thriving community, as distinct from seeking to get richer as an individual and becoming more able to purchase things.

The extremely important point to be made now is that The Simpler Way would not be about reluctantly accepting deprivation and hardship in order to save the planet – it would be a delightful liberation. Because far too much work and producing is done in consumer society, one of the greatest benefits of shifting to a Simpler Way will be that we will have several days a week to devote to arts, crafts, conversation, community activities, gardening, learning and creating. Much of this time will probably go into producing high quality items via slow and enjoyed hand tool production (although there would, of course, still be a limited place for machinery and mass production factories). Many of us would still be highly skilled specialists in a field where we worked for money two days a week, but everyone would be a 'jack of all trades', enjoying the exercise of many skills throughout the day.

The quality and range of our food would be vastly superior to those in conventional supermarket society. The town or suburb would have many gardeners constantly trialling new varieties of plants, and many master chefs who delight in exploring new recipes and ways to preserve.

We would be deeply embedded in a supportive community, conscious of the need to include and to provide for everyone, because everyone's welfare would depend on the level of town cohesion and morale. If these are not high the working bees, committees, town meetings, festivals, concerts and voluntary agencies will not be attended well. We would gain satisfaction from co-operating on projects, sharing, giving and enabling others to thrive. The climate would not be about private and isolated individuals competing for a disproportionate share of scarce resources. We would be immensely secure, from loneliness, dis-advantage, and especially from unemployment and poverty as we would have the sense to eliminate these. A top priority would be to make sure everyone had a *livelihood*, a way of making a valued contribution that would ensure a sufficient income.

We would live in beautiful 'edible landscapes', crammed with gardens, forests, meadows, ponds, animals, little farms and productive public spaces. Within walking distance of your house there would be an inexhaustible range of vistas, ornamental ponds and pagodas, canals, castles and caves, fussed over by all the manic gardeners and landscapers. The town would also contain many little farms and firms to drop into, many familiar people, many animals, and many activities and leisure resources that have been set up by the leisure committee. Your suburb or town has abundant talent to provide entertainment, many dramatists, poets, musicians, magicians, jugglers, acrobats, artists, etc. Many will be able to enjoy performing at the free neighbourhood concerts and art shows. Then there will be the education and culture committee which will organise visiting speakers, educational tours, displays, and the festivals, celebrations and rituals. So we would be living in 'leisure-rich' environments.

The community workshops would include craft areas, recycling and repair operations, art galleries, lathes and drill presses, the community saw mill, meeting rooms and libraries. We would be able to get advice or assistance on almost anything from the many skilled people in the town with the time and the desire to help.

We would be acutely aware of the fact that it is now *our* town. We would run it and we would have the power to develop it the way we want. We would take responsibility for its fate, for identifying problems and dealing with them. We would enjoy thinking about and discussing how the town is going, what we need to attend to, making good decisions, getting our working bees on the job quickly. We would be proud of our town, especially of its capacity to provide for us all regardless of how badly the global economy was performing. The main source of your wealth would not be your bank balance or property but the richness of your town, its gardens, committees, skills, leisure resources, activities, institutions and arrangements, and above all its spirit of comradeship, solidarity and helpfulness.

There are important satisfactions involved in living frugally and self-sufficiently. It feels good to run a household economy effectively and efficiently using as little as you need to, recycling, avoiding waste, and planning and organising the use of the resources you have. When you are producing some of your own food, entertainment, repairs, etc. you have an incentive to save time and materials, and there is satisfaction in being able to organise, use skills and produce well. You will be proud of your well stocked pantry, your safe chicken pen fences, and your well-mulched rows of corn. One of the activities I enjoy is gathering sticks for lighting the open fire. This gives a sense of being able to provide for myself, and not having to use fossil fuels to keep warm. I made the open fire that the sticks light. When I pass one of my neat stacks of fire wood ready for next winter I recognise my wealth, and my skill and good sense in organising this aspect of my 'oikos', my household economy. I like the fact that I have only one pair of 'going-out' shoes, and that my per capita electricity use is about one-thirtieth of the Australian average.

One of the biggest benefits of The Simpler Way would be the peace of mind that would come from the relaxed pace and the freedom from the need to struggle and work hard, the security that would come from knowing that you need not fear being dumped into unemployment by the economy and knowing that you have a community that cares about you. Above all there would be the knowledge that you were not living in ways that cause global problems and that all people could practise. You could feel pride in your town and its citizens for exemplifying a sustainable and just society. As I see it, living in these simpler but richer ways would make life far more interesting and satisfying than the lives of most people in consumer societies today.

Further reading

Trainer, T. 2010. *The Transition to a Sustainable and Just World*. Sydney, Envirobook.

CHAPTER TWENTY-SIX

MINDFULNESS

MARK BURCH

In taking up the subject of mindfulness in the history of voluntary simplicity, I'm adopting an understanding of mindfulness that is broader than the practice of Buddhist *vipassana* (see Burch, 2013: 11-12.). I also want to include any practice which aims to pay deliberate attention to things that matter in the realm of subjective experience. It is the examined life; the contemplative dimension of awareness; the quality of attention we bring to whatever arises in our experience. What distinguishes voluntary simplicity from other ways of living are the things that its practitioners believe to matter, and how these are cultivated.

Looking back over both Eastern and Western history, we might characterise the arc of a human life as following one of three paths. For the unfortunate majority, life is like a minefield every step, which must be negotiated day by day to procure necessities and avoid catastrophic accidents, nature's misfortunes, and the wiles of sharpers and rogues. Along this path may be found respites of comfort and safety, but they tend to be temporary and precarious. Much depends on luck. People living this arc are often understandably preoccupied with material security, envious of those they think have it, and desirous to achieve it themselves. Familiar only with the hazards of poverty, they are prone to think that material affluence is the sole route to security and wellbeing.

For a smaller, more privileged minority, life is much like a candy shop, stocked with many pleasures which are there for the taking, if only one can take them before others do. Commonly, the denizens of candy shops are sharpers and rogues themselves who also own minefields, if only by proxy. Along this path, life is a buffet of material comforts and false security resting on shared delusions of limitless growth, elite superiority, personal entitlement and wilful ignorance of any concerns beyond one's own interests. Life is fun, to be sure, but at its core lies inescapable paranoia and anxiety which candy shoppers try to compensate with systems of state security, institutionalised violence, self-medication and physical segregation – in short, with power and money. The fact that the candy shop *requires* the minefield remains largely beyond the bounds of polite conversation.

The third arc is a way of life different from that both of the mine-fielders and the candy shoppers. Sometimes it has been described as a 'Middle Way' between poverty and affluence, but this really only applies to its material aspects, and even there only superficially. This is the way of simple living. I think what distinguishes it most clearly from life in the minefield or the candy shop is the orientation of consciousness – the worldview, values, and focus of attention – of its practitioners. Of course, how consciousness is oriented manifests at the material level as a different sort of lifestyle, but as Charles Wagner (1895: 17) noted over a century ago:

> *Simplicity is a state of mind.* It dwells in the main intention of our lives. A man is simple when his chief care is the wish to be what he ought to be, that is, honestly and naturally human. And this is neither so easy nor so impossible as one might think. At bottom, it consists in putting our acts and aspirations in accordance with the law of our being, and consequently with the Eternal Intention which willed that we should be at all. Let a flower be a flower, a swallow a swallow, a rock a rock, and let man be a man, and not a fox, a hare, a hog, or a bird of prey: this is the sum of the whole matter. [Gender exclusive language in the original.]

So, in what does this 'state of mind' consist? How is it cultivated? What difference does it make? And what does it have to say to anyone who is not already convinced?

Over the centuries, there have been people who are searching for something more than can be found in the pleasures of affluence; people who find affluence itself burdensome or even morally suspect. Not finding what they are looking for in the realm of fame, fortune, and power, they have turned in the only other direction remaining – inward – and sought their treasure there. Despite the diversity of cultures and historical periods in which they lived, they share many ideas and values.

The most foundational of these, I think, is the common testimony that *how* we think about our lives, and *that* we reflect on them at all, plays a greater role in determining our wellbeing than do our material circumstances or social position. This is not to say that we have no material needs which make legitimate claims on our time and energy, but rather that these claims are in nature modest and easily provisioned in just conditions. The material basis of our lives is more secure than we imagine. What can most deprive us of a good life is not so much material scarcity as it is a host of psychological and emotional habits, delusions and logical mistakes. Moreover, these problems are often created, or amplified, by social customs, institutions, and economic structures which are perverse to human wellbeing. This situation can be remedied if we wish. But the remedy is found only by turning our attention inward, rather than leaving it fixed outwardly on objects of sense, transient attachments, ephemeral pleasures, and empty celebrity. Much depends on where we focus *attention*, and with what *intention*.

Both the habitués of the minefield and the candy shop orient consciousness toward extrinsic, material values with the intention of personal gain, security and pleasure. Precisely because such values are extrinsic and material, they participate in the properties of the material universe making them subject to change, loss, and scarcity. Because we seek permanence, security and abundance where it cannot be found we experience suffering and regret – the very opposite of the sort of life we were looking for. Because we are seldom totally deluded, the contradiction that perishable things cannot deliver secure contentment brings to life a profound insecurity and a surreal quality of bewilderment. Not only that, say the teachers of mindfulness, it brings to life a certain unreality. We miss the boat as we flounder around in the fugue state of consumer culture:

> Will any man hesitate to [embrace simplicity] in order to free his mind from madness? (Lucius Annaeus Seneca, 1996: 114, first century BC)

> Guard also against another kind of error: the folly of those who weary their days in much business, but lack any aim on which their whole effort, nay, their whole thought, is focused (Marcus Aurelius, 1964: 47, second century, AD).

> We do not content ourselves with the life we have in ourselves and in our own being; we desire to live an imaginary life in the mind of others, and for this purpose we endeavour to shine. We labour unceasingly to adorn and preserve this imaginary existence, and neglect the real (Blaise Pascal, 1996: 198, seventeenth century).

> To labour too hard or cause others to do so, that we may live conformable to customs which Christ our Redeemer contradicted by his example in the days of his flesh, and which are contrary to divine order, is to manure a soil for the propagating an evil seed in the earth (John Woolman, 1793).

> The mass of men lead lives of quiet desperation. ... But it is a characteristic of wisdom not to do desperate things (Henry David Thoreau, 1854: 7).

> The cultivation and expansion of needs is the antithesis of wisdom. It is also the antithesis of freedom and peace. Every increase of needs tends to increase one's dependence on outside forces over which one cannot have control, and therefore increases existential fear (E. F. Schumacher, 1996: 10).

So we are ensnared in a kind of nightmare and we remain there multiplying our own suffering and that of others as well, unless we can find a way out – a door hidden in plain sight that can lead us to a more grounded, connected consciousness that offers as much wellbeing as is attainable for mortal creatures like ourselves. But how to find this hidden door?

We begin to discover the exit from our nightmare by withdrawing attention from the 'things' in the material world (money, affluence, power, celebrity, etc.) which until now we thought would bring us security and contentment, and direct attention instead toward nonmaterial values and the inner dimension of our experience. We advance this work further by questioning the importance of fulfilling our desires as infallible means to happiness. And furthermore, we take up the work of discovering, some might prefer 'fashioning', a central meaning or purpose for our lives which is rooted in nonmaterial values. For the ancient Greeks, this was often *philosophy* – the love of wisdom. For many Jews it has been the love of God's law and of righteousness. For many Christians over the centuries it has meant finding the Christ-Spirit within and actively cooperating with the action of this spirit to reshape one's outer life. For Taoists, it has often meant careful observation of the Way of the natural world and aligning one's thinking and behaviour with its wisdom. For many Buddhists this has meant fidelity to the Eightfold Path wherein is formed the right intention to pursue liberation for oneself and all other beings through the acquisition of right knowledge, the exercise of right action, right livelihood, right speech, right effort, right mindfulness and right contemplation:

> To be content with what one has is to be rich (Lao-Tzu, 1996: 124, fourth century BC).

> Nowhere can man find a quieter or more untroubled retreat than in his own soul; above all, he who possesses resources in himself, which he need only contemplate to secure immediate ease of mind – the ease that is but another word for a well-ordered spirit. Avail yourself often, then, of this retirement, and so continually renew yourself. Make your rules of life brief, yet so as to embrace the fundamentals (Marcus Aurelius, 1964: 63, second century, AD).

Our life must be converted into its contrary. We must unlearn those things which we have learned; by learning then we have hitherto not known ourselves. We must learn those things we have neglected: without knowing them we cannot know ourselves. We must like what we neglect, neglect what we like, tolerate what we flee, flee what we follow (Marsilio Ficino, 1996: 280, fifteenth century).

The true felicity of man in this life, and that which is to come, is in being inwardly united to the fountain of universal love and bliss (Woolman, 1793, eighteenth century).

Let man heed well his direction and forces, and keep good faith; and that he may better devote himself to the essential – which is to [moral] progress – at whatever sacrifice, let him simplify his baggage (Charles Wagner, 1985: 14, nineteenth century).

The teachers of simplicity assert that the shift in focus from the outer to the inner perspective, the decision to reserve time to cultivate our inner life, the deliberate adoption of practices that sensitise our intuition and deepen our questioning of all our assumptions and attitudes, the voluntary choice to organise our lives around nonmaterial values that grow through sharing rather than material values that diminish in possession – all these choices help liberate us from having wasted our lives.

If we think of simple living as giving up the affluence we desire, the abundance of material goods and the fawning attention of others, then simple living can only seem like a sacrifice to no good purpose. But even on cursory examination, such a conclusion is absurd. People have never taken up simple living because they thought it would make them worse off. They have never persisted in it if it reduced their wellbeing. But what they have done is place a personal bet on a horse that in mainstream consumer culture is given long odds: namely, that wellbeing will only be found in an entirely different direction from that recommended by nearly every formative influence in our daily lives. Moreover, we have to enter to win.

What relevance could such advice have for people who struggle daily merely to survive (the mine-fielders), or to those who already 'have everything' (the candy shoppers)?

Two issues appear repeatedly in the history of simple living that are relevant here. The first pertains to the idea that only those who first attain affluence can consider simple living. Implicit is the assumption that simple living is mainly about giving up things, and one cannot give up what one doesn't yet have. So acquisition must precede simplification:

> Strive toward a sound mind at top speed and with your whole strength. If any bond holds you back, untie it or sever it. 'But,' you say, 'my estate delays me; I wish to make such disposition of it that it may suffice for me when I have nothing to do, lest either poverty be a burden to me, or I myself a burden to others.'... Doubtless, your object, what you wish to attain by such postponement of your studies, is that poverty may not have to be feared by you. But what if it is something to be desired? Riches have shut off many a man from the attainment of wisdom (Seneca, 1996: 278, 4 BCE?-65 CE).

> 'Just give me a chance,' I hear people say. 'Just let me get my debts paid. Just let me get a few of the things I need and then I'll begin to think of poverty and its rewards. Meanwhile, I've had nothing but.' But these people do not understand the difference between inflicted poverty and voluntary poverty. I prefer to call the one kind *destitution*, reserving the word *poverty* for what Saint Francis called 'Lady Poverty' (Dorothy Day, 1963: 14-5).

> Let us grant that multitudes spend their lives in poverty, or with moderate possessions, without ever receiving the gift of simplicity, which is the beatitude reserved for the poor in spirit. Nevertheless, poverty freely accepted does release people from some of the worst strains of our civilisation, with the complicated forms of unhappiness that these bring with them (Mildred Binns Young, 1956: 18).

So the teachers of simple living urge us to turn our anxieties about simple living upside down and see the choice to live simply in terms of what is to be gained and not what is foregone. For people seeking to escape from destitution (abject, life-threatening poverty), this may consist mainly of setting proper limits on one's aspirations for material wealth. Instead of aiming to escape poverty in pursuit of affluence in material values, thus exchanging one set of afflictions for another, we are urged instead to make for the hidden door that leads from poverty to simplicity. There is no intention here to celebrate destitution as somehow virtuous or admirable. Rather, we aim to avoid a mistake in goal setting.

The second issue implies the invitation to a shift in consciousness among the candy shoppers as well; namely, by interrogating the value we place on material wealth, power, and social reputation. The shift to simple living often implies coming to perceive the value of material wealth differently – a process very much facilitated by mindfulness practice or some other contemplative practice. The intention here is to address not the absolute lack of the material means of sustenance (the daily existential challenge of living in the minefield) but rather to address the spiritual hollowness, the social isolation, and the ecological irresponsibility that often accompanies the pursuit and protection of affluence. Moreover, this is not just an affliction of the 1 percent, but is shared by anyone, regardless of his or her actual 'net worth' (a horrible, but common expression!) who displays the orientation of consciousness characteristic of this group. Paradoxically, it includes a chronic tendency to *undervalue* material things even in the feverish pursuit of them, and which uses the public, visible wastage of material things as yet another way of displaying one's wealth – 'I'm so wealthy, I can afford to abuse and waste this before your very eyes!' The teachers of simplicity would propose an alternative:

> We must daily break the body and shed the blood of creation. When we do this knowingly, lovingly, skilfully, reverently, it is a sacrament. When we do it ignorantly, greedily, clumsily, destructively, it is a desecration (Wendell Berry, 1981: 281).

For these practitioners [of voluntary simplicity], the goal is not ascetic self-denial, but a sort of unadorned grace. Some come to feel, for example, that clotheslines, window shades, and bicycles have a functional elegance that clothes dryers, air conditioners, and automobiles lack. These modest devices are silent, manually operated, fire-proof, ozone- and climate-friendly, easily repaired, and inexpensive. Because they are less 'convenient', they breed a degree of forethought and attention to the weather that grounds life in place and time (Alan Durning, 1992: 139).

For the modern economist this is very difficult to understand. He is used to measuring the 'standard of living' by the amount of annual consumption, assuming all the time that a man who consumes more is 'better off' than a man who consumes less. A Buddhist economist would consider this approach excessively irrational: since consumption is merely a means to human well-being, the aim should be to obtain the maximum of well-being with the minimum of consumption (E. F. Schumacher, 1996: 42).

To have but few desires and to be satisfied with simple things is the sign of a superior man (Gampopa, 1996: 223 – d. 1152).

It has been my aim to illustrate, at least in outline, that mindfulness and that changes in consciousness have been a perennial theme in the practice of simple living. The changes to lifestyle that voluntary simplicity calls forth can appear daunting when attempted without the assistance of a mindful approach to living. When the contemplative spirit is present, however, when we are paying attention in a regular and wholesomely disciplined way, the changes in our way of life are simply logical corollaries, inescapable effects, in fact, delightful manifestations and surprises arising naturally and organically from our new perspective on life. We are all capable of enjoying and being enriched by this transformation.

References

Aurelius, Marcus. (c.180), *Meditations*. Maxwell Staniforth (trans.), 1964. London, UK: Penguin Books.

Berry, Wendell. 1981. *The Gift of Good Land*. San Francisco, CA: North Point Press.

Burch, Mark A. 2013. *The Hidden Door: Mindful Sufficiency as an Alternative to Extinction*. Melbourne, Australia: The Simplicity Institute.

Day, Dorothy. 1963. In: VandenBroeck, Goldian. 1996. *Less is More: An Anthology of Ancient and Modern Voices Raised in Praise of Simplicity*. Rochester, VT: Inner Traditions.

Durning, Alan. 1992. *How Much Is Enough?* New York, N.Y.: W. W. Norton & Co.

Ficino, Marsilio. 1433-1499. (tr.) Virginia Conant. In: VandenBroeck, Goldian (1996). *Less is More: An Anthology of Ancient and Modern Voices Raised in Praise of Simplicity*. Rochester, VT: Inner Traditions.

Gampopa. (d. 1152). In: VandenBroeck, Goldian. 1996. *Less is More: An Anthology of Ancient and Modern Voices Raised in Praise of Simplicity*. Rochester, VT: Inner Traditions.

Lao-Tzu – 4th century BCE. *Tao-Te-Ching*. In: VandenBroeck, Goldian. 1996. *Less is More: An Anthology of Ancient and Modern Voices Raised in Praise of Simplicity*. Rochester, VT: Inner Traditions.

Pascal, Blaise. 1623-1662. *Thoughts*. (tr.) W. I. Trotter. In: VandenBroeck, Goldian (1996). *Less is More: An Anthology of Ancient and Modern Voices Raised in Praise of Simplicity*. Rochester, VT: Inner Traditions.

Schumacher, E. F. 1973. *Small Is Beautiful*. In: VandenBroeck, Goldian. 1996. *Less is More: An Anthology of Ancient and Modern Voices Raised in Praise of Simplicity*. Rochester, VT: Inner Traditions.

Seneca, Lucius Annaeus 4? BC-65 AD. *Epistles*. In: VandenBroeck, Goldian (1996). *Less is More: An Anthology of Ancient and Modern Voices Raised in Praise of Simplicity*. Rochester, VT: Inner Traditions.

Thoreau, Henry David. 1854. *Walden*. New York, NY: Alfred A. Knopf.

Wagner, Charles. 1895. *The Simple Life*. New York, NY: McClure, Phillips & Co.

Woolman, John, 1793. The Journal of John Woolman. In: Phillips P. Moulton (ed.), 1989. *The Journals and Major Essays of John Woolman*. Richmond, Indiana: Friends United Press.

Woolman, John, 1793. A Plea for the Poor, or A Word of Remembrance and Caution to the Rich. In: Phillips P. Moulton (ed.), 1989. *The Journals and Major Essays of John Woolman*. Richmond, Indiana: Friends United Press.

Young, Mildred Binns. 1956. In: VandenBroeck, Goldian (1996). *Less is More: An Anthology of Ancient and Modern Voices Raised in Praise of Simplicity*. Rochester, VT: Inner Traditions.

PIONEERS OF THE DEEP FUTURE

NOTES ON CONTRIBUTORS

SAMUEL ALEXANDER – Samuel Alexander, co-editor of this volume, is a lecturer at the University of Melbourne, teaching a course called 'Consumerism and the Growth Paradigm: Interdisciplinary Perspectives' in the Masters of Environment. He is also co-director of the Simplicity Institute (www.simplicityinstitute.org), publishing widely on issues related to voluntary simplicity, degrowth, post-growth economics, energy descent, and transition strategies. He is author of *Entropia: Life Beyond Industrial Civilisation* (2013) and editor of *Voluntary Simplicity: The Poetic Alternative to Consumer Culture* (2009).

ESTHER ALLOUN – Esther Alloun is a tutor and research assistant in the Department of Resource Management and Geography at the University of Melbourne (Landscape Sociology Research Group), and a contributing author with the Simplicity Institute. She conducts research work around risk and resilience, particularly in disaster contexts. Her research interests also include environmental/animal ethics, eco-feminism, and the 'Transition Town' movement as an expression of community resilience and 'simple living' at the local level.

MICHAEL AUGUSTIN – Michael J. Augustin is a doctoral student in philosophy at the University of California, Santa Barbara. His research focuses on ancient philosophy, and in particular the Presocratic and Hellenistic periods.

DIRK BALTZLY – Dirk Baltzly is Professor of Philosophy at the University of Tasmania. Born and educated in the USA, he worked at King's College London before moving to Australia in 1994. His recent work concentrates on philosophy in the late Roman Empire.

ALBERT BATES – Albert Bates is author of a dozen books, including *The Biochar Solution: Carbon Farming and Climate Change (2010), The Post Petroleum Survival Guide and Cookbook (2006), and Climate in Crisis: The Greenhouse Effect* *and What We Can Do (1990).* He is the co-founder of Global Village Institute for Appropriate Technology (which he has headed for 35 years) and the Global Ecovillage Network. Current projects include a peace-through-permaculture project in Palestine and the Sail Transport Network, moving fair trade goods along coastal routes. In 1980 he shared the Right Livelihood Award (considered an 'Alternative Nobel") for work in preserving indigenous culture. When not tinkering with pyrolizing rocket stoves, he teaches permaculture and climate remediation at The Farm ecovillage in Summertown, Tennessee.

MARK A. BURCH – Mark A. Burch is an author, educator, and group facilitator who has practised simple living since the 1960s, and since 1995, offers presentations, workshops and courses on voluntary simplicity. In 2010, he retired as Director of the Campus Sustainability Office for The University of Winnipeg, and is currently a Fellow of The Simplicity Institute in Melbourne, Australia. He also holds active membership in Transition Winnipeg, Sustainable South Osborne Community Cooperative, and is First Named of the Peace and Social Action Committee of the Winnipeg Monthly Meeting of Friends (Quakers). Mark has published seven books on voluntary simplicity, as well as a series of essays and numerous articles. His most recent book, *The Hidden Door: Mindful Sufficiency as an Alternative to Extinction,* is published by The Simplicity Institute in Australia.

ALLAN CARLSON – Allan Carlson is President of The Howard Center for Family, Religion & Society in Illinois and Editor of *The Family in American: A Journal of Public Policy.* His books include *The New Agrarian Mind: The Movement toward Decentralist Thought in Twentieth Century America* (Transaction) and *Third Ways: How Bulgarian Greens, Swedish Housewives, and Beer-Swilling Englishmen created Family-Centered Economies... and Why they Disappeared* (ISI Books).

DAVID CRAIG – David Craig is Associate Professor of Religious Studies at Indiana University-Purdue University Indianapolis (IUPUI). A religious ethicist specialising in economic, environmental, and health care ethics, he is author of *John Ruskin and the Ethics of Consumption* (University of Virginia

Press, 2006) and *Health Care as a Social Good: Religious Values and American Democracy* (Georgetown University Press, 2014). His other articles and essays explore ethical traditions of human development, economic justice, and environmental sustainability and their relevance for liberal democracies.

WILLIAM DESMOND – Will Desmond is a lecturer in the Department of Ancient Classics at the National University of Ireland, Maynooth. Along with articles and edited volumes, he has authored three monographs on *The Greek Praise of Poverty* (Notre Dame UP, 2006), *Cynics* (Acumen / California UP, 2008), and *Philosopher-Kings of Antiquity* (Continuum, 2011). His main interests lie in ancient philosophy and the history of ideas. His doctorate on classical Greek ideas about wealth was published as *The Greek Praise of Poverty* (Notre Dame UP, 2006), which was awarded the NUI Centennial Prize in Academic Publishing in Languages, Literature & Linguistics (2009). A second monograph, *Cynics* (Acumen & University of California Press, 2008), examines the 'dog philosophers' in antiquity, and their later influence. Philosopher-Kings of Antiquity (Continuum, 2011, pbk. 2013) explores - See more at: http://www.nuim.ie/ancient-classics/our-people/william-desmond#sthash.JqIf3rmg.dpuf

PETER DORAN – Peter Doran is a lecturer in environmental law and sustainable development at the School of Law at Queens University Belfast. His research interests include wellbeing and governance, and using Buddhist philosophy to inform responses to modern challenges in the fields of environment and economy. He is writing a book for Routledge on the 'political economy of attention' and mindfulness as the new commons.

WILLIAM FAHEY – William Edmund Fahey is Fellow and President of Thomas More College of Liberal Arts in Merrimack, New Hampshire. He has taught and lectured throughout the United States and Europe on monasticism and the Catholic social teachings. A founder and Chairman of the Classical and Early Christian Studies program at Christendom College, Fahey earned his Ph.D. in Early Christian Studies at the Catholic University of America. He is a Benedictine Oblate and lives in

New Hampshire with his wife and five children. He is editor of
The Foundations of Western Monasticism (2013).

MARIUS DE GEUS – Marius de Geus lectures Political Theory
and Environmental Philosophy at the Institute of Political
Science in Leyden (since 1976). He has published on many
issues, e.g. the importance of utopian thinking for ecological
sustainability, and the relation between over-consumption and
environmental degradation. His forthcoming book is on the
'necessity of simplicity': how can we simplify our western
lifestyles to deal effectively with the real risks of climate change
and global warming?

MARY GRISBY – Mary Grigsby is an Associate Professor of
Rural Sociology at the University of Missouri-Columbia. Her
research is focused on culture, identity and consumption. She is
author of *Buying Time and Getting By: the Voluntary
Simplicity Movement* (2004); *College Life through the Eyes of
Students* (2009) *and Noodlers in Missouri: Fishing for Identity
in a Rural Subculture* (2012).

SHANNON HAYES – Shannon Hayes holds a PhD in sustainable
agriculture and community development from Cornell
University. She works with three generations of her family
raising grass-fed meats on Sap Bush Hollow Farm in Upstate
New York, and is the author of six books, including the best-
seller, *Radical Homemakers: Reclaiming Domesticity from a
Consumer Culture*. Hayes writes weekly for Yes! Magazine and
blogs at www.shannonhayes.org.

SERGE LATOUCHE – Serge Latouche is Professor Emeritus at
the University of Paris-Sud and a growth objector. He is the
editor of a series entitled *Les précurseurs de la décroissance*
(Forerunners of degrowth). Recent publications include:
News from a growth objector (*Chroniques d'un objecteur de
croissance*), *The age of limits* (*L'âge des limites*), *Ready for
the scrap heap: The unreasons of programmed obsolescence*
(*Bon pour la casse, les déraisons de l'obsolesence
programmée*), and *Toward a society of frugal affluence*
(*Vers une société d'abondance frugale*).

AMANDA MCLEOD – Amanda McLeod, co-editor of this volume, is a writer and historian from Victoria, Australia. She holds a PhD in History and has published widely on consumerism, market research and consumer protection. Her main research interests include: self-sufficiency, simple living, the illusion of consumer choice and mental health and is currently an Adjunct Research Fellow in History at Monash University, Melbourne Australia. She blogs at: www.authenticabundance.com.au.

BILL METCALF – Bill Metcalf is Research Methodologist within Griffith University's Graduate Research School. He is Past President of the International Communal Studies Association, an active member of the Professional Historians Association, Australian Historical Association, Royal Historical Society of Queensland, and National Trust, on the Editorial Board of *Queensland History Journal* and *Communal Societies*, and Editor responsible for all 'intentional community' materials (about 80 articles) in the four-volume *The Encyclopedia of Community* (Sage, 2003) . He is the author of 9 books, 21 chapters in edited books, 7 Encyclopedia articles, and 30 articles in academic journals.

STEVEN NOLT – Steven Nolt of a professor of history at Goshen College, a tertiary school in Indiana, U.S.A. He is an author or coauthor of various books on Amish and Mennonite history and life, including *The Amish* (Johns Hopkins University Press, 2013) and *Amish Grace* (Jossey-Bass, 2007). His PhD degree is from the University of Notre Dame.

WHITNEY SANFORD – A. Whitney Sanford is an associate professor in the Religion Department at the University of Florida. She teaches and researches in two main areas: Religion and Nature and Religions of Asia, and her current work lies at the intersection of religion, food (and agriculture), and social equity. She is currently conducting ethnographic research, exploring how intentional communities translate values around food and agriculture into practices. Her books include *Growing Stories from India: Religion and the Fate of Agriculture* (University Press of Kentucky, 2012) and *Singing Krishna: Sound Becomes Sight in Paramanand's Poetry* (SUNY 2008). Her journal articles have appeared in publications including

JAAR, Journal of Agricultural and Environmental Ethics, International Journal of Hindu Studies, Worldviews, and *Journal for the Study of Religion, Nature, and Culture.*

JEROME SEGAL – Jerome M. Segal is a Research Scholar at the University of Maryland. He holds a PhD in Philosophy from the University of Michigan. Segal is the author of six books, including *Graceful Simplicity: The Philosophy and Politics of Simple Living,* and *Joseph's Bones: Understanding the Struggle Between God and Mankind in the Bible.* Over the last thirty years, his primary focus has been the Israeli-Palestinian conflict.

SHI, DAVID – David E. Shi, president of Furman University from 1994-2010, is a prolific writer and speaker, sharing his knowledge of such topics as American history, sustainability, and leadership. Among other books, he is author of *The Simple Life: Plain Living and High Thinking in American Culture* (2007, revised edition).

TED TRAINER – Ted Trainer is a Conjoint Lecturer in the School of Social Sciences, University of New South Wales. He has taught and written about sustainability and justice issues for many years. He is also developing Pigface Point, an alternative lifestyle educational site near Sydney, and a website for use by critical global educators, which can be viewed at: http://socialsciences.arts.unsw.edu.au/tsw/. His most recent book is *Transition to a Sustainable and Just World* (2010).

SIMON USSHER – Simon H. Ussher is co-director of the Simplicity Institute and a medical specialist based in Victoria, Australia. He is a passionate advocate of the myriad benefits of voluntary simplicity, including those related to health, social justice, and spirituality.

SARA WILLS – Sara Wills is Course Coordinator for the Executive Master of Arts at the University of Melbourne. She is also Associate Dean of the Faculty of Arts and a lecturer of Australia Studies. Sara teaches in an interdisciplinary context, and values humanities and social science approaches in the Arts. Her research interests include migration studies and history. Her doctoral thesis was published in 2006 as *The Greening of William Morris.*

OTHER BOOKS FROM THE SIMPLICITY INSTITUTE

Samuel Alexander, *Entropia: Life beyond Industrial Civilisation* (2013)

Mark A. Burch, *The Hidden Door: Mindful Sufficiency as an Alternative to Extinction* (2013)

FOR MORE INFORMATION, SEE THE SIMPLICITY INSTITUTE

www.simplicityinstitute.org

7961618R00158

Printed in Great Britain
by Amazon.co.uk, Ltd.,
Marston Gate.